Updated Edition

R^{THE}EADING OF THE WILL

A Novel

BY
NWANGANGA G. SHIELDS

ExplOra
BOOKS

EXPLORA BOOKS

700 – 838 West Hastings St. Vancouver, BC V6C 0A6
www.explorabooks.com
Phone: (604) 330 6795

ISBN: 978-1-998394-38-8

Updated Edition

THE READING OF THE WILL

A Novel

NWANGANGA SHIELDS

THE READING OF THE WILL

A Novel

Dedication

To my late mother Esther Mgboro Oti nee Eni.

Table of Contents

CHAPTER 1 1

CHAPTER 2 6

CHAPTER 3 14

CHAPTER 4 23

CHAPTER 5 32

CHAPTER 6 38

CHAPTER 7 48

CHAPTER 8 55

CHAPTER 9 66

CHAPTER 10 74

CHAPTER 11 82

CHAPTER 12 88

CHAPTER 13 93

CHAPTER 14 101

CHAPTER 15 109

CHAPTER 16 114

CHAPTER 17 126

CHAPTER 18 135

CHAPTER 19 147

CHAPTER 20 153

CHAPTER 21 ·· 161

CHAPTER 22 ·· 167

CHAPTER 23 ·· 175

CHAPTER 24 ·· 182

CHAPTER 25 ·· 187

CHAPTER 26 ·· 194

CHAPTER 27 ··201

CHAPTER 28··209

CHAPTER 29 ··210

CHAPTER 30 ·· 221

CHAPTER 31 ·· 229

CHAPTER 32 ·· 234

CHAPTER 33 ··243

CHAPTER 34 ··250

CHAPTER 35 ··256

CHAPTER 36 ·· 266

ABOUT THE AUTHOR ······························· 280

NOTE FROM THE AUTHOR ······················ 280

THE
READING
OF THE WILL

A Novel

CHAPTER 1

Oh my God! Ejituru thought. That must be the reason she's calling. Mama's health must have deteriorated. I must call her back immediately. She dialed Ifeoma's number and waited for the connection. "Hi, I'm sorry I missed your call. We moved east a few days ago, and I have so much to do. Is everything all right?" She felt a bit anxious as she waited for Ifeoma to respond.

After a pause, Ifeoma said, "Sister, is Nduka there? Give him the phone.

I think I'd rather speak to him first." Ifeoma spoke in a hesitant voice.

Ejituru could feel the anxiety and deep sadness in her tone. She knew that Ifeoma adhered to the belief that bad news could be more easily handled by a woman if a man was present when it was given. She was sure that Ifeoma's call held nothing but bad news. She shivered. "He's at work," she said in a small voice. "What is it? Tell me what you have to say." Instinctively, she knew what Ifeoma was about to say, but she couldn't bring herself to believe that it had happened.

"Sister, please don't be sad. Mama passed away last night. I've just come from the mortuary."

Ejituru broke down weeping, unable to say anything.

"Please calm down and let's talk," Ifeoma said, choking on her words.

With shaking knees and still grasping the phone, Ejituru sat down on the leather chair.

"Sister, sister, are you still there?" Ifeoma shouted. "This network!

They've cut us off!" Then the phone went dead.

Ejituru tried to collect herself and calm down. She redialed the number again, cursing the Nigerian network.

"Sister, we got cut off," Ifeoma said. "Please don't be sad. We all knew losing Mama was bound to happen. She's at rest now. It happened last night. The maid found her in distress and called me. Before we could call the doctor, it was too late. Now we need to think of what needs to be done." Ifeoma rattled on, now in control of her emotions.

Ejituru let go of the phone. She moaned, overwhelmed by emotion.

Tears ran down her cheeks.

"Sister, sister, are you there?" Ifeoma shouted.

Half an hour later, after she calmed down, Ejituru called Ifeoma for more details.

"Is somebody in the house with you?" Ifeoma asked as soon as she picked up the phone. "I'd hoped to get you when Nduka was at home."

"It's okay. Nduka is still at work. We can talk. Have you already moved the body? Is she in the mortuary now?" Ejituru tried to picture her mother lying dead in the room in Ifeoma's house in Umuahia, where she'd spent the last four years of her life. Uncontrolled tears poured down her cheeks as her body shook.

"We moved her this morning. I need your agreement on various things. I called Michael, our oldest brother, as soon as it happened. He came immediately from Aba. I'll call you later discuss arrangements. Michael has a specific viewpoint, one that I don't share."

"What's Michael proposing?" Ejituru asked, trying to keep calm.

"He suggested a quick burial, but that won't give those of you abroad time to make travel arrangements."

Ejituru could hear the commotion in the house but was unable to make out what was happening, so she shut down the phone. She stood up and paced the living room, hoping to call Ifeoma again later. She felt she needed to get control of herself first.

She hadn't been present at her father's funeral ten years ago, and she imagined that her half-siblings had already concluded that she would abdicate the burial of her mother to them.

Her mind in turmoil, she said out loud, "I've shared her with all of you these years. How can you think I would let you bury her without me?"

Five days ago, Ejituru, at fifty-three, returned to the Washington, DC, area, where she had lived nineteen years ago. This day, she'd just dropped off her three children at summer school and hurried home to start the arduous task of putting the apartment together. It had rained consistently the previous two days, during which she'd concentrated on unpacking and arranging the family sleeping quarters. She only stopped to fix herself a sandwich or to answer calls from tradesmen interspersed with calls from her local friends who had heard that she was back in the area.

Yesterday, having heard from several sources that Esther—the first friend she had when she first came to United States—was unwell; before picking up her kids, she'd swung by her place. Esther lived in the same apartment building where her first US home was. Thinking of it now, she shuddered, recalling the dank apartment that she was brought to straight from the airport as a bride.

She was surprised at how little the area had changed over the years. When Esther opened her door, she expected to see the usual number of women as before, when the apartment was both a living quarter and a hairdressing salon, but was surprised that the only reminder of those bygone years was the lone hair dryer stuck in one corner of the dining area. Her biggest surprise was Esther herself. She was no longer the strong, determined, opinionated woman whose very judgement was the last word on any subject; but an old, shriveled-up woman who, overwhelmed with emotion, wept uncontrollably.

Ejituru, overcome by this spectacle, was speechless, and had helped her settle down. Esther, she learned, had no relatives in the area, since her three children had moved away from the area because of job requirements or because of marriages. Although her children would like her to relocate nearer to them, she'd chosen to live in this area. Unfortunately, as she aged, it had become difficult for her to manage without help. Ejituru tried to tidy up the house, and before returning home, she picked up a few tins of soup and other supplies for her from the supermarket. Ejituru left determined to help improve Esther's situation with her children and until then, to visit as often as she could.

Back in her house and seeing the many boxes still remaining to be unpacked, she thought of the move. The move was precipitated by a generous job offer to her husband, Nduka Dike, from a prestigious hospital in the area. For a month after the offer was made, they'd agonized over what they should do. When she previously lived here, she was the wife of Ignatius Ngwu, and Nduka didn't want to bring her back to a place that held so many bad memories. Unwilling to let him sacrifice his career for her, she'd instead consulted her dearest friend, Cece, a civil rights lawyer in this area, who helped her identify possible openings for her in a pediatric practice in the area. Within a week, she'd heard of several possibilities. She sent out her resume, arranged for interviews, and found a match with one in Silver Spring, Maryland. It all worked out, and now the family had relocated.

Ejituru couldn't believe she was living in the apartment building she had admired as a young bride during those awful years with Ignatius. She remembered her visits to the apartment of Mary, Cece's friend, and how she'd begged Ignatius to find a similar apartment so she could move away from that dank and smelly place they were living in.

She heard the buzz of her cell phone and wrenched herself from thoughts of the past to the present. She found her phone, but by the time she answered, the caller had rung off. She hurried into the living room, dropped her handbag, and proceeded to the kitchen to unpack the last of the kitchen boxes. Before starting, she scrolled down and found that the caller was her forty-three-year-old halfsister, Ifeoma Obi, in Nigeria. She wondered whether Ifeoma had tried the Dallas landline and had learned that it had been disconnected. She hadn't told many people that they were moving to the DC area. The only ones in the know were her most trusted friends, Cece and Mary.

Her cell phone number wasn't generally known because she'd tried to keep the number hidden from her family in Nigeria since most of the calls would be demand for money. However, some time ago, she'd given Ifeoma the number with strict instructions that she only use it when it was absolutely necessary to get in touch with her given Nkechi's deteriorating health. This was the first time Ifeoma had used this line.

CHAPTER 2

Ifeoma, the last of the five daughters of Nkechi, wasn't Nkechi's natural-born child, like Ejituru was. But she had never been treated differently from Ejituru. Nkechi survived Ifeoma's birth father, Nwakama, by ten years. Onyeka -her birth mother, died two years after that.

Ifeoma married a young man from a socially prominent local family, and had followed Nkechi's dictum that the best profession for a woman was teaching. She chose a teaching career and had retired as an inspector of schools. Even in her retirement, she had from time to time been called upon to administer national examinations. Ifeoma's husband, on the other hand, was not a good student, and though offered positions because of his family's social standing, he couldn't hold onto any of them. Like Nkechi, Ifeoma was the main breadwinner in her family.

Ifeoma had become Nkechi's caregiver, and Nkechi had lived with Ifeoma at her house in Umuahia. It had been a period full of ups and downs. Ejituru had helped by sending money every month for Nkechi's maintenance and for the purchase of any equipment and drugs needed. Udo, another sister who lived in London, would give a paltry sum whenever she visited, but unlike Ejituru, she wanted to be given an account of expenditures.

Upon Nkechi's death, it fell on Ifeoma to contact her immediate siblings and to make all the arrangements for Ejituru, who was the woman's only natural child. Nkechi, the glue that held the family together in her lifetime, never gave preferential treatment to any of them. She regarded all of her husband's children as hers with no exception.

Not knowing Ejituru's financial situation, Ifeoma wanted to give her time to prepare. Before calling her, she'd called Michael, the oldest of her three brothers, who lived in Aba. When Michael finally arrived that morning after Nkechi's body had been moved to the mortuary in Umuahia, they'd had a face-off regarding the timing of the funeral. Given Nkechi's social position, the funeral was going to be expensive. She'd proposed a six-month waiting period, as this would give Ejituru time to prepare. She needed agreement on this before calling Ejituru and others.

But Michael, knowing he had the full support of his younger brothers, angrily said, "Why is this an issue? Isn't she our mother? Those of us here in Nigeria should make that decision. We fix the date, and the others decide whether to come. If those living abroad cannot come, they can send money. After all, it's not the first time we've had a funeral."

Ifeoma, still in shock and trying to come to terms with the death of a woman who meant so much to her, stared hard at her fortyeight-year-old brother sitting in the dining room of her Umuahia house eating cornflakes. Normally, as the temporary head of the family, his decision would be final. But in this case, it would be unfair to let him make that decision alone.

Fuming, she'd retorted, "Nkechi was Ejituru's mother, and we should leave that decision to her."

"Oh, for goodness' sake," Michael had said. "She may not even come to the funeral."

"What are you saying, Michael?" Ifeoma shouted, unable to believe what she was hearing. "Her mother is dead! Give me a break."

"As far as I'm concerned, that would be the best outcome, because we could bill her for a lot more money than we actually spend," Michael said. "It's the only way we can extract money from her. The funeral will cost more than a million naira, and this should be nothing to her since she's a doctor married to a specialist and living a sumptuous life in the US."

"Michael, do you hear yourself?" Ifeoma, overcome by emotion, wiped her eyes. "Nkechi is dead—the only mother we, the children of Onyeka, knew." Ifeoma wanted to remind Michael that Nkechi never differentiated between Onyeka's children and Ejituru, her only natural-born child. They owed it to her to contribute toward her funeral, even though Ejituru would be largely responsible, given their financial situation.

To bolster his case, Michael slammed his palm on the dining room table. "Have you forgotten that Ejituru never came home for our father's funeral, though Nkechi said she sent money to help defray the cost? Who knows whether the reason given was really as stated?"

"What are you implying?" Ifeoma lashed out. She also pounded the table. "You know very well the situation with her marriage."

"She probably didn't want to face her ex-husband's family," he replied, while getting up and washing his hands in the washbowl placed in the corner of the dining room.

"Nonsense!" Ifeoma exclaimed vehemently. "I can't believe what's coming out of your mouth! Our father would be turning in his grave to hear what you've said. Ignatius lied about his situation. Ignatius was probably carrying on with the woman who gave him a child all the time he was still married to Ejituru. Ignatius was to blame for the failure of the marriage."

"Are you sure?" Michael asked, raising his eyebrows.

"Our father knew that, or he wouldn't have accepted the bride price and payment from her current husband's family," Ifeoma retorted. "She didn't come to the funeral for reasons given. Full stop." Overcome by emotion, she fell down on the floor, weeping.

Nkem, Ifeoma's husband, a normally mild-mannered man, sat in a chair near the door. Seeing his wife so distressed, he stood up, walked up to Michael, and poked him in the chest. "Oga, listen," he said, in a voice full of venom. "If you aren't careful, I will let it be known among our kinsmen that you are a worthless son who's never contributed even a single kobo to defray the medical costs of the woman who did so much for you. Shame on you." He straightened up. "Tell me what you've ever done for Nkechi. She protected you all your life. She's not yet cold, and you're already thinking of how you can make money from her death. You have no shame. I've tolerated you all these years because of Nkechi, but now I want you out of my house immediately."

Ifeoma had to restrain him from fighting with Michael. When everybody calmed down, she said, "Brother, let's leave the decision to Ejituru. It's her mother who died."

Unfazed, Michael said, "You all seem to have forgotten that Nkechi hated keeping the body in cold storage for any length of time. She would prefer to be buried immediately, depending on the church's timetable. And six months in the mortuary would add to the expense of the funeral."

Ifeoma tried to tune out what was happening and to once again focus on what needed to be done. Nkechi's death wasn't entirely unexpected. She'd been ill for the past four years, and under Ifeoma's care for the better part of that period. That was the cause of estrangement from Michael, who felt that Nkechi was removed from his house because Ifeoma wanted to deprive him of the financial support that Ejituru gave for Nkechi's care.

Michael was just trying to flex his muscles and using Nkechi's death, she thought. She'd call Ejituru back and come to some agreement about the immediate expenses.

But Michael had struck a raw nerve, and it made Ifeoma examine her own feelings toward their father. She felt that she hardly knew him. He was the provider of the seed that brought her into this world and nothing else. She couldn't remember anytime during his life that she'd had an intimate discussion with him. She often puzzled over what he actually thought of Onyeka, the woman who gave birth to his children other than Ejituru. As far as she could see, she was just a vehicle for producing children. He never showed any affection toward her. He treated her as a servant and nothing more. He respected and deferred to Nkechi in everything. She was his confidant and, of course, his private purse.

She tried to think of any gift she had received from her father, but couldn't remember anything, except of course her arranged marriage with Nkem; if she could call that a gift. She was told about the arrangement, and she had to acquiesce, but she was happy about the choice, unlike Ejituru with Ignatius. Poor her! To be blamed for her absence at the funeral of the father who forced her into an unhappy marriage.

The fight with Michael was still fresh in her mind when she picked up the phone and redialed Ejituru.

∼✦⟨◊⟩✦∼

When Michael, the oldest son, got the news of Nkechi's death at five in the morning, he was in a quandary.

Ifeoma's call had come an hour after the event. "Come immediately to Umuahia," she said without any preamble.

"Ifeoma, it's five o'clock in the morning," he said, irritated. "Can't whatever it is wait until later?" He had gone to bed late and had other plans for the day. "Did something happen to you?" Maybe Ifeoma had been robbed, given the prevalence of armed robberies in Umuahia.

"It's not me, but Mama," Ifeoma said, weeping. "Is she in the hospital?" he asked.

"We found her dead an hour ago. I need you to come help me with the arrangements."

"Oh my God!" cried Michael. "I wasn't expecting it to happen now. I'll come immediately."

Michael's worst fear was that Nkechi would die just when he had no job and not a penny to his name. All eyes would be on him to fulfill his obligation to the woman he owed his life to. He shrugged off his pajama shirt, all the time thinking of his next step. First things first. He needed to find the money for his fare, since Ifeoma had said his presence was required before the body could be taken to the mortuary.

Wiping the sleep from his eyes, he tried to concentrate. He stood up, walked the few paces to the door leading to his small kitchen, and washed his face in the sink. He should call Ifeoma back to say he couldn't come before nine o'clock, when the bank opened. This ruse would give him time to find a moneylender, since he would be expected to share the cost of the mortuary. Shaking his head, he discarded this line of thought. Nkechi had not only raised him but was responsible for his education, and she was the person he could always rely upon to bail him out whenever he needed help. She'd had high hopes for him from the time he was born. After all, having him was the very essence of her life. It justified everything she did. It justified her position within her husband's family. He must go to Umuahia immediately, he decided.

He looked for his bag and brought out his wallet. He saw a fiftynaira note in it. That should be enough to get him to Umuahia, but after that he would have to lay his hands on more money. Ifeoma would require immediate cash for the mortuary in advance, and he had none. How would he be able to survive the resulting ridicule that he, Nkechi's firstborn son, could not afford to bury this woman who loved him so much and sacrificed so much for him?

Several times during the past months when Nkechi's health was deteriorating, Michael had hoped death wouldn't claim her until he was able to get himself together and be in a position to give her a suitable funeral. But her death had occurred at the most inopportune time for him.

His third wife had taken her three children and fled to the north, where her rich brother had promised to get her a job and settle her as befitting his only sister. He hadn't told anybody of this new event in his life. He was still hoping that she would see the evil of her ways and return to him. Now he couldn't even depend on the money she earned from her trading and her weaving business. She had dismantled the loom, packed up her clothes and that of her teenage children, and left. She didn't even have the courtesy to warn him beforehand of her intentions. He had come back home from his job search to find the flat empty of her things. He'd covered her absence by saying that she had temporarily gone to visit her sick brother. But how long would he be able to hide the truth? he wondered as he opened his front door to check the weather. It had been raining when he went to bed.

Michael wished he was living in the old days when there was no mortuary, and the only thing preventing a person from immediate burial was lack of a house. Funerals in those days were a simple affair, unless you were a chief; unlike now when funerals cost so much.

He had no money in the bank. It was only yesterday that one of his sons from his second wife had unexpectedly shown up to demand money for school fees and uniforms. He had scrounged around and found 1,000 naira left under the bed. He was grateful that his third wife had forgotten that she'd hidden the money there, or it would have gone like her to the North. The money had saved him from embarrassment. He'd asked his son to accept 950 naira and to ask for a delay in paying his school fees. Now he was grateful that he at least had 50 naira for transport to Umuahia, knowing that if he didn't answer Ifeoma's call, her husband would make sure that all the extended family knew about it, and he would be a pariah.

Thoughts of money always led him to remember that Ifeoma had robbed him of the opportunity to benefit from caring for Nkechi. Ever since, pressured by Ifeoma, Ejituru—his father's first daughter and Nkechi's only natural child—removed Nkechi from his care, he'd ceased to receive any money from Ejituru, nor to have contact with her. Ifeoma was her only line of communication and the beneficiary of her financial help. He remembered that during the call from Ifeoma, she had mentioned that because of the time difference, she had delayed the call to Ejituru until after the mortuary visit. He wondered whether Ejituru would be able to come for the funeral. She hadn't come for their father's funeral, but then Nkechi was still alive and financially capable, so the funeral expenses didn't pose a problem. Would she come for her mother's funeral?

Perhaps, given that it was her mother's funeral, she should bear the full responsibility. This line of thought temporarily freed him from any responsibility.

Feeling extremely restless, he walked around his tiny bedroom, realizing that he was fooling himself by thinking that he had no financial obligation, since all eyes would be on him, the first son, the family prince. He pulled on his pants, grabbed his batik shirt hanging on the peg on the wall, slipped on his flip-flops, locked his front door and went to the motor park, hoping to find a taxi bound for Umuahia.

When the taxi carrying him finally arrived at Ifeoma's gate at 7:30 a.m., he asked Ifeoma to pay the fare, pleading inability to get to the bank at that time of the morning. Later, at Ifeoma□s, smarting from his altercation regarding the timing of the funeral, he was glad that his two brothers would be arriving soon so they could support him on the timing of the traditional death announcements to the kindred. He was particularly happy because this task involved being given a substantial sum from the money Ejituru had sent for that purpose.

CHAPTER 3

In Silver Spring, Maryland, a suburb outside of Washington, DC, Ejituru paced her living room frantically. Just as she was about to redial Ifeoma, the phone rang. Controlling herself and remembering that decisions had to be made, she said into the phone, "Sister, when do you think will be appropriate for us to have the funeral? I know she hated the idea of a long stay at the mortuary."

"Michael said the same thing, but I think his idea is motivated by his own greed," replied Ifeoma.

"Why do you say so?" Ejituru asked, her voice full of concern.

"Oh, sister! Let's not go into that. Don't mind his foolishness. When do you think you'll arrive? That will determine when we can set the date. Of course, we still have to consult the church. Nowadays, funerals are booked in advance."

"Perhaps you're right, and this isn't the best time to talk about Michael. I think I should be able to come a week before the funeral, but I'm not sure about anything now because we've just moved here. I don't even know who'll take care of my children. I'll let you know when I can be there after I consult Nduka. Oh dear, I need to call him. He needs to know. Shall I call you later?" Ejituru began to sob.

"Sister, please hold yourself together," Ifeoma said into the phone, trying not to cry. "We need money right away. There are arrangements to be made."

Realizing that Ifeoma's immediate concern was monetary, Ejituru replied, "Sorry, Ifeoma, I'm not thinking straight. I wasn't expecting it to happen so soon, and I'm all alone in the house. Will two thousand dollars be enough to set things in motion?"

"Yes," Ifeoma answered, sounding relieved. "That should be sufficient for now."

"Let's agree on that then, my dear sister. I'll go to the Western Union to wire the money to you. I presume you'll have to let Udo and others know about it, and please let me know whether they intend to come home for the funeral." Ejituru paused for an intake of some air, feeling she had said too much. "Ifeoma, my sister, I'm sorry to pile this on you. I'll never forget it as long as I live. I'll let you know soon what the control number is," she added as an afterthought. Overcome with anguish, she rang off.

She tried to call Nduka, her second husband and her rock, but was told that he was in surgery and to leave a message. She decided not to.

Putting down the phone, she ran out of the house to the nearest Western Union on Thayer Street, only to realize that she had left her wallet at home. Back in her apartment, she called Nduka again but still couldn't reach him, so she went back to Thayer Street to wire the money.

When she called Ifeoma to give her the control number, she could hear the noise in the background, and she wished she was there in the midst of family to comfort and be comforted by them. It was the first time since she had left for the United States that she missed her extended family.

As if reading her mind and feeling the sadness, Ifeoma said, "Sister, both Nwankwo and Emeka are here, and we're just telling funny stories about Mama. By the way, I've spoken to the reverend, and the funeral will be in eight weeks. I hope that will give you enough time to plan."

Ejituru couldn't immediately respond because she was extremely agitated.

To fill the empty air between them, Ifeoma said, "Hold on, everybody wants to talk to you."

Ejituru made small talk with each of them before ending the call.

With her elbows on her dining room table and her hands on her face, she thought of her mother, Nkechi, who believed in the importance of education and, in particular, American education. "Mama!" she cried aloud. "I didn't have to come to America to become a pediatrician. I would have made it in Nigeria, but to you it would have been an inferior education for your daughter."

I agreed to that first marriage because I shared your belief in American education, and I was determined to get it by any means, she thought.

"Mama, wherever you are, I know you're happy that I did you proud," she murmured.

As if from far away, she heard the sound of the telephone. Her first thought was that it was a reminder from the school to pick up the kids. Instead, it was her husband returning her call. Hearing his voice, she burst into tears.

"I'm on my way, and will pick up the kids," he said.

She looked around the room but lacked the energy to resume unpacking. She lay flat on the sofa, weeping, and it was there that, thirty minutes later, her husband and children found her.

They enveloped her in their embrace. "Mama, don't be sad," the children said.

Lifting her tear-stained face, she saw the love in their eyes and was comforted. She gently got up to embrace each one of them, then went and washed her face. She came back and drank the tea that her husband had prepared while the children told her stories about their day.

Later in the evening, when the children had gone to bed, Ejituru and Nduka sat down as they did most nights to share the events of the day quietly. Lost in thought, she was brought back by Nduka's touch and his voice saying, "Was it Ifeoma who gave you the news?"

For a moment, she looked at his strong face, full of emotion. She noted the small strands of white hair in his eyebrows and his hair gradually graying. Then she nodded and said, "She also needed money for the mortuary, among other things that she has to do."

"I presume she has to inform all the extended family on both sides," he said.

"Yes. But I must tell you that my mother's death made me think of the event leading up to my previous marriage. I'd always blamed my father for the wasted years and the hardship I suffered because of my mother's belief that American education justified all the suffering of my first marriage."

"Ej. I thought we agreed to put all that in the past," Nduka murmured. "Yes, but I have given this some thought, and I feel I could not totally blame my father. His need to free himself from his financial dependency on my mother through alignment with rich inlaws played a major role in his decision. But I also think that he genuinely believed he was securing my future."

"In a way, he did."

"Yes, but not in the way he envisioned, since the marriage brought me to the United States. While it took longer for me to obtain my medical certification, the fault was not entirely his." She paused to take a breath while her eyes sought his agreement.

Nduka coughed and added, "I tend to agree with you. Like everybody in the village involved in the marriage arrangements, he was hoodwinked by your ex, who presented himself as something he was not. How could they have known that he was a taxi driver and not an engineer as he said?"

Ejituru thoughtfully replied, "Having lived all these years in the US, I've come to know the various lies and half-truths Nigerian immigrants tell their relatives in order to appear successful. My father should not bear the blame alone. I should have fought most forcefully with my father. There were times during that fateful summer that I could have stood my ground. But my dear Nduka, the lure of going to America was such that I felt I could do nothing but acquiesce."

Nduka, laughing, said, "The marriage was doomed from the start."

She nodded, adding, "Besides, how could the family have known that he had no intention of helping me pursue my dream?"

She gazed at him and thought, We were meant to be together.

Otherwise, how could one explain our running into each other in the quadrangle at Howard University, of all places, after ten years of separation? She remembered the shock she had felt at seeing him again after all those years. She'd left the medical program at Nsukka without saying goodbye. Although, come to think of it, she never had given him any hope of marriage, even though she loved him and knew he loved her. If she had acknowledged that love at the time, she knew she would have run afoul of her mother, who wanted her to achieve the highest education level possible before any thought of marriage could be contemplated. To her mother, Nkechi, education was very important, and being a doctor the ultimate prize.

Returning to the moment, she said, "I talked to my half-brothers today." "Did they call you?"

"Oh, no. They were at Ifeoma's in Umuahia, where Mama died." "How did that go?" He enfolded her in his arms.

"What could we say to each other?" she whispered. "I'm not close to any of them, although it was always Mama's wish that I should have a closer relationship with all my half-siblings."

Just then they heard the footsteps of their eldest daughter, fourteen-year-old Nneka, going to the bathroom. Nduka let go of Ejituru and went to make sure that the children had finally settled in for the night. When he came back, he sat facing her.

"I'm really dreading going home to face my siblings," she said. "We've never been close."

"I've noticed that," he said in a voice full of emotion. "Why is that? I often wish I had many more brothers and sisters, but as you know, it's just my brother and I."

"I really don't know why. I sometimes feel that it's because we were competing for Mama's affection. You remember her last letter to me before she became ill?"

"You mean the one you read bits of to me? I remember the part that said she hoped that all of you, her children, would get on, or something like that. Perhaps that letter would help you come to terms with your siblings."

"I've been thinking of it since I heard the news because Mama was the glue that held all of us together," Ejituru said. "With her gone, we've no need for each other. But I don't want to take the letter with me and read it to everyone. It wouldn't solve anything. Besides, it's a private letter sent to me, and it contains information I don't want to share."

Wiping away her tears, Nduka tried to comfort her before resuming the conversation. "I've always been curious about how your mother, an educated woman, was willing to share your father with another woman."

Before answering, she conjured up in her mind all the bad feelings associated with having half-siblings who despised her. She had always avoided having to deal with them whenever she visited. Could she avoid them this time? During such moments, she cursed her mother for bringing Onyeka into the house. But on one level, she understood her need for a male child, so she said glumly, "My mother needed the security a male child brings to a marriage, especially when one is constantly treated as a stranger by the inlaws. She had three miscarriages before having me, her only child, and after my birth, she had an ectopic pregnancy. The doctor told her of the danger she faced if she tried again." "How sad for her," Nduka murmured.

Ignoring the interruption and bent on telling her story, Ejituru said, "She realized she couldn't have any more children, so on the advice of my father's sister and confidant, she chose a young girl, Onyeka, from a poor rural family, as her wife, whom she could mold to do her bidding."

"My experience is just the exact opposite. My mother had sons, but her biggest fear was not having a daughter, but having a daughter-in-law she couldn't get along with. It must have been hard for your mother to make such a decision, especially since polygamy is forbidden by the church." Shaking his head, he studied her face.

Ejituru laughed. "You talk as if you don't know that polygamy is still widely practiced. Some rich men pick one wife as their official wife, even though they're married to others."

Nduka looked into her eyes. He remained silent, allowing her to continue.

"As far as the church was concerned, my mother was the official wife. In any case, from Nkechi's perspective, Onyeka wasn't my father's wife but her wife, chosen to produce children for her. It was she who was marrying Onyeka. This was a better arrangement than having my father take on concubines. In this case, my mother had control over who he brought into the household." She got up and went to the kitchen to get some snacks and juice. When she came back, she searched his face, hoping that he would have some positive things to say.

Instead, he remained silent, as if he was still processing what she had said. When she sat down, he asked, "How old was the chosen one?"

"At that time, Onyeka was fourteen years old. It was agreed that when the girl turned eighteen, the marriage ceremony would be completed, and Onyeka, as Nkechi's wife, would be presented to Nwakama as someone with whom he could have children. Nkechi was happy with the services provided by Onyeka and had begun to give her more responsibility in the management of her small garrigrating operation, the income from which augmented her small teaching salary."

"I'm surprised your father agreed to such an arrangement. My father, who unfortunately you didn't meet, would have found the arrangement unthinkable, even though he longed for a daughter. Surely your father must have had a say about who should be chosen."

"You've forgotten that my mother held the purse strings. My father wouldn't have been able to support a second wife. However, my mother's pursuit of education hastened the process." Ejituru laughed mirthlessly as she spoke. "A year after Onyeka's arrival, she enrolled in a course to earn a diploma in education at Nsukka and left her in charge of me, who at that time was three years old, and of her business. In the beginning, my mother came home frequently on weekends, but as her course work became more difficult, she sometimes would stay away for more than a fortnight. At the end of the year, she found out that Onyeka was pregnant." "Bound to happen," Nduka chuckled gently.

Telling this part of her mother's story lifted Ejituru's spirits, and she could see how the choice her mother made precipitated the outcome, so she said, "I was just three years old then, and I can only tell you my mother's version of the situation."

Nduka stopped laughing for a minute before saying, "I didn't mean to make fun of it. I'm really interested in knowing how you became part of this large family that you feel apart from."

Visibly upset, Ejituru kept silent for a second before saying, in a voice reflecting her sadness, "Apparently, at first Onyeka wouldn't disclose the name of her partner until Nkechi threatened to send her back home and cut off all ties with her, since she couldn't be expected to take on another man's child. Onyeka confessed, and accused our father of being the culprit."

"Fireworks!" Nduka said with a straight face. "Boom!"

Ejituru ignored the sarcasm and continued her story. "Faced with the truth, my mom confronted her husband, who in turn blamed her for putting her ambition before his needs. She felt that her husband had preempted her, forcing her to hasten the process of marrying Onyeka." Overcome with emotion, Ejituru rubbed her eyes, but before Nduka could react, she recovered her composure and continued. "My mother didn't want Onyeka's child, if it turned out to be a boy, to be a bastard. She had no choice but to hasten the process and marry Onyeka. That was how Chinyere became my little sister. Onyeka would go on to produce for her two more daughters and three sons. All children from the union were treated as Nkechi's natural children. The much-sought-after son, Michael, came two years later, after Chinyere."

Sitting there with her husband holding her, Ejituru again wept for her mother, whose only wish was to secure her family's future by giving her husband what he desired most: a male child.

CHAPTER 4

For the next five weeks, Ejituru set aside her grief. While she concentrated on the task of setting up the household in a new city, she kept in touch with Ifeoma on the progress of the various arrangements that needed to be made for Nkechi. She found a housekeeper, a woman from Honduras recommended by her nanny in Dallas, who'd been with her since the birth of her first child, Nneka, and had seen her through the birth of the twins, Rosaline and Godwin, now twelve years old.

Leaving the nanny in Dallas had been a hard decision, since they had become close, but she knew that if she were in difficulty at any time, this wonderful lady would come to help her out. She'd considered asking her to come to Silver Spring for the period she would be in Nigeria, as this would soften the impact of her absence on the children. But with her own family in Dallas, the nanny had rejected the idea. However, the new housekeeper had bonded well with the children, and Ejituru had made Nduka promise that if the occasion were to arise, he wouldn't hesitate to ask her to help out temporarily.

She arranged with her clinic for a temporary pediatrician to sub for the duration of her stay in Nigeria. The week before she was due to depart, she came home from work and found the house strangely quiet. Normally, Nduka had no surgery on this day of the week and would be supervising the children's homework, but today, she heard not a sound from any one of them.

Dropping her bag, she went into the kitchen and found the housekeeper preparing to leave. "Emelda, you're still here? Are you almost done? Where is everybody?" She fired off each question without waiting for a reply.

"Oh yes, the doctor came early and took the children out. He said to tell you they'll be back soon. He said not to cook."

Shaking her head, Ejituru left the kitchen area and rapidly proceeded to her bedroom to remove her work clothes. Shortly after, she heard the arrival noise of the children and the loud bang of the door.

"Mama, where are you?" Nneka called. "Come and see what Daddy has.

I bet you'll be surprised!"

Ejituru silently walked to the living room and saw a set of suitcases for her journey. They were what she needed, and she'd been planning to buy some on the weekend. She was touched, and unintended tears filled her eyes. In addition to buying the suitcases, her husband had made reservations at a French restaurant for the family that evening. It was a typical Nduka thing to do, and she again was grateful that she had him in her life.

Later on, when they were alone, he said, "Ej, would you like us all to go with you? We could arrive the day before the funeral, in which case the children wouldn't miss much."

For a second, Ejituru wanted to say yes, feeling that she would need the comfort of this man by her side, but then reason took over, and she remembered that they'd examined carefully how much this funeral would set them back financially. She shook her head and said, "It would be selfish of me to insist that you all come with me. Realistically, I think we've made the right decision. I'll go alone."

"Have you been able to find the last letter you received from Nkechi? Remember, we talked about it." He crossed his arms as if he was about to say something difficult. "I know you said you didn't want to, but I think it would be nice if at some opportune time you could share her thoughts with your siblings. It may be what you need to draw the family together. With Nkechi gone, the tendency will be for you all to go your own way."

"You know I really don't want to read the letter," Ejituru said.

Holding her hand, he said, "Ej, you should at least have a gathering of the family before you travel back to the States. This will give you closure. Your conscience will be clear, and you'll feel that you've somehow carried out your mother's wishes. Think about it."

Ejituru kept quiet. She didn't want the evening to end on a sour note. But on the day of her departure, the letter was with her passport and travel documents.

~∽✧❀✧∾~

In spite of the lingering heat and occasional breeze, Ifeoma had been waiting at Port Harcourt International Airport for over an hour for the arrival of Air France from Paris. The waiting area was unusually overcrowded and noisy, and she had to strain to hear the announcements. Sweating profusely, she wiped her face with the tail end of her top wrapper. Every now and then someone would tap her shoulder, seeking information regarding the plane's arrival. As the arrival time drew near and there was no sighting of the plane, Ifeoma felt a knot in her stomach marking how anxious she was that something might go wrong and Ejituru wouldn't arrive in time for the proposed family meeting the next day.

Relieved to see the plane approach and land, she strained to discover whether Ejituru was among the disembarking passengers and was relieved when she saw her. It took almost an hour for the passengers to start trickling out of the exit.

As Ejituru muscled her way through the crowd, she heard someone calling her name and looked ahead to see Ifeoma's lit-up face.

"Sister!" Ifeoma shouted. "Thank God, you had a safe journey. Welcome home." Ifeoma rushed toward Ejituru and embraced her while her driver handled the suitcases.

Shocked by Ifeoma's unexpected presence, Ejituru tried to mask her irritation. "Ey ee, I wasn't expecting you to come for me. You already have a lot on your plate without taking me on." She'd intended to spend the night at the airport hotel and to travel the next day in time for the proposed family gathering to complete the financial arrangements for the funeral. To this end, she'd made arrangements for a taxi to meet her at the airport. "When I called to tell you my plans, I only needed your address for the taxi I intended to hire from here. The taxi must be here somewhere, since Nduka arranged for it with a friend of his in Owerri."

Just then a tall, skinny man wearing light-blue brocade trousers and a shirt bearing a placard with her name approached them. "Ej, you've not changed. I would have recognized you immediately," said Philip, who'd been designated by Nduka to meet Ejituru's plane. Philip had been in the same medical program at Nsukka as Nduka and had a practice in Owerri.

Ejituru shook his hand and said in a contrite voice, "Philip, thank you for coming out to meet me." She nervously rubbed her palms together.

Ifeoma beamed and offered an effusive greeting.

"There's been a bit of confusion," Ejituru said. "My fault entirely. I wasn't expecting my sister, but she's here with a car. I'll go home with her instead of to the hotel as previously planned."

Phillip, who had already surmised the situation, said, "I fully understand. The taxi driver is very trustworthy. He'll come for you tomorrow in Umuahia and will be with you during your stay in the country." Then he turned to Ifeoma and said, "Mama Ifeoma, it's a pleasure to meet you. Please give the driver your address. By the way, if you all have time, perhaps we can go to the airport bar and have a drink before you head off."

Ifeoma turned to Ejituru. "It's getting late, and we have at least two hours to drive. I suggest we skip the bar."

Pleading with her eyes, Ejituru said, "I'm concerned for Phillip, since he'll be returning to Owerri tonight."

"No," said Phillip, waving his hands dismissively. "I have business here in Port Harcourt tomorrow."

Relieved, Ejituru chitchatted with him about the journey and his future plans. She again thanked him for being so understanding and left to accompany Ifeoma to her home.

⚜

Finally alone with Ejituru, and just as the luggage was being stored in the trunk, Ifeoma, who all the time couldn't restrain herself, posed the question she'd been bursting to ask. "When is Nduka arriving? Everyone will be expecting him."

Thrown off balance by this question, Ejituru was confused, then recovering, she bristled. "Why was he expected? Are those expecting him paying the airfare?" She took a breath and caught herself as the car exited the car park and moved on to the airport road. In a more conciliatory voice she said, "At first, we thought all of us would come, but that proved too expensive, knowing how much the funeral itself would cost us," Ejituru said. Staring at the food stands and shacks lining the road as the car entered the junction from the airport road to the road to Aba, she said in a faraway voice, "Besides, one of us has to be at home for the kids. I'm sure Mama would understand." By this time the sun had long set, and at six o'clock in the evening, the streets were crowded with shoppers.

Ifeoma sighed. "I understand, but I mentioned it because the rest will capitalize on his absence."

"Let them think what they like. You visited us several times in Dallas, and you know the problem of getting help in the US. We don't have unlimited resources, contrary to what people think, to pay for an expensive funeral and to pay for five people to fly over from the US at the same time. My only regret is that we were trying to save enough money for the children to visit Mama next year, even though we knew that, with her Alzheimer's, she wouldn't know who they were." Tears trickled down her face as she spoke.

The tears made Ifeoma regret her question. She looked out of the window and could see a line of small shops lit with paraffin lamps and knots of people haggling with the shopkeepers, and a young girl being berated by an elderly woman she thought must be her grandmother. She felt that she too had just dealt a blow to Ejituru and at that moment, she heard her sister's calm voice ask, "Who else will be coming?"

"Udo called to tell me she arrived yesterday. She traveled with Sarah. I invited them to stay at my house, but not surprisingly, they declined. I understand they're at a hotel in town."

By this time, the car was passing stretches of road where one could see narrow paths leading to small villages separated from the major road by small strips of palm groves. Looking out of the car window, Ejituru could see dots of light reflected by the paraffin lamps those on these paths were holding. She wondered what their day had been like and what type of welcome they expected at home. Then she heard Ifeoma in a faraway voice, as if remembering a difficult conversation, say, "You know I had a falling out with her?"

Wrenched back to the present, feigning surprise, she asked. "What happened?"

"She often sent money to me for Mama's care, as you're well aware," Ifeoma replied, with a serious expression on her face, her voice rising as she adjusted her headdress. "But what you don't know is that she always insisted on an itemized list of expenditures. Believe me, sister, I would have gladly given her the list, but I resented that she would predicate the gift by letting me know that as a single mother, her life in London was not a bed of roses, and she had to allocate her resources carefully."

By this time, the car was passing a stretch of road where there were thickets of palm trees as far as the eye could see, and bunches of palm fruits waiting to be picked up by lorries in the morning. Ejituru, fascinated by all the development on the road since she'd last visited, gradually tried to refocus on what Ifeoma was saying.

"Calm down, Ifeoma. That's in the past, and there's no need for you to get heated up now." She patted Ifeoma's hand.

"I know, sister, but it really bugged me. Last year, do you know what I did?" Before Ejituru could answer, she plunged ahead. "I lost it, and sent back the money with a note saying that there was no need for her to deprive herself of necessities just to assuage her guilt over not caring for her mother." "You didn't!" exclaimed Ejituru.

When Ifeoma saw the effect her words had on Ejituru, she tried to soften her expression. "Yes, I did. Tomorrow will be the first time we've met since then."

Ejituru took her hand and softly massaged it as she asked, "When are the boys arriving?"

"Tomorrow morning, by public transport," Ifeoma replied.

Still holding her hand, Ejituru said with a voice full of concern, "Sister, to be frank, I, too, am dreading meeting everyone, especially Chinyere. Is she coming?"

For a while there was complete silence in the car. When they entered Aba, the car slowed almost to a halt as they were bombarded by vendors trying to entice them to make a purchase. Ifeoma, distracted by the vendors, didn't reply immediately. But when she did, she said, "To be frank, I've never been close to Chinyere. I know nothing of her life since she left home."

Ejituru looked askance at her. "But I thought you stayed with her on your way to visit me some time ago."

Ifeoma adjusted her position on the seat. "It was a visit that I will never forget." Her voice reflected her frustration. Shaking her head as she tried to recollect what happened, she continued. "Chinyere spent the whole time I was with her telling me about all the ills that family members, especially Nkechi, did to her and our biological mother, Onyeka. It was torture being in her house, and I was glad to get out of there." Turning to face Ejituru and realizing that her attention was elsewhere, she paused. Then, she said in a determined and slightly raised voice, "Sister! To answer your question, we've not heard anything from her. I did call her to tell her of the meeting tomorrow, but so far, there's not been even a peep from her."

This got Ejituru's attention, who replied in a voice tinged with sadness, "Why did it all go wrong? She was my little sister, whom I adored, and I thought she adored me. Mama's plan was for her to follow me to Ibiaku. Mama loved her, and sometimes I was a bit jealous of that love, but that was before the arrival of Michael."

By this time, the car entered the Aba-Umuahia road where there was a lot of activity at the junction. The noise was deafening as the music from each vehicle competed with one another. People milled around trying to haggle with the traders in the dim light cast by the paraffin lamps. Their passage was blocked by a lorry whose passengers were intent on buying some snacks for their immediate consumption. The drivers blew their horns as a way of attracting the attention of the errant lorry driver. Ejituru rolled down the window to lessen the heat in the car but this attracted moths and gnats drawn by the light in the car, as well as several youngsters, anxious to make trades, towards their car. Since Ifeoma had no intention of buying anything at this junction, she quickly urged the driver to roll up the windows.

After a quarter of an hour sitting in the sweltering car, the errant driver blew his horn and finally drove away. Once on the road, except for the taillights of cars or lorries preceding them, the pale light of the moon cast a mysterious haze on the world outside the car. Ifeoma scrunched up her face in an attempt to remember things that happened a long time ago.

"I was perhaps six years old at the time of Chinyere's pregnancy, and I can remember the ruckus over her refusal to go to Ibiaku. It was the only thing we talked about at home. We were all shocked that she'd refused to go to such a prestigious school, especially since Mama had lobbied very hard for her to be accepted. She claimed she wanted to live at home and be near her friends. Mama was very upset."

Sitting there in the car, Ejituru wondered why Ifeoma was dwelling on the past. Then she decided to humor her. Shrugging, she said, "I can just see Mama, with eyes blazing, castigating Chinyere for ruining her future. We all know how much Mama valued education."

"Who can blame her?" Ifeoma vehemently responded. "She wanted all of us to get at least a secondary school diploma." She scowled as she remembered the incident. "Mama used her influence to get her into a day secondary school, and you know what happened there."

"I missed all that." Ejituru reluctantly turned away from the road to face Ifeoma. "Did she ever say who Sarah's father was?"

"To be frank, sister, it was all hush-hush," Ifeoma recalled, all the time swiveling in her seat "It was one of those things that was never openly discussed. If asked about Chinyere, we would say that she was in Jos with a relative."

"It must have been hard for all of you to keep such a secret," Ejituru interjected.

"It really was, but we knew that Mama was ready to punish anyone who broke the rule. She did not tolerate gossip, especially when it involved family members." Ifeoma breathed heavily.

"I remember that Sarah was passed as Onyeka's daughter for Nkechi, and that practically silenced any gossip." Ejituru, finally animated, warmed up to the story. "I wonder how many people actually believed that lie."

"If they didn't, nobody said anything openly." Ifeoma shook her head as she spoke.

"I can't understand why Mama allowed her to keep the baby," Ejituru said. "Da Erima, our beloved aunt, apparently wanted the pregnancy terminated so that Chinyere could complete her education. She was, after all, only thirteen or fourteen, I can't remember which." Her heart swelled with emotion.

Ifeoma, steepling her hands as if in prayer, thoughtfully responded, "I think Mama was conflicted. She must have remembered her own struggle with pregnancy and the many lives lost through the hands of incompetent midwives. She wanted to protect Chinyere's future."

"What future?" Ejituru exclaimed, not caring whether the driver heard her.

"I presume that's why she decided that the best scenario was to send her to live with Onyeka, away from prying eyes, until the child was born. A conjecture on my part, since I wasn't privy to that decision." Ifeoma sniffled and wiped her nose.

Ejituru nodded, staring out of the window to the outside now lit by electricity, heralding that they had entered Umuahia. "You're probably right. But I wonder how Chinyere sees it, and whether she feels it was the best thing for her. This may partially explain why she hated Mama so much."

Ifeoma blew her nose with the handkerchief she'd tucked in the side pocket of her handbag. She hesitated before saying, "Perhaps not. It all began with an incident at school when she was in third grade. One of the kids got in a fight with her and mocked her by telling her who her mother actually was. Until then, she believed she was Nkechi's child and your full sister."

"Come to think of it, perhaps being rude to Mama was her way of dealing with the situation," Ejituru thoughtfully replied. "What do you think?"

Ifeoma cleared her throat. "You're definitely right in your observation. I confronted her once about her attitude toward Nkechi, and she vehemently said that Nkechi needed to be put in her place, since she never was able to give our father a male child."

Before Ejituru could think of a response, the sound of the car horn was announcing their arrival.

The gate opened, and the car entered Ifeoma's yard.

CHAPTER 5

Chinyere, the fifty-one-year-old daughter of Nkechi from Onyeka, arrived in Umuahia early that morning from Lagos. In her youth, she was considered a beauty, having inherited her mother's rich, brown skin and dreamy eyes. Slightly under five feet, now fat and shapeless, she never lived up to that promise. The first thing one noticed about her was the fleshy rim of skin on her neck. Having lost most of her hair due to overprocessing, she wore a loosely tied head scarf, the same color as her long, wide buba.

When she first received the message about Nkechi, she had responded,

"Good riddance. I'll never have to deal with her or her daughter ever again." That evening, at dinner, she'd mentioned it in passing to Phillip, her husband, and was surprised at his reaction.

"When did it happen?" he asked, his voice full of emotion. "What's the big deal?" she said. "She meant nothing to me."

The next morning, she refilled his prescription, since he'd been ill with acute malaria. When she returned home, he told her that he'd called Ifeoma to express his condolences and to inquire about the arrangements. When the date was fixed, Ifeoma would let him know.

A fortnight before the event, he summoned Chinyere to the bedroom. Without waiting for her to sit down, as was normally the case when they discussed important family issues, he said, "You're going to your mother's funeral. I'd like to go, but my health isn't good, as you know."

She looked at him in disgust. She hadn't seen Nkechi since her father's death. Knowing how much she hated Nkechi, why would this man dare to make such a suggestion? Gathering herself together, she stared at his face, wrinkled and yellowed by malaria, then lashed out at him. "Not in this world!"

He raised his hand to slap her but restrained himself. In a calm, strong voice, he announced, "I'll not brook any objection. You're going to pay your respects to this great woman who has done so much for you."

Shocked at the vehemence of his words, she was speechless. She breathed deeply. After a few minutes of silence, she responded, "I don't intend to ever see her or her daughter again."

"You're going, and you're going to contribute to the funeral expenses," he retorted. "No argument." He banged the table for emphasis.

It had become a sore point between them until two days ago, when she finally bought the bus ticket. He'd given her twenty thousand naira as their family contribution to the funeral expenses.

Now Chinyere stood in the Umuahia bus station, being bombarded by the noise of car engines and horns and the sound of touts trying to corral passengers for buses or to sell them some food to aid them on their journey. Struck by the throng of people who had risen at the crack of dawn to catch the buses for faraway places or to meet loved ones arriving at that hour; she wondered why she was at this place instead of her home in Yaba with her husband, who had saved her from the ogre and whatever plans Nkechi had for her after the birth of her illegitimate daughter, Sarah.

She recalled the anguished discussions between her father and Nkechi about what to do with her when her pregnancy was discovered. She'd always maintained that Nkechi was more concerned about preserving her name and position in the church than she was with her. It was the reason she'd sent her away from home to live with Onyeka in the farm village. She remembered how much she'd hated the six months she'd spent there. She'd come home after the experience of giving birth feeling like a stranger. She was forbidden to touch the child, who immediately became Onyeka's child for Nkechi.

Lost in thought, she forgot where she was at the moment and was only reminded of it when she was pushed by a wheelbarrow full of sacks of onions.

A man yelled, "Woman, move out of the way!"

Apologizing, she picked up her bag and moved toward the taxi stand. She couldn't go to Ifeoma's house directly from the bus station. She needed to tidy up in order to look her best when those jackals in her family laid eyes on her. She decided to pay a short visit to a friend from elementary school who she knew lived in the area.

As the taxi carried her along the streets of Umuahia, just starting to come to life after the night, she thought of the day she had left home after her return from giving birth. It was the happiest day of her life. She was leaving to start afresh.

She remembered fondly the family she stayed with. The head of the family, a teacher at the Catholic secondary school in Aba, was Nkechi's relative. As a favor to Nkechi, he had agreed to take her into their house and to enroll her in a secretarial school managed by his wife. They treated her as a family member, letting her out of some housework so she could practice her shorthand.

When they found out that she was having a secret relationship with her now husband, they'd cautioned her but had never threatened to report her to Nkechi. Phillip had struck up a conversation with her at the gate of the school and had immediately taken a shine to her. He'd bought her peanuts and oranges from a vendor near the gate and made her promise to come to the hotel where he was staying to see him. At first, she didn't accept his invitation, but when he came again to the school, he had asked about her.

Until then, no man had ever shown any true interest in her. Her pregnancy was not a result of love for the boy but because she was extremely reckless in those years, having become sexually active at a very young age.

She recalled how it all started. She was sharing a room with Udo, and one night she'd fallen out of bed to the floor, where the young male servant was sleeping. The next thing she knew, he had had sex with her. Chinyere didn't see any harm in having sex with him, and she had felt alive to have someone close to her who was regarded as a troublemaker in the house. Not having reached puberty, she had no fear of pregnancy. She had eagerly anticipated the next night and had deliberately fallen down to sleep with him, hoping it would happen again. But it never did, because he was afraid of being discovered and losing his job because of it. Each night, she had deliberately fallen down to sleep with him.

She looked out the window of the taxi and saw a young man whose face reflected his fear of crossing the road amid all the cars and trucks jousting with each other for advantage. It reminded her of the face of that young man on the morning after, afraid their secret would become common knowledge. She'd used this knowledge to manipulate him to do her bidding. Shortly after, he'd left to go back to his Ibibio village, ostensibly to help his parents. She wondered what had happened to him.

She'd often felt that her promiscuity was Nkechi's fault in that she created a situation that brought it about. She shouldn't have had a young man sleeping in the same room as her daughters. Why didn't she put him in precious Ejituru's room, where Ifeoma slept? She didn't expose Ejituru to that. Why her, then? It was Nkechi's fault that she'd quickly progressed from that to other boys in her secondary school, believing that she would never become pregnant. Her pregnancy was a result of a dare by her girlfriend, the very one to whose house she was bound, who never believed that she was promiscuous and had dared her to have sex with her boyfriend in her presence to prove it. The act itself meant nothing to her at that time. She wouldn't even have remembered it except for the consequences.

She looked around at the men and women going about their early morning business, and she wondered what they were all thinking and where they were going.

Living in Aba, she was thrilled that such an important man as Phillip, a retired military officer and a businessman, had noticed her. He was there to meet with clients, and happened to have met her outside the secretarial school, chatting with friends. He'd persuaded her to accompany him to his hotel, and that was how it all began. After several such rendezvous, he'd invited her to quit the secretarial school and follow him to Lagos, where he would send her to a better school and help her find a suitable job.

Giddy with love, she ran away with him to Lagos. Of course, this had resulted in a schism between Nkechi and the family in Aba, which was only recently healed. Her marriage was only recognized after the birth of her son, when her husband had come to her family to carry out the bride price, which legitimized the marriage. Her only regret was that she never told him that Sarah was her child but had introduced Sarah as Nkechi's last-born child. Later in their marriage, she'd felt that he knew about Sarah but had decided to keep this knowledge private. She had always been grateful to him for having given her a purpose in life and a family that accepted her, so perhaps going to this funeral was a small price to pay for his enormous gift to her.

Chinyere disembarked from the taxi and the gateman took her bag and ushered her into the yard, where Kate, her friend from childhood, welcomed her. It was the first time they'd met since her father's funeral, though they'd talked many times on the phone and she'd been helpful when her son was in secondary school in Umuahia. She was struck by how beautiful and fresh Katie looked. Seeing Kate made her realize what her life would have been if she hadn't recklessly thrown away her chance at secondary school. Kate had gone on to university and was now a principal of a secondary school in Umuahia.

Watching her, Chinyere saw herself as perhaps a secondary schoolteacher and, like this woman, making her life better for her birth mother. Then she flinched, arguing that her life had been good. She'd married a nice man. She loved her children, who had excelled in school, and she had nothing to regret.

"Nkechi's death is a great loss," Kate said. "Please accept my sympathy. I saw Ifeoma yesterday, and she said Ejituru was arriving this evening by Air France."

Chinyere nodded and embraced her friend.

"Have you heard from Udo or Sarah?" Kate asked as the two moved toward the door. "When will they arrive?"

"Now that you mention it, Udo often overnights in my house on her arrival from London, but this time she didn't. Perhaps she isn't coming." Chinyere entered the living room, which was sumptuously furnished with imported furniture.

"Have you heard recently from Sarah? You're on good terms with her, aren't you?"

"I won't say we're friends, if that's what you mean. She was pleasant enough when she came for her interview at the American embassy. But since she left, we've not heard from her. With that one, you can never tell what's in her mind." She rubbed her eyes. "To answer your question, she doesn't know I'm coming."

"What of Ifeoma?" Kate asked. "She deserves to know that you'll be there, given that she's borne the brunt of your stepmother's illness and it's in her house you're all meeting." Kate opened the drapes to let in the early morning light.

"Nobody knows," Chinyere said. "Ifeoma telephoned Phillip to tell him of the arrangements, but she doesn't know of my arrival. I want my arrival to be a surprise." She laughed hilariously. "What an unexpected shock that'll be!" She stretched her arms as they sat down on the sofa.

Kate looked at Chinyere's tired face. "My friend, you're full of surprises. Come, have a bath and rest a little before going to fight your next battle." With a mock laugh, she led Chinyere to the guest bedroom.

CHAPTER 6

When Udo, Ejituru's sister from Onyeka, called to give her the news of Nkechi's death, Sarah was devastated. She was about to leave her apartment in Bowie, Maryland, to catch the bus, when the phone rang and it was Udo. She'd only given her the phone number a week ago.

Growing up, Sarah, now thirty five, knew no other mother than Nkechi. Although she'd met Chinyere during the few times she'd visited, she regarded her as an older aunt in the same situation as Ejituru, living far away and visiting from time to time. But unlike the other aunts, Chinyere never tried to get close to her and would do her utmost to avoid her. In contrast, Sarah felt adored by Udo and Ifeoma, who both treated her as their little sister, always showering her with gifts. During the few times that Ejituru visited, she, too, would make sure that she gave her some money, explaining that she thought she would prefer to choose her own gift.

However, during her last year in primary school, Sarah found out that she was Nkechi's granddaughter, not her daughter. It was during one of Chinyere's fleeting visits, when a dear friend of Nkechi visiting the family during Nkechi's absence made a passing comment. "You're looking more and more like your mother every day. Is she in? I hear she's visiting."

Who else should I look like? Sarah thought. "Mama Nkechi isn't here. She just left for the compound."

The woman looked hard at her and said, "I meant Chinyere."

Sarah couldn't understand why the woman would mistake Chinyere for her mother. She'd tried to dismiss it from her head, arguing that older women are sometimes universally called Mother.

But it gnawed on her like a toothache, so much so that, at an appropriate time long after Chinyere had left, she'd gone to Nkechi and asked her outright if Chinyere was her mother.

"Yes," Nkechi had said without prevaricating. "She had you very young and couldn't take care of you, so I adopted you." She rubbed Sarah's nose in a playful way. "It makes no difference who gave birth to you. You're both my daughter and my granddaughter."

It was a very emotional moment for her. Nkechi's comforting words and actions helped her forget all the times Chinyere had ignored her very existence whenever she visited. From that day on, she locked her anger against Chinyere in the inner recesses of her heart, where, from time to time, it still surfaced.

The news of Nkechi's death hit Sarah hard. She was incoherent for a while. When she calmed down, Udo asked if she thought she would go home for the funeral.

"Of course," she said in the midst of her sobbing. "Is there any doubt? She's the only mother I knew. I have to pay her this respect. Let me call you back. I have to let the office know I'll be home today." She lay in bed weeping the rest of the morning. When she called Udo back, she asked, "When is the funeral?"

"In two months' time," Udo said. "They're giving us time to get ready for it. Ifeoma said there's a lot to be done before then. Incidentally, have you contacted Ejituru to let her know you're now in the US?"

The question hung in the air while Sarah tried to find an appropriate response. She coughed and cleared her throat, and then said, "No, I intend to do so once I'm settled. But please don't give anybody my telephone number. Promise you'll let me know the date as soon as possible." Sarah wept uncontrollably as she let go of the phone.

The news couldn't have come at a worse time for Sarah. She'd been living in the US for a year, having won the diversity visa lottery, and had been struggling to stand on her own two feet. She'd had problems finding an affordable apartment and had lived with various friends until two months ago. The last place she lived, she'd had a falling out with the owner's wife, who accused her of trying to take her husband. Despite Sarah's denial, the woman had insisted that she move, or else she was going to make a public announcement about her at the indigene meeting the following month.

To avoid any unpleasantness, the man in question had found a permanent place for her to rent. The apartment was only furnished with a bed, and she was hoping to buy some additional furniture at the end of the month, since she'd just managed to pay off her credit card bills. But now, she had a new worry—finding the money for her airfare and her contribution toward the funeral.

Sarah sat down on her bed in her little apartment and looked out the window. The rain, which had begun the night before, was still falling. It looked like teardrops being shed for her dear mother by God, acknowledging her sorrow. She thought of her financial situation. In the past, Udo had always been her last resort, but she'd tapped that palm tree many times, and it might not have any more palm wine flowing from it just now.

The last time she saw Udo was after she won the lottery and went to her house to beg for financial assistance to attend the green card interview at the US embassy in Lagos. She'd implored Udo to help her because she would lose the once-in-a-lifetime opportunity to live in the US if she failed to show up for the interview. She only needed money for her airfare, she'd said, since she was hoping that Chinyere would put her up for the duration of her time there. Could Udo also help by informing Chinyere to expect her?

Udo was very gracious and had, without asking too many questions, agreed to help her out. This was the second time since she'd left Udo's house that she had asked for help, and she knew in her heart that Udo would regurgitate everything in due time to show what a burden she had to bear for the family.

The first time was six months after leaving Udo's house, when she found out that she was pregnant. She didn't want the baby, but abortion was very expensive. She forced herself to call Udo, who she knew was still angry with her since she'd left her home without warning and had kept her whereabouts a secret.

Udo had listened to her request, and without judgment, had given her a check for the amount she'd needed. Sarah's insistence that it was a loan was met with, "Okay, pay when you can. I just want you to be safe."

This second time, Udo had hesitated at first and reminded her that she still hadn't paid back her initial loan. Nonetheless, she called her travel agent and charged the fare to her credit card. Udo had also given her a check for a hundred pounds for her incidental expenses in Lagos.

Sarah felt she couldn't ask Udo again for financial help but would fund her travel using her own credit card and getting loans from various friends.

By the time Udo called back, everything had fallen into place, and they'd agreed to travel together from London to Lagos.

⁓✵⁓

Sitting in their room in the Rest House after dinner on the day of their arrival in Umuahia, Sarah looked across at Udo, who was on speakerphone with Ifeoma because she wanted Sarah to be privy to the conversation. Ifeoma had called, very upset that they had chosen to stay at a hotel instead of at her house.

Udo told her they didn't want to inconvenience her, and it was better that they stay in the hotel. Then she asked, "When is Ejituru arriving?"

In the background, they could hear Ifeoma shouting at a servant to bring water. When she came back to the phone, she sounded harried. "She's arriving today through Port Harcourt. I'll be picking her up at the airport, and she'll stay here."

After that conversation, Udo turned to Sarah. Scrunching her face, she said, "I'm actually dreading meeting Ifeoma."

"I thought you were on good terms with her," Sarah said. "What happened?" This family! she thought. Nothing is as it looks.

"We had a falling out six months before Mama died, and her call was the first time we spoke."

"Was it something to do with Mama's care?" Sarah asked, confused. "She took offense because I asked her to tell me how she used the money I sent for Mama's care." Udo continued to put away her toiletries and tidy her space. "I felt it was my right to know, since I worked hard to save that money, and I wanted to be sure it was used for the purpose it was meant."

"Did she comply with your request?" Sarah watched Udo's attempt at being busy. She tried to keep her voice neutral, without exposing her feeling on the subject of Udo and money.

"Of course she didn't. But she sent back my money with a curt remark. Since then, we've not spoken."

At a loss for words, Sarah remained quiet. After a short silence, she asked, "When is the meeting?"

"Tomorrow noon," Udo replied, while folding her pajamas in anticipation of the room servant's arrival.

"I'm not looking forward to it," Sarah said, grimacing. "I don't want to see Chinyere. The last time I was in her house, it was just awful."

Udo raised her eyebrows. "When was that?"

"During the time I had the green card interview in Lagos." "What happened?" Udo asked.

"To begin with, I shared a filthy room with her daughter, who was home for the holidays." Sarah shook her head in disgust. "And her children thought I'd come with bags of money. Each time we went out, they expected me to buy food and anything they fancied. I kept on saying that I had no money, but they didn't believe me."

"What did you expect?" Udo said, laughing out loud. "You're from the land of milk and honey."

"Auntie!" Sarah exclaimed heatedly, extremely worked up. "I was trying to keep the little money I had for a visit home to see Mama. Can you believe it; when I was leaving for the airport, they each gave me their bank account number so that I could send them money when I returned to the US!" She blinked and spoke in an angry voice. "They'd forgotten that their mother abandoned me and had never given me even a penny."

"Sarah, calm down. Perhaps they didn't know that you were their sister, and even if they did, I doubt they would have behaved differently." Udo shook her head. "They probably thought you were one of their aunts, and coming from the US, you must be rich." With a mocking laugh, she added, "You are Chinyere's well-kept secret from her family. I doubt even her husband knows. If he does, he's never disclosed it."

"I wish she wouldn't show up," Sarah said angrily, wiping her eyes furiously.

"I doubt she will," Udo answered as she examined her nails. "She hated Nkechi."

⚘

At breakfast on the morning of the meeting at Ifeoma's, Sarah was in a better mood than the day before, having had a good night's sleep. Sitting at a spot overlooking the parking lot, Sarah turned to Udo, who had ordered a large omelet with onion and tomato and a side order of fried plantain, and said, "I presume Ejituru has arrived."

"Yes, I should think so, or we would have heard otherwise," Udo said. "The meeting is at noon. We need to get ourselves organized for the checkout." Udo momentarily took her eyes off the motor park, where two drivers argued over a space.

"What will we do with our suitcases?" Sarah asked, cocking her head. "After breakfast, I'll arrange for the Rest House to keep them. I don't think we should carry them to Ifeoma's, since we'll be leaving from here. I've made arrangements with a friend to pick us up here at about four o'clock."

Sarah left Udo finishing her breakfast to return to her hotel room to pack. The room was smaller than the hotel room she had stayed in during the one time she went to Paris with her London college friends. The two beds with their thin mattresses reminded her of the dormitory in her secondary school. She wondered why the hotel couldn't afford to install proper beds in the rooms. Framed photographs of Ibo and Ibibio dancers graced the wall, and a television set on the credenza covered part of the mirror. She looked around the room and noticed Udo's toiletries neatly placed on the bedside table, her packed suitcase nearby. She looked out the window toward the street, where women sold oranges and bottled peanuts. She sat down on one of the beds and thought of Udo. Their relationship hadn't always been good. There were stretches of time when she never felt like contacting her or telling her of her whereabouts, even though she was instrumental in bringing her to the UK and was expected to look after her, by Nkechi in particular.

When she wrote to Udo to say she had completed her secondary education but didn't score high marks that would qualify her for university, Udo had replied that she didn't want Sarah wasting away in the village, helping run Nkechi's numerous businesses, and perhaps getting married to an unsuitable man who got her pregnant. She wanted to save her from all that.

At that time, Udo was a secretary to the head of a technical college in London. Miraculously, she was able to convince her boss, a bleeding heart, to help her rescue her niece from the evils that awaited her in the village.

Sitting now in the hotel room, Sarah imagined herself as an impoverished young girl who needed to be rescued from the clutches of illiterate parents who were offering her to a potbellied, corrupt businessman looking for a young virgin in exchange for cash to meet their immediate needs. She laughed out loud at this vision of Nkechi and Nwakama.

But Udo was willing to do anything to bring her to the UK. Her boss had believed her portrayal of the family and had suggested that Sarah should apply to study accounting, and her admission would guarantee issuance of the necessary entry visa by the embassy in Nigeria.

It had worked, and she found herself in London living at Udo's.

At first, Sarah was grateful to Udo for her efforts, but living with Udo wasn't easy. Udo had a tiny apartment and two daughters who were in middle school. She wanted Sarah to work on weekends for her pocket money, and Sarah resented this because she saw weekends as the days she was free to socialize with her college friends. Udo bought her only the bare essentials and expected her to pitch in with housework, unlike her daughters, who were given time to study and who would sometimes go out to the movies or shopping with their school friends.

Sarah felt that Udo had treated her unfairly while she lived with her, that she had treated her like a maid. Udo shouldn't have made her work and pay for her education.

Whenever she had any issue with Udo, Udo would tell her that she should realize that she, Udo, was a single mother of two young girls and was sacrificing a lot to help her obtain an education, and she needed to pull her weight. Sarah tried to ignore Udo's constant nagging until she graduated.

Once she had the certificate and had her first job, she'd moved out of Udo's apartment. Udo thought that her move without prior warning indicated ingratitude, but at the time, Sarah didn't really care what Udo thought. She hoped Udo would eventually understand.

Didn't Udo move out of Uche's house without warning? she thought, trying to justify her action.

She later found out that her first-year fees and maintenance were paid by Ejituru, who also paid for her airfare to London, so Udo's moaning and groaning wasn't justified. She didn't contact Udo for three years, and then it was only because she needed money to terminate an unwanted pregnancy.

Sarah looked around the room and wondered if she should form a close relationship with Udo. That would mean having to ignore Udo's irritating habit of recalling every ill done to her, imagined or real. Sarah had no connection to anybody in the family except Udo. What would become of her relationship with the rest of the family? She expected that this probably would be the last time she would see some of the family members.

She was glad when the door opened and Udo announced that it was almost time to head off to Ifeoma's.

In the taxi, Sarah noticed that Udo was unusually quiet. She turned to her and asked, "Auntie, is something wrong?"

"Not really," said Udo, "but I'm not looking forward to the next few days with my brothers."

What next? Sarah thought, but aloud she said, "How come? I thought you enjoyed being with them."

"My last visit home without Mama's presence left me with a sour mouth."

"Tell me what happened."

"Do you remember New Year's Eve when Papa was alive?"

"Yes, I often wish it was possible to recreate those days when everyone would gather in the upstairs parlor. At the stroke of midnight, Papa would offer prayers and toast the new year, and we would rush out and ring the bell and shout Happy New Year to each other before going to bed." Sarah's face shone in remembrance of those days gone by.

Udo's eyes misted as she remembered her pain. Then she said in an anguished tone, "Well, during my last Christmas here, I tried to bring that period back. I bought several bottles of alcohol and spent the afternoon preparing platters of beef and chicken, expecting that my brothers and children would celebrate with me. Do you know that I waited in the parlor until almost midnight, and none of them appeared?" She wiped her eyes and looked out the taxi window.

Sarah, incredulous, said, "I find that hard to believe. Didn't they know your plans?"

"I did tell them. But you've not heard the worst." She paused and watched Sarah's concerned face. "As midnight approached, I went downstairs and noticed that there was a party at Michael's to which I had not been invited. In frustration, I went upstairs, sat down, looked at my food, and started crying. I cried for Nkechi, my mother, and for Nwakama, my father, and for my children who were in the UK without me. It was there that my brother Emeka found me."

"I'm so sorry. Why didn't they let you know of their plans? You could have had a combined party." Sarah shook her head.

Udo looked out the taxi window. "We're almost there. Let's hope that everyone will pull their weight."

CHAPTER 7

M eeting at Ifeoma's house was partly due to convenience. Ifeoma lived halfway between Aba and the family's hometown, and her home could easily be reached by public transportation from either the airport serving Port Harcourt or the one serving Owerri.

It was also partly nostalgic. After all, Nkechi had spent the last few years of her life there, and besides, every member of the family was related to Ifeoma.

When she arrived, tired from her flight and the long drive to Umuahia from the airport, Ejituru was taken straight to the room Ifeoma had dedicated to her use only. Ifeoma had set the room aside for her when she was building the house and had solicited Ejituru's help.

Due to a power outage that day, the room was lit by a kerosene lamp. Without electricity, the fan didn't work. The heat was unbearable, and Ejituru noticed that Ifeoma had had the foresight to leave a bottle of cold water in the room. She drank as much as she could, hoping that she wouldn't have to seek the bathroom during the night. A faint smell of mildew permeated the room. She wondered how she would survive the night without fresh air. The room obviously needed a thorough airing.

She tried desperately to open the windows to let in fresh air, but her efforts proved fruitless, either because the windows had been bolted shut to keep out intruders or because they weren't meant to open. In the dim light of the lamp, she could see suitcases piled together on one side of the room and a table on the side nearest to the door, on which lay heaps of exercise books, Bibles, and hymnals. A rope strung across the room held assorted blouses and skirts, singlets, and underwear. The room had a double bed covered with a white bedsheet.

A knock at the door brought her back to the moment. Her bath was ready. Not fancying having a bath in the dark, she groped her way in the shadowy light cast by a lamp at the end of the corridor to the bathroom opposite the room and washed her face and arms. She went back to her room, where she quickly changed into her nightwear and lay on the bed. Sleep eluded her, and she tossed and turned until daybreak, when finally, she fell asleep.

She grudgingly got up at 9:00 a.m., when Ifeoma came to announce that her younger brothers had arrived and she should get ready for the arrival of the others.

The first person Ejituru saw upon entering the dining room that morning was Emeka, the second of Onyeka's sons. He had aged since she last saw him and looked older than his forty-one years. His small head had sprinkles of white hair, and his face had thinned out a bit. She remembered that he'd had a very promising childhood. He was bright and did well in elementary school, and was expected to go on to secondary school, as did his siblings. He was verbally versatile, and as a result, Nkechi had expected him to be the lawyer in the family.

On the month he was to enter secondary school, he'd fallen from a tree and hit his head hard. That was the beginning of the change in his personality. He lost interest in further education. He became introverted, and would sit for hours staring vacuously into space. As he grew up, he became even more introverted, preferring to stay in his room for hours with his only companion being the radio, which he had removed from the parlor of his father's house to his room, where he could listen to it uninterrupted by anyone. That period lasted for almost two years.

Then one day, he saw a broken-down car left on the premises by a relative of Nkechi. He found out it was abandoned and decided to take the engine apart and study it. He became adept at diagnosing car problems. He made a career of engine repairs and was sought after by car owners. At twenty, with Nkechi's help, he'd obtained a position in the transport division of the Ministry of Works in his hometown.

He'd always been Ejituru's favorite. During one of her visits home, when her father was still alive, she'd given him the shortwave radio she'd brought, and this had become his most precious possession, since it enabled him to listen to radio news from all over the world.

The BBC was his favorite source.

"Emeka, how are you?" Ejituru asked.

Busy spreading jam lavishly on a slice of bread he was preparing to eat, Emeka didn't immediately know what to say. He hardly knew her. He had grown up when she was already out of the house and in boarding school and then at the university in America. She often sent him money when he least expected it. Only three months ago, he had rejected a gift from her of new furniture for his room. He'd felt that he had no need for new blinds, a new bed, and a new wardrobe. He remembered that Ifeoma had used this gift to furnish another room in the house. He often wondered why Ejituru chose him to help. She never gave anything to Nwankwo, saying that Nwankwo was being supported by Udo. She seemed to forget that he, too, was being helped by Udo and didn't require any help from her.

It wasn't the same when Nkechi was in good health. In those days, Ejituru's primary concern was Nkechi. But once Nkechi was taken away because of her illness, she began to send money occasionally to him through Ifeoma.

Frightened that she was about to berate him for his refusal to accept a gift from her, he murmured, "Fine, Ma."

Before Ejituru could say something else, Ifeoma blew into the room like an unexpected wind, carrying a tray with a pot of tea and a plate filled with tomato omelets and fried plantain. "You must be hungry," she said in a staccato voice as she placed the contents of the tray on the table. "Eat something. Nwankwo is here, too, but he doesn't want anything. Emeka, do you want tea?"

Before she could frame a response, Ifeoma was already out of the room. Ejituru could hear her voice instructing the maids to make sure there were enough seats for her guests. Ifeoma had said that the meeting would be held in the shade abutting her house. Due to the power outage, the outside was much cooler than her house at that time.

Ejituru looked around the room at the photographs of Ifeoma's children displayed on one wall. An enormous side cupboard occupied one side of the room, and a stand with a basin of water and a towel stood near the door that led into the living room.

She stood up to wash her hands, wondering how many people had done so that morning. The water was clean, and after washing her hands, she sat down facing Emeka. The eggs were still warm, so she ate some and drank the tea, which by now was almost bitter since she had added no sugar and it had been steeping for some time. Realizing Emeka's embarrassment at having to face her at this time, she asked again in a kind voice, low enough for him only to hear, "Really, how are you, Emeka?"

Emeka hated being beholden to anyone, and wished that Abia State would meet its obligation to him by paying him regularly instead of owing him six months' salary. He didn't immediately respond. Ejituru's unexpected money gifts had been his lifesaver. He was grateful to her, but wished he wasn't beholden to her.

Lifting his head and swallowing the last bit of the bread he'd been eating, he murmured, "Fine. The Lord always provides when you least expect it."

Further conversation was cut short by the arrival of Michael from Aba.

Not prepared to face Michael at that time, Ejituru got up and left the room. On her way out, she could hear Nkem, Ifeoma's husband, ask, "Where is Ej? Wasn't she with you?"

Not waiting to hear a response, she moved quickly along the corridor to her room, passing five other bedrooms on the same side of the corridor as the master bedroom, until she reached the kitchen.

She entered the kitchen and looked around. It was a busy time, since preparation was afoot for the family gathering. She could see various covered pots simmering and fried turkey and chicken legs piled on platters ready to be brought out. A young girl was busy pounding yams. As if on cue, the girl stopped what she was doing and looked at her.

Stunned by the amount of food being prepared, Ejituru looked for another exit. One exit led to the part of the compound where Ifeoma had added several small rooms for use when the need arose, and it was in one of those rooms, she remembered, that Nkechi had lived out the final years of her life. The other door led to the back of the house, and this was the exit she chose.

She descended the steps and found herself gazing at a huge garden, where Ifeoma had various food plants growing. There were rows of yam plants neatly staked, and as she walked on, she saw okra, pepper, and assorted vegetable plants. On one side were the usual pawpaw, banana, and plantain plants in abundance. Afraid that her flip-flops wouldn't withstand further wandering, since last night's rain had left small puddles everywhere, Ejituru turned back and walked toward the room where her mother had stayed. It was here that Ifeoma found her sitting on the bed. "Has everybody arrived?" Ejituru asked reluctantly.

"Only the boys," Ifeoma answered.

"Let's sit here a little before going to the parlor to meet Michael," Ejituru said in a voice tinged with sadness. She had come to this room seeking refuge and hoping that in here, she would find the courage to face her siblings. She wasn't happy to be found by Ifeoma, but then, she couldn't send her away. Reluctantly, she brought herself back to the moment. She raised her eyebrows. "Did Michael's wife come?"

"No. I should have told you that his wife left him and took the teenage children still in the house with her." Ifeoma shook her head in disgust.

"Isn't she his third wife?" Ejituru asked as she adjusted her bottom on the seat. "I thought this one would really last forever. Where are the other wives?"

"The second wife, I've heard, lives in Port Harcourt," Ifeoma replied in a low voice, as if afraid she would be caught gossiping. "She has her children. The first wife lives in Umuahia, and I run into her from time to time. She's remarried, and the husband is fairly comfortable and has been a good father to the children."

"I liked the first wife, and I often felt that Mama was the cause of the breakup," Ejituru said in a flat voice.

Ifeoma adjusted her head tie. She lifted her eyebrows. "Sister, not quite. Why would you say that? He committed adultery with his maid. I wouldn't have stayed with him under such circumstances."

Ejituru laughed and said, "She would have forgiven him if she felt that Mama had accepted her. But Mama never did because she was upset that he married from outside. Mama never trusted her. Remember all the problems they had when she was living with Mama when he was sent to France by his company for six months?"

"I remember, but all the same, I feel that what he did was bad," Ifeoma said heatedly. "And you know he repeated it again with his third wife, and that was why his second wife, too, left him."

"I agree with you, but what's so unfortunate is that he lost his children," Ejituru said, extending her hands as if asking for forgiveness. "None of them are close to him. Is he working now?"

Ifeoma laughed. "He hasn't worked since his second wife left. It's as if he's been cursed. He couldn't hold a job. Mama was supporting him, and after her illness, he used to come here when he needed money. I must say that his third wife was very industrious. She really kept him afloat. That's why I'm concerned about how he'll subsist now that she, too, has given up." "She must have been fed up being the sole provider for the family," Ejituru said thoughtfully. "He shouldn't look to me for money." She gazed at Ifeoma in admiration. "Ifeoma, you are incredible. This is a huge estate. I should go back to the room and change into something comfortable. I've been walking around your garden in the back."

"Sister, you know that I, too, am the sole provider for the family, so I have to dabble in many things to make sure that our needs are met," said Ifeoma as the sisters stood up and moved toward the main house.

CHAPTER 8

When Ejituru finally emerged from the bedroom at Ifeoma's, she'd washed her sweat-covered body and had changed into a caftan and combed her hair, which she'd kept short.

Power had been restored by the time she made her way into the parlor, where her brothers were busy drinking beer and eating akara balls. She greeted them warmly. As soon as she appeared, Ifeoma directed everybody to a place adjoining the house, where a circular dining table had been set up. On the side was a rectangular table loaded with covered bowls of food and assorted juices and liquor. Ejituru chose a seat that gave her a clear view of the yard and from which she was able to observe her siblings.

Outside in the yard, several hens and two roosters strutted around pecking at the dirt. Three goats, tethered near the gate, chewed at a bundle of straw placed beside them, and a dog on a leash opposite them was dozing off. The yard had been swept, and one could see the patterns on the dirt made by the broom. Every now and then, the goats would bleat, and the dog would make a lazy effort to catch a chicken.

Ejituru looked at Nwankwo while slowly sipping the ginger ale she had been served. He wore only a long-sleeved shirt and khaki shorts. She had difficulty believing that he was almost forty. He looked younger. Unlike most men of his age, he hadn't developed a big pot belly or the dried-out skin and limbs of many of the villagers who struggled to make a living. He had inherited his father's build and Onyeka's light-brown complexion. He looked as if he had just woken up. Crow's feet radiated from his eyes to his chin on both sides of his face, and his hair was uncombed. She attributed his look to having gotten up so early this morning to catch the Umuahia bus.

Her eyes gradually shifted to Michael, who looked troubled and was worriedly massaging his temple. She covertly watched him and saw him shrug. She wondered what was going through his mind as he sat there waiting for the arrival of the others. Was he worrying about money? It was generally known that Nkechi subsidized his lifestyle until her illness. Was he worried that he would be expected to contribute toward the funeral expenses, since this meeting was for family members to pledge money for the funeral? Ifeoma had let it be known that the advance she gave for initial expenses was given to him.

As if he knew she was watching him, he got up, grabbed a beer from the beverage table, and took a quick drink. Just then, they heard the loud jangle of the gate bell, followed by the creaking sound of the gate being opened. Udo and Sarah stepped out of a taxi, and Ifeoma rushed out to welcome them.

Ejituru tried to reconcile the Udo she remembered from four years ago when they were both visiting at the same time with the Udo she saw now. This Udo looked younger than her forty-six years, was svelte, and dressed in a fitted pantsuit. Gold-toned earrings dangled from her ears. Her makeup was impeccable. She wore a wig of a rich brown color, which at first sight could pass for real hair. On her feet were high-heeled sandals. The whole effect was that of some thirtyyear-old rich woman. Ejituru felt underdressed beside her.

After the initial shock, Ejituru stood up as Udo approached and they embraced. Behind Udo she saw Sarah, who at thirty looked tired, with puffy eyes.

Sarah embraced each of the men in turn before settling down beside them. She ignored Ejituru, who remembered that Sarah had the reputation of serially targeting each family member as her enemy.

I'm the designated enemy today, Ejituru thought. However, releasing Udo, she said, "Hi. Nice to see you."

They stared at each other for a few seconds, each daring the other to be the first to look away. Sarah blinked and opened her mouth to speak, but her response was lost in the loud chatter around the table and Nwankwo's voice saying, "Has anyone heard from Chinyere?"

The silence following this remark lasted about a minute before Ifeoma uncovered the bowls and asked each person to help themselves to their favorite food. With everybody in place, Emeka called for silence and offered a prayer.

Amid the clatter of forks and knives, Ifeoma said, "Let's start, as some of us would like to travel today for the final preparation, since the funeral will take place a week from now." She handed out a printout showing the details of the proposed expenses. "As you can see, the budget is for approximately 1.5 million naira, but it might exceed that." She paused and looked around the room.

Ejituru, who had been sitting quietly in her chair nibbling on a piece of chicken, glanced at the paper in front of her. She lifted her head and said, "Hi, everyone. I'd like to say that this meeting is unnecessary, since I'm prepared to fully fund the funeral. I don't require any contributions." She turned back to the chicken she was eating.

The resulting silence was broken by Udo. With blazing eyes, she said, "Nkechi was not only your mother, she was our mother. You alone can't claim her." She banged on the table and looked pointedly at Ejituru, who grimaced. "I may not have as much money as you have, but I came prepared to give whatever I can. Nkechi sacrificed a lot for each one of us gathered around this table." Her fury turned into tears as she heaved and cried. With her mascara running, she frantically wiped her face with a napkin.

"Wow!" Emeka exclaimed. "She did indeed, and we all know that we're appreciative."

"No doubt about that," said Ifeoma.

Ejituru got up, went over to Udo, and held her. "I don't want to stop anyone who wants to contribute from doing so. What I should have said is that anyone who feels like giving should, but that no one should feel obligated to give."

Ifeoma immediately spoke up. "My view is that every one of us— Nkechi's children—should contribute as much as we can. Mama was our only true mother." She looked around the table at each one before adding, "I have here forty thousand naira as my contribution." She put the money on the table.

Udo, already worked up and ready for a fight, pulled out 200,000 naira, which she placed on the table, making sure that everybody knew how much she was giving. Sarah, who was sitting quietly and listening to the argument, said that she could only afford 50,000 naira, which she added to the amount on the table.

Ejituru tossed a questioning look at Udo at the amount Sarah was pledging and shook her head before saying, "Sarah, are you sure you can give that much? You're only beginning life. We expect a lower pledge from you."

Sarah bristled. "She's my mother, too, and I want to contribute."

Both Nwankwo and Emeka sheepishly said they had no money to pledge but would give their labor.

Shamed, Michael opened his mouth and closed it. With all eyes on him, he finally said, "You all know my situation, but as Udo said, Mama belonged to all of us."

Udo stopped him short before he could say anything more. "Ha!" she exclaimed. "Stop whatever you're thinking of saying. Situation or not, you have to pay your share of the cost." She stared at him, as if daring him to disagree.

The sound of a chair scraping caused everyone to look at Sarah as she got up and moved toward the table piled with food. After filling her plate, she turned and looked at Michael. "Uncle Michael, it would be a terrible shame if you left all the expenses to us." Pointing at him, she raised her voice. "Tell us what you have ever done for anybody in this house. As long as I can remember, you've always used your situation to evade paying for anything. Don't you dare do that this time!" She sat down, ignoring the impact of her statement, and continued eating.

Ejituru, nonplussed, tried to avoid looking anyone in the eye. She put a finger to her lips to stop herself from saying anything.

Michael, looking confused, stared at his plate. "That is unfair, Sarah!" he croaked. "You've spoken out of turn. You have no idea what I intend to do." Raising his face from the plate, he added softly, "I will pledge twenty thousand naira, but I don't have it with me now. I'll give it to sister Ifeoma when we get home."

Just then, as if on cue, the gate bell rang, and everyone sat up a little straighter. Michael's jaw jolted forward as it did when he was feeling defensive. Sarah shuddered, as if an electrical current had passed through her body. Ifeoma put down a jug of water she was holding. Both Ejituru and Udo were stunned into silence midway through their discussion.

All eyes were trained on Chinyere as she walked toward them. At fifty-one, Chinyere had added a lot of weight. She had changed out of her travel clothes and now wore a long batik skirt and matching fitted blouse and a scarf tied over her wig. The fitted blouse accentuated her bulging tummy.

Ifeoma was the first to recover. Putting down what she was holding, she walked up to Chinyere and embraced her warmly. "Sister, you're right on time. We've just started the discussion, and everyone has said what they're giving. Come and sit down. Eat something."

Chinyere looked smugly around, pleased with the emotion she saw on their faces. She chose to sit near Nwankwo and took her time selecting what to eat and drink. Meanwhile, the temporary silence on her arrival had turned into chatter as each person nervously resumed the interrupted discussion.

Ifeoma again called everyone to order. "So far, we have on hand two hundred ninety thousand naira, with Michael pledging to give twenty thousand later. The budget is for 1.5 million naira."

All eyes turned to Chinyere, who finally stopped eating. "Unfortunately, since my pension hasn't been paid, and my husband has wound up his business, we're financially strapped, and I have nothing to give." She'd just that minute decided not to pledge the 20,000 naira her husband had given her.

Ejituru looked around the room. Before she could speak, Sarah exclaimed, "Ungrateful bitch!"

All eyes swiveled toward her, but Ejituru, quickly using her fork as a drum, brought everybody's attention to what she had to say. "In that case, I will cover the rest of the budget and any extras." Ejituru considered divulging her planned get-together to her siblings at that time, but decided against it. She'd hoped to call for a one-time gathering to establish a relationship with them, but now she was unsure how to proceed. Having decided that this occasion was not the best time for it, she stood up and left, followed by Udo, who wept uncontrollably.

Sarah stood up, glared at Chinyere in disgust, and wandered away into the main house to visit with Ifeoma's husband. Chinyere was left with her brothers listening to her talk about the hardship of traveling by bus from Lagos to Umuahia.

Ejituru left the dining area looking for Udo. Instinctively, she felt that she would be in Nkechi's room, where she herself was a few hours ago, and she found Udo there, sobbing. Her heart went out to her. She sat down next to her and put an arm around her shoulder, trying to comfort her. In a corner, she noticed the wheelchair she had bought when Nkechi was no longer able to move around without pain.

She remembered the visit she had made a year ago. Nkechi's caretaker was pushing her around outside the gate when she arrived. She'd gotten out of the taxi expecting Nkechi to be glad to see her, but instead of a welcome, Nkechi had asked her who she was and where she was coming from with those suitcases. Nkechi couldn't connect her to her daughter in the United States and had spent the whole time she was there talking about that daughter and wondering when she would come to see her. The whole visit had been a nightmare, and even though Ejituru realized that the disease had robbed her mother of her memory, she could not be consoled.

Sitting there with Udo crying, she could think of nothing to say except, "She loved you very much, and was happy to have visited with you in London."

Udo gulped some air. Wiping her eyes, she said in a teary voice, "I feel so guilty."

Surprised, Ejituru asked, "Why? You have nothing to feel guilty about.

Please don't punish yourself."

"You don't know half the story. I blackmailed her into agreeing to me going to London with Uche, and when everything went bad, I was too ashamed to let her know about the situation."

Ejituru held her breath. Whatever Udo wanted to say, she wasn't ready to hear it.

But Udo whispered, "I thought foolishly that being a maid would provide me with a path to a better education."

"But it did. Look at you. You should be proud that you've supported yourself all these years. Mama was very proud of your achievement."

"But at what cost?" Udo asked. "I caused a rift between her and Uche's family, even though I tried for a long time to avoid that."

"Sister, you exaggerate," Ejituru said convincingly. "There is no rift."

But Udo would have none of that. "Yes, there is. I tried to avoid causing a rift by not getting in touch with family members for several years, but when I did, I allowed everybody to blame me for leaving Uche's protection without warning." It was as if Udo had opened a floodgate and couldn't stop the water from flowing.

Ejituru got up and closed the door. When she sat down again, she said, "If it will make you feel better, you can talk to me, and whatever you have to say will be between us. But whatever you think you did is in the past, and my advice is that you should forget it."

For a short while it seemed as if Udo had exhausted whatever was on her mind, but just as Ejituru made a move to get up,

Udo said, "I really suffered when I was with Uche. Nothing was as it was supposed to be. But I can't blame anybody for it, because it was my decision."

"In what way?" Ejituru said, feeling that she had to ask.

"What you people didn't know was that I was kept a virtual prisoner, not allowed to see or talk to anybody except the family I was living with," Udo said in between weeping.

"That must have been terrible. We all thought you were attending evening classes."

Udo, uncorked, continued to spill out her story. "As God would have it, I befriended a Yoruba woman in the park, the one time I was allowed to go there without either the husband or wife. Even when she sent me an application for evening classes, I couldn't send in the form because Uche wouldn't pay for the application fee or guarantee that I would have free time for classes. He always used the financial burden for his wife's training and his children's needs as an excuse."

Feeling hot and thirsty, Ejituru looked around the room and saw a pot of water and a cup nearby. She offered Udo some water, which Udo gratefully accepted. After she'd had a drink of water herself, she asked, "Why didn't you write and tell Mama, knowing that she would be worried?"

"I was ashamed, and didn't want to confess that I had been wrong in my assessment," Udo quickly retorted.

Nauseated by what she was hearing, and feeling sad for Udo, Ejituru moved nearer to her and held her hands in comfort. "How did you manage to get out of the situation you found yourself in, with no family members or friends to confide in?"

Udo smiled weakly and said, "That, too, was a miracle." She wiped her eyes. "Uche left me alone in the house while the family went to Paris. I called my Yoruba friend to talk to her. She suggested that we meet, and she sent her husband to pick me up." Fidgeting and lacing her fingers, she continued. "She connected me with another woman from Aba who was working as a nanny to an English family." Udo brightened up and breathed a sigh of relief. "My nightmare ended that weekend because the Aba girl luckily knew of a nanny vacancy with a family who had lived in Nigeria. I had an interview with them and was hired. To make the long story short, I went back to Uche's and searched the house for my passport. With that in my possession, I left to stay temporarily with my friend." By this time Udo was breathless, and took another drink.

Ejituru tried to digest what she had heard. "What a story! We were told by Uche that you ran away with no justification."

Udo shrugged her shoulders. "When I told Mama about my situation, she couldn't bring herself to blame Uche, but there was a story on the BBC about a girl in the same situation as I was who had reported her master to the police for enslaving her. It was then that Mama felt perhaps I was telling the truth." Udo lifted her tearstreaked face, seeking support from Ejituru.

Ejituru nodded for her to go on.

"I told Mama that Uche got off easy. I was urged by my friends to report him to the authorities and to claim payment for services rendered, but I thought of home and decided to forgo doing so."

Ejituru wouldn't let go of Udo's hands as she told her story. She thought of her own struggle to pay her way through medical school. Breathing deeply, she said, "People think we've had it easy living abroad. They have no idea how we came to achieve what we have." She shook her head. In a gentler voice, she said, "Come stay with me in my house at the new extension. You'll be comfortable there. The driver will take you to our family house each morning for whatever needs to be done." Ejituru adjusted her position and looked at Udo's tear-stained face.

Udo raised her head and looked at her with eyes brimming with tears and said in a firm voice, "I prefer to stay in my father's house, thank you."

Taken by surprise at Udo's tone, it was on the tip of Ejituru's tongue to say, "You mean my mother's house," but she decided it wasn't the time to fight that battle.

～✴❀✴～

As the family began to disperse, Ejituru went back to the room to repack and call her family in the States. She was surprised when the door opened and Michael stood there. "Do you need a ride home?" she asked him.

In lieu of an answer, he looked at her sadly. "How are you, sister? We haven't been able to talk to each other since you arrived. How are you bearing up?"

Taken aback, she thought it was very kind of him to think of her in this way. "I'm okay. It hasn't really sunk in yet." Then she abruptly changed the subject. "How have you been keeping? Will any of your family be at the funeral?"

"I don't think so," he replied, nervously scratching his thin hair. "My wife is visiting her brother in Abuja. The children went with her. I can't afford to bring them back for the funeral."

Ejituru, already aware of the situation, feigned ignorance. "Will any of the other children come? It's been a while since I saw them." She lifted her eyebrows and looked at him.

Sitting on the bed, he stretched his legs while constantly rubbing his face, a movement which ran counter to the pose he was adopting. "I think my children from my first wife will come to the funeral ceremony. I spoke to their mother, and she said they'll definitely come but won't spend the night."

Ejituru, who had continued to pack throughout the intrusion, stopped briefly and looked at him. "How old are they now? They must either be in secondary school or in university."

"The oldest girl is in her last year at Ibiaku," he replied.

"It will be nice to see them." She snapped shut her suitcases.

He offered to help her take them to the car as she made a move to leave the room.

"Thank you," she said. "You take one, and I'll follow you as soon as I call Nduka. He'll be expecting my call."

By the time her call was through to her husband, the children had already left for school and she could only talk to him since it was one of the days he had a late start. He wanted to know how she was feeling after meeting with her family.

"Chinyere came," she said. "I still can't believe it."

"Perhaps she had a change of heart," he said as the phone crackled. "Don't obsess over it." He must have sensed the irritation in her voice as they continued to chitchat, since out of the blue, he said, "Don't forget, I love you very much. I wish we were there with you. Try not to fret too much. But have you considered what we talked about? Are you going to call a family meeting to resolve some of the issues?"

Ejituru remained silent for a moment before saying, "I almost did that today, but I had second thoughts. I think after the funeral will be better."

"I'll be thinking about you. Call when you have a chance." He rang off.

Comforted, she carried the remaining suitcase outside for the journey home. The hired driver had come, and her travel companion would be Ifeoma. She reluctantly agreed that Michael could accompany them. The wake would be in a week's time, and until then, she would stay in her house.

CHAPTER 9

The days before the funeral were very difficult for Ejituru. Alone in her house, with only the driver and the temporary maid Ifeoma had found for her, Ejituru sought solace in the Nollywood DVDs she found piled on top of the TV table. At first, she wondered when she had bought them, but then it occurred to her that perhaps Ifeoma might have used the house on occasions when she needed extra rooms for her children or friends visiting the town for an event.

For two days she wandered around the house, with no interest in going to the house where she grew up. Often, she would be found sitting on a couch trying to solve sudoku puzzles. She'd bought the little book with a hundred puzzles and answers, and she'd found solving the puzzles a way of temporarily fighting her boredom whenever she visited home.

Sometimes, she would read one of the novels she had on her Kindle and temporarily live the lives of the protagonists in those novels. Ifeoma dropped in every day to keep her abreast of activities around the compound. Udo had hired workmen to repaint the parlors and the outside. Her mother's room had been cleared of furniture, since her grave would be there. Their father's grave outside had been washed and cleaned. Ejituru would make appropriate noises, though she had no real interest.

Ifeoma always ended every visit by saying, "Sister, the driver should bring you to the house to see what's happening. At least come to my house to eat. People think you're ill. You know how villagers talk."

Ejituru felt she needed time to get used to seeing the house without her mother's presence.

On the third day of her stay, Ifeoma came midmorning. Surprised that she was visiting so early in the day, Ejituru reluctantly invited her to the upstairs parlor, where she had been reading. The room was airy, with the overhead fan whirring. It had windows on one side with bars and mosquito netting. The batik drapes, the only furnishings for which she had had a say, were drawn. On one side was a half-wall from which one could see anyone coming up the staircase from the public sitting room downstairs. This large room was sparsely furnished, with only a large couch and two matching chairs, two ottomans, and two lampstands placed on the opposite side of the couch next to a wall opposite the rail. Apart from the television stand, there was a small round coffee table in the middle on which the maid had placed a tray with two bottles of orangeade, a bottle opener, and two glasses. There were no pictures on the wall because the windows left no space for them, and besides, she had always regarded this place as a temporary home. She'd only actually stayed here for a total of five weeks since it was built nine years ago.

Ifeoma explained that she had business at the government offices but had stopped by to check on her.

Ejituru knew she liked to talk about the preparations for the funeral. As they sat drinking orangeade, she turned to Ifeoma. "I'm puzzled by something."

"What?" Ifeoma asked, her voice reflecting her concern as she searched Ejituru's face for an explanation.

"Do you know where I can find Mama's bank account records? It's something that's been worrying me since I arrived. Did you know that Mama, before her ill health, refused any financial help from me, saying she had enough?"

Ifeoma didn't immediately respond. She pursed her lips and squinted her eyes as if in deep thought. Then, looking directly at Ejituru, she said, "I wish I knew. You ought to direct such questions to your brothers."

"I almost raised this issue during the family meeting, but we've not previously talked about it."

"You should have," Ifeoma said, straightening her posture. "If you had, it would have been an opportunity for the men in our family to give account of their wickedness."

Ejituru shook her head. "What do you mean?"

"Perhaps you didn't know that before we were aware of her condition, Nwankwo, in collusion with Emeka, gradually sold off her jewelry and wrappers."

Ejituru shook her head. "I have difficulty believing that Emeka colluded with Nwankwo."

"Believe it or not, that's what happened. The rest, I believe, were taken by Michael when he took her to live with him. I know this because I've seen his third wife wearing what looked like our mother's jojis."

"Did you ever confront them?" Ejituru asked, her hands wrapped around her body as if to stop it from exploding. Overcome with despair, she began to cry.

Ifeoma tried to console her but she, too, was weeping. "Is Udo aware of the situation?" Ejituru asked.

Ifeoma said, "I'm not sure she knows. My inquiries have been met with denials from both Nwankwo and Emeka, but I have witnesses."

"Why didn't you report them to the compound court as you did with Michael when he sold the land?" Ejituru asked incredulously.

"What would have been accomplished?" Ifeoma responded vehemently. "We wouldn't get back what was sold, and besides, the witnesses would refuse to come forward." Calming down, she said, "When I collected Mama from Michael's in Port Harcourt, her suitcase contained only her clothes. There was no bankbook there or in her handbag. I asked Michael, who feigned ignorance." She paused to swallow. "Only the other day, Udo also asked me the same question."

"That shows that we're all on the same wavelength." Ejituru sarcastically interjected. "Sorry, go on."

"She said it was Mama's wish to pay for her funeral from her own resources," Ifeoma said in an almost inaudible voice. "She said in her anguish over the death, she forgot to mention it during the meeting, and since she came back, she's been looking for the book." "And?" Ejituru asked.

"Udo expected to find the bankbook in one of the trunks, but when we cleared the room, the trunks were empty and contained only a few of Udo's and your letters. Udo was shocked to tears." Ifeoma wrung her hands.

"We can find out who cashed it out by going to the bank," Ejituru said angrily.

"But then, sister, we would be washing our dirty linen with outsiders. The bank wouldn't keep our inquiry secret. People would talk!" Ifeoma extended her hands to pat Ejituru.

"I absolutely don't care," Ejituru said, shrugging her off. "You know the bank manager. Let's go there tomorrow. I want everybody to know the culprit."

"Sister, calm down. We'll not only shame our brothers, but our family will be ridiculed. The brothers are the burden we have to bear. Let's leave it at that." Unable to control herself, Ifeoma started crying loud sobs, loud enough to attract the attention of the maid, who rushed into the living room with cold water bottles.

"Here is cold water," she said. "Please calm down. You'll make yourself sick."

Sipping the water, Ejituru turned to Ifeoma and asked, "Is there anything we can do? I thought normally the daughters get the clothes and jewelry of the deceased mother."

Ifeoma thought briefly and said, "That's what should happen, but the boys have preempted us. We can't take them to court because we would be washing our dirty linen outside."

They sat, each lost in her own thoughts. The silence was broken by Ejituru, who said sadly, "Perhaps we can't blame them. Both Nwankwo and Emeka depended on Mama for practically everything, and once she was removed, they had no fallback position. I presume that's why they sold her things. But Michael! He has no excuse." Ifeoma shook her head and stood up to take her leave.

The next day, Ejituru decided to visit her parents' house to show interest in what was going on, and perhaps seek answers to questions in her mind. But just as she was closing her front door, she heard a car horn. The gate opened, a blue Peugeot passenger car drove in, and out stepped her friend Stella. Although Ejituru had attended elementary school in the area, she couldn't remember any friends she had in elementary school. On the other hand, she did remember friendships she had formed at secondary school and university. One of them was Stella. They'd met at the Ikot Ekpene bus station the very first time she'd left home for boarding school, and they'd forged a close bond throughout their boarding school life and at Nsukka University. Stella was her best friend, and the only one she had kept in touch with over the years.

During this period at home before her mother's funeral, she'd often thought of Stella and wondered whether Nduka had informed her of the tragedy. This was the one person she had longed for since arriving from the US, and here she was in front of her. Perhaps it was all a mirage conjured up by her thoughts.

She stood there holding the door handle, transfixed, unable to move until Stella got out of the car and approached her.

"Is it really you, Stella? You're supposed to be in Atlanta!" Ejituru sobbed as she hugged her. "I can't believe it's you!"

"My mother-in-law is ill," Stella said as they entered the house. "I came to look after her and make sure she's well taken care of. Then I read the announcement of your mother's funeral and surmised that you would be home for it." Stella dabbed the tears from her face.

They sat on the wicker chairs of the public sitting area and for some time just stared at each other.

Then Ejituru asked, "How did you find me? Did you go to my parents' house?"

"We left Owerri early this morning and should have been here two hours ago, but the road was very bad. I remembered your parents' house from the last time I was here, so we went there hoping to surprise you. Your brother Emeka gave us the directions."

~≈⊙⊹⊙≈~

"You're not going back today, I hope. I'll die if you say you are." Ejituru's voice reflected her concern.

"I intend to stay," Stella replied. "And if you'll put up the driver, too, we'll stay with you until the morning of the wake." She looked around. "This is a big estate, dear friend. Has Nduka seen it?"

"Not yet," Ejituru said, shaking her head. "He'd hate it, just as I do." With her arm around Stella's shoulders, she added, "I built it to please my father."

"How come?" Stella asked as they walked toward the house.

"Shamed by my father in order to hold onto the land he had fought for, I agreed to spend the little money I had to lay the foundation. At the time I was building it, it seemed like a good idea, but it was the biggest mistake of my life."

Stella shook her head and said, "You're not alone. We're all forced to build houses we hardly use."

"But," continued Ejituru, "I honestly thought I would use my experience to help the people here. It didn't quite turn out that way. My first attempt to start an industry that would provide employment to the villagers exposed all their hatred against the family."

"What happened? We also tried to start something that would give employment to villagers."

"I had a plan to start a fishpond that I hoped would eventually provide employment to village women. I asked family members to get the requisite permission from the village council. Unfortunately, the message that went out was totally different from what I had in mind."

Stella laughed and said, "I bet they thought you were out to enrich your family."

"Exactly!" Ejituru burst out laughing. "They thought it was an attempt by my family to expropriate communal land for the benefit of one family."

"Our experience is different. We actually succeeded in starting a business at home. It's being managed by my husband's brother," Stella said shrugging her shoulders.

Ejituru added wistfully, "In any case, let's not talk about it. It's in the past. Come, let's hear about your plans." She called out for juice and snacks as they climbed the stairs to the upstairs parlor.

Ejituru was happy to have her there. Her presence, she felt, would lessen the loneliness she had been feeling since she had arrived. No other friend would come all that way just to cheer her up.

During that week, Stella made the visits to her parents' house less painful. They took long walks around the neighborhood, marveling at all the big estates that were only inhabited, at most, one month during the year. They went to places she'd never dared to go, and one day they drove the dirt road toward Itu and branched off to visit a fishing village on the Cross River—or was it one of the many creeks emptying into it? Ejituru wasn't quite sure. They bought crabs, assorted fresh fish, and snails.

Later, they sprawled on the floor mat in the downstairs parlor, joined by the drivers, the gateman, and the maid, tearing out the flesh from the boiled crabs and the broiled fish until only the bones were left, and downing everything with fresh palm wine they'd managed to obtain on the way back home. The drivers entertained them with stories of their experiences with the politicians they drove during the elections and their antics at election rallies.

Both of them laughed until tears rolled down their cheeks, and they temporarily forgot the reason for the visit. Then, satiated, they stumbled up the stairs to the upstairs parlor, turned on the television, and watched the latest Nollywood movie.

Another night, they both cracked up with laughter at the portrayal of the mother-in-law as someone who would deploy all types of juju to ensure that her son remained under her control. Ejituru had turned to Stella and said wistfully, "I often wish for a mother-in-law. Ignatius met me long after his mother had died, and the same applied to Nduka, who lost his mother in a tragic accident years ago, before our reunion. What is your relationship with your mother-inlaw? I seem to remember that she was opposed to your marriage and had forbidden her son to marry you."

Stella carefully chewed her last helping of food while they ate sprawled on the floor in front of the television. As if conjuring up a difficult time, she said, "I worked hard to gain her confidence and to overcome her initial objection. Our relationship is now that of mother and daughter. She was especially helpful to me after my mother's death. She visited many times to help care for the children, and I got to know her very well. That's why I felt obligated to be with her immediately when we heard she was unwell. My husband is presenting a paper at a conference and couldn't come."

"Nduka often said that if his mother was alive, she would have regarded me as the daughter she never had and loved me as such. He said that his parents had longed for a daughter but never had one." Ejituru got up to wash her hands.

Ejituru was sad when the time came for Stella to leave. She also had to make the journey to Umuahia to bring back her mother's body for the wake that night.

Just before she left, Stella asked, "Dear friend, what do you intend to do after the funeral? I noticed the animosity between you and your siblings, and I don't see anything binding you to this place."

"Sadly, you're right," Ejituru responded. "I've been thinking about it. I thought I would try one more time to reconcile with my siblings, but even if I achieve my objective, this place holds nothing for me. My place is with Nduka, and this is probably my last visit."

Since Stella had mentioned that her family, too, would be moving to the Washington, DC, area in the spring of the following year, they both looked forward to resuming their friendship again.

After seeing her friend off, Ejituru drove to Ifeoma's house for the journey to Aba to retrieve Nkechi's body from the mortuary.

CHAPTER 10

At 5:00 a.m. on the day of the wake, Ejituru stood outside their family home preparing for the drive to Umuahia to bring back Nkechi's mortal remains. It was a beautiful morning. Last night's rain had left puddles of water on the uneven path leading to the road from the house. On the road outside, early risers were already making their way to the stream or the farms. The air was damp, and the trees were heavy with dew. The damp air kept the gnats and mosquitoes at bay. The moon of the night before had long set, and the sky was covered with clouds of various hues of gray. In the far eastern side of the town near the Cameroon Mountains, the sky held the promise of the sun, which had still to show its face.

She huddled together with her family facing the hearse, which had been hired by Ifeoma for transporting the body from Umuahia. The hearse, a converted pickup van, could seat five, including the driver, with two sitting with the coffin.

Pointing at the hearse, Ejituru said, "Some of us will have to stay behind." She raked the faces of each one present with her eyes.

"I have to go whether you all like it or not. I want to clothe my mother," Udo immediately stated in a voice that brooked no question.

"Someone has to stay behind to complete the arrangements for the wake keeping," Ifeoma stated. Nwankwo, fearing that a fight was brewing, excused himself, since he had to complete the arrangement for the grave.

Immediately, Udo, in a raised voice drowning out the whispering between Michael and Ifeoma, said, "As far as I can see, Ifeoma and Michael have to go because they made the arrangements for the mortuary. I presume Ejituru would want to go for obvious reasons.

As far as I'm concerned, the rest should stay back to help prepare for the evening."

Sarah, extremely irritated, said, "I have the same right to go as you, Udo. You cannot deny me that." Listening to the siblings bicker, Ejituru decided to intercede and said, "Sarah, I will gladly give up my place for you."

"No way!" Michael and the others shouted.

Waving them aside, she said, "We still have a lot of things pending before tonight, although Ifeoma has arranged most things. But we need someone other than Nwankwo to contact the providers of various things to remind them of what they'd promised. Please, Sarah, stay behind and help."

Annoyed, Sarah stamped off, not before Udo said in a contrite voice, "Perhaps Chinyere can help you, since she has already opted out."

As the last-minute decisions were being made, Emeka said, "On second thought, I will stay behind. I have to see about the order of service for the funeral and to make sure the brochures are delivered to the church."

The trip to Umuahia took more than two hours because ten miles of it were scarred with gullies that had been temporarily covered with planks to make the road drivable, and some of the planks had split due to the weight of the passing vehicles. Once they approached the Bende junction, the driver was able to pick up speed.

In Umuahia, the hearse moved along in traffic more chaotic than Ejituru had ever seen before. There were horns honking and drivers yelling at each other. Bicycles, lorries, cars, and scooters weaved through the gridlock, almost colliding. Pedestrians and small boys darted from one car to another, selling cold water and assorted goods, urging passengers to buy. Inside, the hearse was hot. The driver said he had been very busy and hadn't had the chance to repair the air-conditioning.

Although the windows were down, Ejituru wiped her brow and realized that her blouse was saturated and sticking to her skin. She felt sorry for Michael and Ifeoma, sitting at the back where there was no window. She wished she had given up her seat for one of them. After all, they had borne the brunt of her mother's illness.

When they finally arrived at the building that housed the mortuary, parking was difficult. The surrounding area was crowded with families trying to retrieve the bodies of their loved ones. There were knots of people standing or sitting around and cars with blaring horns trying to find parking spots. It was like a market with hawkers of food, handkerchiefs, water, peanuts, roasted corn, and assorted goods plying their trade.

When the driver finally found a spot, Michael and Ifeoma went in to settle the bill and finalize the paperwork for the release of the body. Only then would it be necessary for Ejituru and Udo to join them if they wished. Ejituru, already feeling nauseated, declined to view the body inside the mortuary, and opted to sit in the car during the long wait before they could be attended to. The scene reminded her of the time she'd left home for secondary education at Ibiaku, except there were no touts rounding up passengers for buses. As cars or lorries left, their places were taken by new arrivals. Snacks were in high demand, and business was brisk.

Ifeoma came back shortly with the news that it would be an hour before the body would be released. She offered Udo and Ejituru bottles of cold water. "Michael is grabbing something to eat, but I'm not hungry. What about you?" Ejituru shook her head.

Udo, who had been sniffling since they arrived at the mortuary, said, "How can anybody feel like eating at a time like this?"

"Why not? Many people here left home very early in the morning without breakfast, so what do you expect?" Ifeoma said.

Ejituru kept silent as she surveyed the place. Every now and then a coffin would be carried out, and the family associated with it would gather together and proceed to their hearse.

Finally, Michael came back and said it was their turn.

Udo and Ifeoma went into the building, but Ejituru, fearing that she would break down at the sight of her frozen mother in that condition, sat quietly in the car. When the coffin was placed in the hearse, Michael opened the coffin for her. She wept.

At one point during the journey back to their hometown, the hearse broke down. After investigating the problem, the driver reported burst tires. Ifeoma looked at him angrily, but before she could say something, he said remorsefully, "The road is bad."

While the tires were being repaired, Ejituru and Udo sat on a log at the roadside, each lost in thought. Udo broke the silence. "We're going to be late for the scheduled ceremony at home. This is the type of thing Mama hated."

It took Ejituru some time to frame a response. Finally, staring into space, she said, "True. Poor Mama, lying there, must be steaming because she can't tell the stupid driver off—or Ifeoma, for that matter, for hiring him."

"She did hate being late for anything," Udo replied, smiling. "We sure are going to be late this time."

"That's a pity," replied Ejituru. "But I presume people at home are used to delays."

"That may be so, but shouldn't he have checked the vehicle to make sure that it was in good condition before we left home?" Udo asked, shaking her head in disgust. "This is typical of everything here in Nigeria."

"He has a good excuse. This road has always been bad, and the condition hasn't changed from when I was young and traveling to Ibiaku."

"You're right," Udo said. "No amount of intercession with the government has led to any improvement." She swatted a fly with her hand as they drank some water from the bottles they were holding.

It took about an hour to fix the tires and resume their journey. Once the hearse entered their hometown, it proceeded to the birthplace of Ejituru's mother for the ceremony marking the closure of her life cycle. Despite its late arrival, a crowd had gathered in anticipation. It was a simple ceremony during which libations in honor of the ancestors were poured, kola nuts broken and shared, and kinsmen given the opportunity to heap praises on the loved one.

Ejituru accepted the condolences of her kinsmen and women and thanked them for their support. From there, they proceeded to the family house, where the viewing and the wake would take place.

The wake itself was in the house where Nkechi had lived with her husband. The downstairs parlor had been cleared of furniture and a queen-size bed placed there. The walls had been covered with many yards of beautiful lace material matching the cover of the canopy above the bed. On this bed lay Ejituru's mother, beautifully clothed and made-up. Ejituru wished she could ask her to get up and walk away. She was unsure of what to do, having been living outside the country for more than twenty years. Her visits had always been very short, and in all those years, she had grown apart from her contemporaries in the village.

Rather than go around to welcome the guests, Ejituru chose to sit with her aunt on the mat placed opposite the bed. Long lines of people circled the bed, dancing and singing the songs the band was playing, and occasionally, someone would come and touch her hand as she sat there, impervious to what was happening.

She didn't recognize any of the people there. There were so many faces that she couldn't put names to, but everybody seemed to know her.

As they touched her, they called her by the affectionate name she was known as. "Ej, wipe your eyes and be strong," they urged.

Three hours into the wake, her aunt said, "Ejituru, go and lie down." She shook her head, and her aunt didn't press her. At about 2:00 a.m., the place started to thin out, and Ifeoma came and sat beside her, holding both her hands.

"We all have to lie down for a few hours," she said, trying to keep her eyes open. "The funeral is at 9:00 a.m. today, and we need a rest. I'm going to my house and will be here at 8:00 a.m. I've asked the driver to take you home."

Ejituru shook her head and said nothing. An hour later, when most people had left and the place was being cleared of the remains of the celebration, her aunt nudged her. "Ej, I think I'll go home to prepare for the burial service."

At first, it seemed as if no response would be forthcoming. Then finally, as if she was speaking from a very deep pit, she said, "I think I'll just stretch out here, and when Ifeoma returns, I'll go home to change for the church. Let the driver take you home."

When most people had left the wake, Ejituru chose to sleep on the mat where she had been sitting during the wake. At six o'clock on the morning of the funeral, she went home, rested a few hours, and was back at the house for the procession to the church about half a mile from there. The ceremony was at 9:00 a.m.

At the church, she sat in the front seat with family members. The church was full, with standing room only. Although the family had printed multiple copies of the brochure, many people had to go without.

During the ceremony, both Emeka and Michael served as lectors. The pastor praised Nkechi in his eulogy for her community and church work, and exhorted the family to take comfort in the fact that she had lived a good life. The service concluded with the singing of "Amazing Grace."

Although it was a beautiful service, Ejituru felt like a zombie, unaware of what was happening. She could hardly stand up for the songs and had to be supported by Emeka, who stood by her throughout the service.

At the end of the funeral service, the family lined up to follow the hearse home for the burial. On the way, Chinyere, fuming since morning, moved near Ifeoma, shoving her on her side, she hissed loudly, "Look at you, Ifeoma. You're wearing brocade while you gave the rest of us cheap cotton. We look like your poor relatives. Shame on you, peacock." She was upset over the uniforms the family members wore. Ifeoma had taken measurements from family members and had bought the material in bulk and had them made.

For a second, it appeared as if a fight would break out. Udo, who overheard the remarks, joined in. "Chinyere, I can't believe I'm agreeing with you, but this is not the time for it. We'll settle the score with her at an appropriate time."

Michael also joined in with a voice dripping with hate. "I'm surprised we're dressed the same as Ejituru. For once, she lumped all of us together. Perhaps Ejituru will at last notice."

Ifeoma, who during this time was trying to keep her cool, hissed, "Remember where you are and respect your mother. I will deal with each one of you later."

Accompanied by the band and the choir, the hearse proceeded to the house for the final rites.

During the burial, given the size of the room, with many people squeezed into the space, there was not enough room for family members to witness the burial and pay their last respects to their loved one, Udo, visibly upset, shoved a woman who was preventing her from seeing the action in order to make space for Ejituru. Ejituru, who was standing next to her, tried to hold her back but couldn't stop the woman from stumbling into the pastor. She almost toppled the pastor, preventing him from completing the rites of burial. The pastor was forced to stop midstream just when he read, "Earth to earth—"

Udo could be heard shouting, "Can't you allow us to bury our mother? Get out of here!" Ifeoma, noticing the confrontation, moved forward and gently led the startled woman out of the room. It was then that the ceremony was completed, and the family left the room as the grave was filled with dirt.

Ifeoma marched to where Udo was standing with Ejituru. "What is wrong with you, Udo? She's my friend, and also a pastor. She had every right to be here." She wagged her finger at Udo. "I invited her here to comfort us."

"What comfort?" Udo shouted. "She was a nuisance, not a comfort!"

Ejituru looked at Ifeoma's angry face and said, "You should've told us about your arrangement. I, too, was upset to see a stranger in our midst at such a critical time. I wanted us as a family to bid goodbye to our mother. In any case, that's water under the bridge, and Udo, we should let it go. By the way, who is responsible for keeping details of all the gifts from visitors?"

Ifeoma, still angry, said, "Michael has the notebook. He's responsible.

Sarah said she would help."

Surprised, Ejituru said, "Are you sure he's the right person for the task?

Couldn't you have designated Emeka?"

Ifeoma thought for a moment before saying, "I know that we're taking a risk asking him to be the recorder, but what could I do? He had to be assigned a task."

Ejituru shook her head. "I have to go home to get something. I'll see you in a while." She made for the road.

At home, she had a quick wash, changed out of the ill-fitting funeral uniform into a navy-blue skirt and blouse, and recombed her hair and dabbed eau de cologne behind her ears before driving back to the repast.

CHAPTER 11

E jituru returned to the repast to find a mass of people, many of whom lived outside the area but who had come home to celebrate her mother's death. That surprised her.

How did my mother know all these people? she wondered.

They couldn't have all come just to pay respects to her. It had been more than twenty years since her mother served as a member of the women's group that raised money for the new church building.

Ruminating on this, Ejituru was struck by the idea that some of the mourners weren't there for her mother, but for her sister Ifeoma, as well as her brothers, who were important members of the society. How could she then explain the presence of school choirs from Aba and Umuahia, where Nkechi never at any time lived?

Amid the sea of people at the funeral, first in the church and afterward on her father's lawn where the funeral feast was held, she felt that she did not belong. There was nobody she could say was her friend. Having lived most of her life away from this place, she felt alone, and would gladly have slipped away to her house in the new extension just to get away from the crowd. But she instinctively felt that she could not do so. She had to move around and greet the guests.

She came to a table occupied by a group of women reminiscing about their various experiences working with her mother. After retiring from teaching, Nkechi had put all her effort into starting a dressmaking business to supplement her pension. It was a natural choice. Ejituru remembered the dresses her mother made for her when she was in primary school, her school uniforms, and the church dresses much envied by her contemporaries. A smile spread over her face. At first, Nkechi was jeered at for thinking she could make a living from sewing when dressmakers were a dime a dozen. Couldn't she find a more suitable undertaking? she was asked. Like everything else she put her mind to, she was determined to succeed. As soon as she got her gratuity, she bought several sewing machines, hired competent tailors, and set about looking for clients. She quickly found a niche making uniforms, not only for schools but for funerals, weddings, and every occasion.

As soon as Ejituru sat down, a woman said, "Nkechi taught us well. The catering for this function is a tribute to her. Nobody had ever thought of catering for events before her."

Ejituru remembered that it all began at the funeral of Nkechi's dearest relation, when she witnessed the squabbling among the village women over the preparation of the food to be served. She decided to take control and organize the catering. With the money allotted, she bought the ingredients, informed the women that they would be paid for their services, and hired servers. After that, she began by offering her services as a caterer for funerals, and later on, for weddings and any event requiring the provision of large quantities of food. She had a coterie of village women she could pay to help whenever the need arose. With her numerous contacts, she became a wholesaler for Heineken beer and soft drinks. Only the other day, Ifeoma had informed Ejituru that the caterer for this event was a woman trained by her mother, and she had repaid the debt by charging less than her normal price.

Ejituru remembered how amazed she was at the transformation of her mother when she came home before starting her residency. Her mother was so busy she could hardly spare the time to sit and carry on a conversation with her. The only time they could have an uninterrupted discussion was very early in the morning when she would creep into her mother's room and snuggle beside her. That was when she was able to tell her mother that she was thinking of remarrying, and Nduka was the one.

She remembered that visit, and how frightened she was that her decision to marry Nduka would cause a strain in her relationship with her mother. What helped was the visit from Stella, her college friend, and finding out that Stella faced a similar situation, fearing that her family would disown her for marrying outside her social class. She'd had a heart-to-heart discussion with Onyeka, her mother's wife, who suggested the best time to approach her mother. She'd followed the advice of both and had, before the end of the visit, opened up to her mother both about her life in the US and her love for Nduka. With her mother's support, any objection from her father melted away. They'd both convinced her father that Nduka was the right person for her, and he should expect a visit from his people to legitimize the marriage. Before she left home for her residency, she felt happy that she had her family on her side.

Illness had made her mother give up all her businesses, only to become dependent on handouts from her children in her later years. In her lifetime, she touched so many lives, helped so many people, and contributed enormously to the development of the place. Perhaps the number of visitors to her funeral was indeed a tribute to that.

At one point during her meandering and greeting the guests, Ejituru saw Udo in an argument with Sarah. Having convinced herself to intervene, she moved toward them, arriving just as Sarah ran crying into the house. Udo was left standing there, looking unhappy and unable to decide what action to take.

Ejituru said in a comforting voice, "What's the problem, if I may ask?"

Shaking her head, Udo said, "I might as well tell you, since you're also part of the problem."

"What have I done now?" Ejituru asked in a bemused voice.

"Nothing really, but Sarah is upset because the printed brochure listed her as a daughter instead of a granddaughter, and she's having second thoughts regarding her contribution.

She felt that as a granddaughter, she didn't have to contribute anything."

Ejituru laughed. "That's utter nonsense. She contributed voluntarily.

Remember, I tried to restrain her." "I reminded her of that," Udo said.

"Besides, isn't her name Sarah Oji, our maiden name?" Ejituru asked, extremely irritated.

Shaking her head and looking very dejected, Udo said, "For thirty years, she's been Mama's child, and now she wants to be Mama's granddaughter. Incredible."

"Don't worry about that. If she wants her contribution back, she should raise the issue when we meet to finalize the expenses. Let's try and see this repast through."

Ejituru continued greeting the guests, and as she moved from one table to another, she overheard the villagers praising Ifeoma for organizing such a sumptuous send-off for her mother. "That woman, she is one to be reckoned with. She is truly Nkechi's daughter," was the refrain.

She bumped into Udo as she walked around observing people eating and chatting.

Udo said, "I feel as if I don't exist. When people see me, their first question is, 'Where is Ifeoma? We want to pay our respects.' I feel as if she's hijacked this event. We might as well not be here."

Ejituru grabbed her hand. "Don't think that way. You've forgotten that of all of us daughters, Ifeoma is the only one who lives here. The rest of us don't really count in the scheme of things, since we can't reciprocate or pay back any acts of those who've come to the funeral."

Leaving Udo, she noticed that there were tables where she was met with silence, either because she was the subject of the discussion or because the topic was unfavorable to the family. Instinctively, she knew she was often the topic, since her history was well known among the villagers. She spied her ex-husband's family sitting at a table with their friends. She briefly considered approaching them but decided not to. She felt that Okoro, Ignatius's uncle, must be happy that Nkechi, his nemesis, was no more.

But just as she turned away from the table, Okoro and his wife stood up and walked up to her. Embracing her, Okoro said, "Your mother was a great woman. No one can replace her. Please remember that. Ignatius couldn't come because he had some important business in Lagos, but he sends his regards. Again, accept our condolences."

Ejituru felt very small beside them. Here she had been feeling guilty all these years and dreading this meeting. As she started to walk away, she reconsidered, turned around and embraced them, and wished them luck. Glad for the closure, she moved on to the table where the chiefs sat.

Next, she ran into Chinyere, whom she'd been trying to avoid throughout the week. Chinyere gazed at her as if she was a stranger. Without any preamble, she said in a spiteful voice, "Some of us can't wait to get out of mourning. We're already fashionably dressed. Haha."

Ejituru could see the look of expectation on the occupants of the nearby table. She wouldn't give them the satisfaction of witnessing her anger, so she simply stared hard at Chinyere before she turned and left.

"Don't you have anything to say?" Chinyere shouted. "Idiot."

Ejituru fumed as she walked away, but just as she entered the main house, Nkem, Ifeoma's husband, came to tell her that the kinsmen had gathered at Michael's house for the clothing of the dead.

"You're summoned to appear before them," he said.

She followed him to the place where about nine men from her father's compound and her brothers were sitting and drinking. On the middle table were several pieces of joji and Dutch batik, and bottles of schnapps and gin. She noticed a pile of naira notes on the table. She greeted each person and sat down, wondering why she had been summoned.

The oldest person in the group said, "Your kinsmen have each already clothed your dead mother. We've waited for your husband to do his part, but we haven't seen any of his kinsmen yet. That's why we called you."

Ejituru checked the faces of her brothers sitting there, looking sheepish. She felt a rage coursing through her body, but she tried to repress it. Finally, when she felt that she was in control, she said, "Mazi, thank you for coming to my mother's funeral. Nduka, my husband, partially paid for this funeral. As I explained to my brothers, he couldn't come—not out of disrespect, but because it was important that I come, and he had to stay home to look after the children."

"Nonsense!" shouted one of the chiefs. "You could have brought the children to say goodbye to their grandmother. This is atrocious!"

Ejituru looked around the room and finally said, "Mazi, I'm not going to repeat myself. My husband and I paid for the funeral. You asked why my husband wasn't represented at the funeral. My brothers know that Nduka's parents are dead, and I think those of you who came for the ceremony of our marriage know that, too."

"That's not the point!" shouted an old man sitting in the corner. "He could have found acquaintances in his village to come here and stand for him. Nobody is an island in the village. His family has connections there."

Controlling her anger and ignoring the remark, Ejituru said, "Secondly, his only living relative, a brother, lives in England. He had no one in his village to arrange the visit."

The kinsmen rejected her excuse and imposed a fine of a cow, a piece of joji, and a bottle of schnapps. However, through the intercession of the head of the kinsmen, a confidant of Nkechi, this fine was finally reduced to a goat and a bottle of schnapps.

Ejituru felt that she had no option but to appease their anger by paying the fine. After doing so, she stood up and looked at each person sitting there. "I thank you all for coming, but I have to go back to attend to the other guests." Leaving them, she entered the house and went to the room where her mother was buried to vent her anger. Then she left the repast and went back to her house. Calming down, she called her husband in the States to talk about the events of the day.

CHAPTER 12

As the repast wound down and the guests began to drift away, Ejituru and Ifeoma had left for their respective houses. Sarah sat in the upstairs parlor with five of her siblings and their closest friends, rehashing the events of the day. They discussed the funeral, comparing it with past funerals in the area, the ill-gotten gains of some of the attendees and their lavish spending on big houses with swimming pools located in the new extension, and of course, the sexual exploits of the men in their age group with multiple wives and girlfriends. Every now and then, someone would get up to step outside to seek a bushy area on the side of the house to get rid of the excess beer they'd been imbibing. Sometimes multiple men would exit the room for that purpose. At that point, there would be a slight pause in the conversation, only to be resumed when they returned.

She spied Udo in a corner, scowling. No doubt Udo would have preferred to be asleep in her bed in the room next door. But how could she sleep with the raucous conversation going on? Sarah shrugged her shoulders. She felt that Udo was better off sitting where she was rather than in her room, irritated and tossing and turning the whole night.

She looked around the room, which was twice the size of the living room in her Bowie flat. Her attention centered on

Chinyere, who was about to tear into a fried chicken leg, her eyes slightly closed and her lips parted in anticipation. The dim light cast by the single bulb dangling from the ceiling revealed her bulk squeezed into a chair too small for it. Sarah flinched in disgust. Her eyes moved to Emeka, who sat in the corner occasionally nodding, as if dozing.

The conversation at that point centered on the sexual exploits of adulterous husbands in Nigeria. She glanced back at Udo, who now stared angrily at Michael. Though shocked by the anger, Sarah wasn't surprised when Udo lashed out, wagging her finger at Michael.

"How can you sit here and gossip about others? Are you better than those people you're gossiping about? You, who have married three wives?"

The outburst temporarily halted the conversation. Several eyes turned to look at her in shock.

"Let's talk about you," Udo continued. "Where is your third wife?"

Finally, Michael found his tongue. "I told you that she went to visit her brother in Abuja," he whispered. "Why are you raising that now?" He looked at her combatively. "I'm not a polygamist. I divorced each one of them."

"That was what he said, and we should believe it." Nwankwo glared at Udo.

"I, too, would like to know, sister," said Chinyere, who had stopped chewing and was laughing loudly with her mouth wide open. "This brother isn't any better than the men he was condemning a while ago. The only difference is that he's the son of the sainted dead person, the golden boy who saved her marriage."

Sarah could see pieces of chicken flesh stuck in between Chinyere's teeth and a smear of palm oil on her upper lip. She shuddered in disgust. Sarah felt that she should try to defuse the atmosphere, so she coughed gently and said, "By the way, I'm glad that your children from your first wife came today. Where are they staying?"

Relief washed over Michael as he nervously wiped his face. "The arrangement was for them to go back to Umuahia today, but they chose to stay at Ifeoma's with their cousins."

"I must say, I like their mother, and wish you had stayed with her."

Sarah's comment was interrupted by Chinyere. "You know exactly who was responsible for that," she cried, waving her hands for emphasis. "Your precious dead woman. She drove her away because she was a competitor for the affection of her son, the one thing that saved her marriage."

This turn in the conversation energized those in the room. Until then, they had assumed that Chinyere was dozing off in the corner, since she had been tossing off bottles of beer. The room geared up for a fight.

"Wow! Wow!" cried Nwankwo. "She did no such thing. Michael drove his wife away by sleeping with his maid. He alone is to be blamed. You've forgotten that Mama tried to get Michael to apologize, and she even offered to look after the maid's child after the birth."

"I bet she did." Chinyere laughed. "She was an expert at taking other people's children as hers. Ha-ha." Everybody started snickering.

Chinyere wouldn't quit. "Here we are having a celebration for the woman who usurped our mother's place, whereas our mother's funeral was uneventful. She was more or less dumped into the grave at the back of the house without anybody knowing. We were never given an opportunity to mourn her."

There was total silence, with everybody in shock.

"Sister, you're wrong. Those of us in the house saw what was done when Onyeka died. She was given a good burial. I bet if you had been told of her death, you wouldn't have come!" shouted Emeka, who had been silently listening to the conversation and totally ignored by everyone until then. Breathing heavily, he added, "Nkechi looked after her while she was sick. She got her the best treatment.

You can't fault Nkechi, our mother."

Chinyere wouldn't let it go. "You're still calling that woman our mother.

Onyeka is our mother!" She slammed the coffee table for emphasis.

"It depends on your definition of mother!" Udo angrily shouted. "To me, Nkechi was my mother."

Sarah, unable to keep quiet any longer, stared at Chinyere and pointedly said, "A better mother than some people we know in this room."

As Chinyere tried to get them to think of their real mother, Onyeka, who was buried in one of the rooms in the back of the house, Sarah saw Udo get up.

Udo pounded the table. "Let me tell you, Chinyere, I've never regarded Onyeka as my mother. What did she ever do for any of us?" Heatedly, she answered her own question. "She was an illiterate woman, one of the maids, doing the laundry, carrying firewood, or bringing cassava from the farm and grating it to make garri, unable to make enough to support her children." She stopped and looked around the room, challenging the siblings to object. But when no objection came, she tearfully said, "Nkechi was the mother I knew, comforting her children when they had nightmares in the night, taking them to the doctor, caring for them when they were sick, sharing hospital beds with them, pushing them to do well in school, and sharing their successes. Nkechi always welcomed us lovingly whenever we visited. Without Nkechi, none of us would be where we are today." Tears poured down her face as she tried unsuccessfully to wipe them away. Amid her sniffling, she added, "This visit without Nkechi has shown me what the future will look like."

"Stop right there!" Chinyere interjected with blazing eyes. "True, Onyeka was illiterate, but Nkechi did nothing to help her obtain survival skills. Her only use was pumping out children for her and helping her run her household and nothing else." She stood up, retied her wrapper's top, and adjusted her head tie before sitting down and glaring at them all.

"Rubbish!" shouted Udo. "She was not a slave. She was free to leave the house if she so desired, and she had many opportunities to do so." She paused to swat at a mosquito buzzing near her. "I for sure know that Nkechi gave her trading money as a way to make her independent, but she wasn't able to handle that." She pounded the table with her right hand for emphasis.

Her brothers nodded their heads in agreement.

Then, in the same high voice, she said, "Remember!" She gazed at the faces of Chinyere and every one of the siblings, as if trying to jog their memories of the past. "Remember that Onyeka went to Da Erima to beg to come back to the house as before. Let's be honest in our assessment, Chinyere."

Sarah could no longer keep quiet. "If Chinyere thinks that Onyeka was oppressed, what did she do over the years for her precious mother? Come to think of it, Chinyere, you were supposedly married to a rich guy. Tell us the number of times you sent money to your mother, Onyeka. Tell us."

Udo laughed and clapped her hands. "Sarah, I should have thought of that. Thank you. Dear sister, answer her question. Why didn't you, Chinyere? You're the oldest of her children. Why not rescue her from the clutches of this woman you hated so much? Tell us."

Chinyere looked confused, as if blindsided by Sarah, and for the moment had no response.

"Talk is cheap," Sarah said, as everybody waited for Chinyere to respond.

The brothers sitting there looked around sheepishly. Michael got up to bid goodbye to his friends, looking surprised and embarrassed at the turn of events. With nothing more coming out of Chinyere, Emeka and Nwankwo looked bemused.

As Udo stood up to leave the room, she looked at Sarah and said, "Some of us like to sanitize our lives. But those who grew up with them knew better, Sarah."

Sarah stood up, feeling physically upset. She looked pointedly at Chinyere and muttered, "You, idiot." She flounced out of the room and made her way downstairs to the room she shared with Chinyere, wishing she was going somewhere else.

CHAPTER 13

Early the next morning, Ejituru stood in front of her father's grand house staring at the lawn and observing the servants and the hired help removing all the detritus and vestiges of the two-day party to celebrate the death of her mother, Nkechi. It was a period before the morning's wave of visitors would arrive to pay their respects and congratulate the family again for staging the best sendoff for their mother. They would, of course, be expecting any leftovers from yesterday's feast.

She had left her house at the new extension three miles from here before the first cock crowed, ostensibly to make sure any borrowed items were returned to their rightful owners.

In actual fact, she'd been unable to sleep, her mind replaying over and over the events of the past two days. After rising, she'd considered waking the temporary maid to boil hot water for her bath but decided against it. She'd quickly dressed, splashed cold water on her face, picked up the key of the rental car, and driven herself here. Driving as fast as she could, given the potholes in the road, she passed the Nkwu Iso junction, where, during her school holidays from Ibiaku, when she was young and carefree, she had often lingered with friends on their way to the stream. She continued past the primary school she had attended from the age of four. She didn't notice the men and women who, like her, had risen early and were on their way to the farm, or the young children with water pots on their heads returning from the stream, anxious to get the water home so the adults could bathe before stepping out to do their errands. Her one thought was to get to her father's house as soon as possible.

She was aware that her mother's funeral yesterday had won the acclamation of the town. Each grandchild had given a cow, and not many people had ten cows slaughtered for their funeral feast, apparently. On the whole, Nkechi was sent off in style, everyone agreed. They said it was a well-deserved funeral, the best ever send-off. The family spared nothing to ensure that she was sent off as befitting a queen, and the funeral repast was the most elaborate. Nkechi must be looking down on the celebration with pride. These were the verdicts of the villagers as they discussed Nkechi's funeral.

The night before, as the people were beginning to disperse, the family had made sure that each attendee left with a coffee mug engraved with Nkechi's photograph, the dates of her birth and death. Ejituru recalled that Nkechi herself had been the beneficiary of more than a hundred such mugs, which were stored in the closet in her room, only to be brought out when a visitor was served with tea. At such times, the mug served as a reminder of the person whose image was engraved on it. The ensuing conversation would cover the deceased person's character and achievements while alive and end with a hope that she or he had gone to a better place.

Sometimes the discussion would center on the shenanigans of the family left behind. Someone would say, "Did you hear that her youngest son is selling off all her jojis?" Then the conversation would turn into either a discussion of the character of the son or the number of jojis the woman had acquired during her lifetime. "The other day at the women's gathering, I saw her eldest daughter wearing her matching earrings and necklace. You remember, the one she always wore at Christmas?" Everyone in the room would nod in agreement, and someone would say, "I'm glad she was able to grab those, given the disorder in that family."

Ejituru sighed, wondering what would be said of Nkechi and this family whenever anyone drank from the mug. Thinking about it brought up the bile from her stomach as she burned with indignation, not against the villagers, per se, but because of the gossip. She knew only too well what people were saying about her: that she was an ungrateful bitch who used her ex as a stepping stone to attain her primary objective. She was all too familiar with the vapid chatter, the usual tittle-tattle, the nonsense people say that strangles the truth. But what did she care? Villagers could say what they liked. She would not be here to hear it.

Throughout the funeral, she'd been troubled by the amount of money spent. Was it worth it? she wondered. Wouldn't it have been

better to use the money to provide for the living instead?

Of course the villagers wouldn't have forgiven the family, since it was a strongly held belief that one should be sent off to the beyond in a manner according to their stature while alive. Nkechi had never subscribed to this belief. To her, such ostentatious display was unnecessary, given the abject poverty of many in the villages. It wasn't as if she was begrudging the villagers their enjoyment at her expense, but she had always argued that it would be better to spend the money on the parents while they were alive than to spend so much to celebrate their death. Others argued that it was their life that was being celebrated, and the money spent at funerals should be regarded as the living honoring the life of the dead.

It never used to be like this, Ejituru thought.

In the past, her mother had told her, the dead were buried with as little fanfare as possible, except of course if they were traditional rulers. The current type of extravaganza had been imported after the civil war, when Igbo migrants to other parts of Nigeria came back and introduced burial customs they'd witnessed in those areas, such as the wearing of uniforms. She herself had made sure that her mother's final days on Earth were comfortable. She regretted that when her father was alive, she gave him very little financial assistance, arguing that he never contributed anything toward her upbringing, or for that matter, the upbringing of any of the other children. Their upkeep and education had been totally borne by Nkechi, who was the acknowledged breadwinner in the family. Besides, she never actually forgave him for arranging her marriage with Ignatius and for ignoring her wishes.

Yesterday, she'd been taken aback to see members of her exhusband's family at the repast. At first, she had thought they'd come to gloat over the death of Nkechi, whom they blamed for the failure of the marriage. But both the uncle and his wife had come up to her to express their condolence before joining their cronies at the tables set up for the rich and famous members of the society. Even so, she couldn't help but wonder what their actual thoughts were when they saw her. Later on, she'd wondered whether Okoro was one of those people who'd instigated having the members of the compound query her about the absence of her husband at the funeral.

Thinking of the event during the clothing of the dead, she was surprised at the angry words used to describe Nduka's absence and people from Owerri, where Nduka came from. She'd tried to explain Nduka's regret that he had no living relatives in Nigeria or anyone from Owerri to represent his part of the family at the funeral. His distant relatives were scattered all over Nigeria. How could they expect him to leave the position he had only recently assumed after one month? Besides, who did they think would look after the children while she was burying her mother? But then, why would they understand? Their lives had always been bound by custom, and any deviation from the norm was unacceptable. During the family meeting to plan the funeral, she had patiently explained to her brothers and sisters that the cost was being borne by both Nduka and herself. She'd explained that he wanted very much to be with them, but the timing was bad, and besides, one of them had to be at home for the children.

Obviously, they'd chosen to hide the truth from their friends, or perhaps she should give them the benefit of the doubt. Maybe they never saw the need to explain his absence or that of his Nigerian family.

The elders wanted to impose a huge fine on Nduka for insulting the memory of his illustrious mother-in-law by not personally paying his respects or sending a representative from his village in Imo State. She was surprised at the evil things said during the meeting. Although she was seething with anger, she tried outwardly to control herself. She wanted to tell them to go to hell and to follow that by walking out. Instead, she had, in her most humble voice, reminded them of the facts they'd forgotten. She almost lost it when her children's absence was mentioned. Knowing that all overseas Nigerians were assumed to be filthy rich, she had replied that Nduka had helped pay for the funeral, and they couldn't afford the airfares as well as the huge cost of the funeral. Through the intercession of an elderly man—a confidant of Nkechi, the fine was lowered, and she'd reluctantly paid it.

Ejituru had had difficulty holding back her tears and had fled to her mother's room with her grave to calm down before going home to her house.

Her mind swung to the events leading up to her inauspicious marriage to Ignatius. She couldn't totally blame her father. After all, he thought he was securing her future. In a way, she felt, he did secure her future, though not in the way he envisioned it. The marriage had brought her to the United States, and while it took longer than expected for her to obtain her medical certification, the fault wasn't entirely his. Like everybody in the village involved in marriage arrangements, he was hoodwinked by Ignatius, who presented himself as something he was not. How could they have known that he was a taxi driver and not an engineer, as he said? How could they have known that he had no intention of helping her pursue her dream? Having lived all these years in the US, she'd come to know the various lies and half-truths that Nigerian immigrants told their relatives in order to appear successful. Her father shouldn't bear the blame alone. She had often blamed herself for not putting up a fight.

There were times during that fateful summer when she could have stood her ground, but the lure of going to America was such that she could do nothing but acquiesce. She did often blame herself, especially during those years when it was a struggle to enter medical school and to keep her grades up while working. Now she patted herself on the back.

When her mother's health deteriorated and she wasn't able to keep her businesses, she'd made sure that her mother had a monthly stipend. Her mother didn't want it, but she wanted to maintain her social status. Ejituru had never begrudged her anything, and never asked her what she did with the money she sent to her every month, even when she heard rumors that she was handing it over to the oldest son, Michael. Shame on him. Despite the money spent on his education, he couldn't support his family, let alone his father and the mother who, even though she didn't carry him for nine months, did care for him from birth. In any case, what needed to be done had been done, and she need not cry over spilt milk.

As she stood outside the house, with so many thoughts skittering across her brain, Ejituru observed the used paper napkins and tablecloths and the soiled plastic cutlery being unceremoniously dumped into big cardboard boxes, and the empty Coca-Cola and soft drink bottles being placed in the crates, along with the empty beer bottles. Tables and chairs were being folded and placed on the lorry standing by. Leftover food on the plates was dumped into its own separate cardboard box, and the lawn was being restored to its prefuneral look. The lawn wouldn't be the same, having been trampled upon by so many feet in those four days. But then, it didn't really matter anymore. She would soon return to Nduka and the life from which she had only taken a temporary leave.

During the years of separation from Nduka, she had heard from friends that he was very upset and depressed because he had hoped that on graduation they would get married. He did eventually move on, from what she heard. According to her confidant, Stella, who by this time had married her professor and was living at the main campus of the university, he had gone to Russia for further training. Then he had come back to set up his practice. She had had no inkling that he wasn't in the US, nor of the tragedy he suffered losing his mother and his girlfriend at the same time. During those years, she was consumed with her own situation and how to get out of her marriage to Ignatius. She remembered when Nduka told her his story, how her heart ached for him. At that time, she wanted nothing but to make his life from then on, a happy one, to get him to forget all the bad things that had happened to him.

She thought of her own life before that day when she reconnected with him. It had not been a bed of roses. She had married the man picked out for her by her father, a man she did not love because she had already given her heart to Nduka, even though she had never told Nduka that she loved only him.

I married my ex because I really wanted to study in United States.

That was the dream of all of us girls at the secondary school we attended. Ignatius was my ticket to achieve all that I had wished for.

A bad mistake, as it turned out. He was uncouth and lacked ambition. Too old to change, he wanted a traditional, subservient wife who would bear him children and work to support the family. He didn't understand her ambition to make something of herself. Nobody understood that but Nkechi, who had instilled in her from birth that education was the only thing in this world that mattered because it would open all the doors for her.

She thanked God she had met Nduka when she did because he gave her the strength to leave that marriage and encouraged her to pursue her dream. It was wonderful being married to someone she loved and to have that love reciprocated by a person with whom to share so many things and create beautiful memories.

How I miss him. Waking up in the morning without him is hell, and not being able to talk to him face to face since coming here has been really hard.

They'd discussed the possibility of coming together, knowing full well that this was impossible given that they had nobody to leave the children with, and they were just settling into a new place.

She shook her head. Standing in this place at this particular time, she realized she needed to heed Nduka's suggestion and try to build a bridge with her family. She needed to find out if there was any hope of a relationship with them before heading home to her house in Maryland. She'd been dodging the effort, but now she could no longer put off her planned final meeting with her siblings. This event was her responsibility, and in all the hustle and bustle of the funeral, she'd forgotten to alert her brothers and sisters of it. Or maybe she just hadn't wanted to. Before returning to her house in the new extension, she would talk to her trusted sister Ifeoma, who would relay the message to all the others.

CHAPTER 14

When Ejituru entered her father's house, the first person she saw sitting in the parlor was her youngest brother, Nwankwo. He wore only a wrapper around his waist and looked as if he'd just woken up. He obviously had yet to shower. Who could blame him for oversleeping? The funeral had been strenuous. On the other hand, apart from standing around and greeting friends, he'd contributed nothing to the event. But then, how could he, not being able to keep a job throughout his forty-odd years?

Ejituru debated whether to tell him of the event she'd planned for tonight. It was a throwaway thought, and one she never intended to act on because she didn't trust him. He would most likely spread the news in garbled form, adding his thoughts and presenting them as if they were what she intended to convey. She would talk to Ifeoma, and Ifeoma alone would be the messenger.

He startled as she entered the room and murmured a greeting. "Ma, Ibo la chi. You are here early. Are you traveling today?"

Irritated because of the implied suggestion that she would leave before the memorial service, she sharply replied, "Odighi, not today. I wanted to make sure that the place got tidied up and all the borrowed tables and chairs returned to the school.

I also thought I would catch up with Udo and Chinyere to find out what their plans are." She stared at his confused face. "Where are they? With so many people around yesterday, it was very difficult to keep track of everybody."

He locked eyes with her before lowering his gaze. "Did you look for them at Michael's house next door?"

"Actually, that never occurred to me. In any case, I'll be here for several hours and will catch them when they return—that is, if they've gone out. But I did notice that Michael's house looked unattended."

Nwankwo rubbed his face uneasily. "Sister, that was a grand funeral.

Everybody enjoyed themselves."

For a short period, both sat lost in their own thoughts.

After a time, Nwankwo spoke, his thoughts still on the missing presence of the sisters. "I only saw them fleetingly. You're probably right. Perhaps they've gone to the compound."

Ejituru nodded. Then she asked, "How's the shoe business?" Because of her parents' insistence, Ejituru had spent an inordinate amount of money to get him trained in whatever skill her father hoped would provide him with a livelihood— shoe repair, mechanics— to name a few. At one point when he showed interest in shoe repairing, she'd financed the construction of a workshop in front of her father's house for him, including the purchase of equipment and initial material.

He looked at her as if wondering about her concern. "Ma, times are hard.

The sewing machine needs repair, and I haven't been able to repair it."

Feigning surprise, she asked, "Aren't you able to do those things that don't require stitching?"

He looked at her as if surprised at her persistence. "Ma, that isn't how it works. Without the machine, I can do nothing."

"Are you working now?" she asked, staring him in the face. As if embarrassed, he laughed and looked away.

Ejituru felt her original concern dissipating and quickly dismissed him from her mind. He was not her concern. To her, he was a simpleton born when Onyeka was in her late forties.

Startled at this thought, she quickly regretted it. Her parents had worried about his inability to concentrate in school. Unlike his siblings, he was a poor student and had dropped out after three years. They could never understand why he couldn't finish his primary education. Throughout his life, his father worried about what would become of him. He wasn't interested in farming or trading, preferring to lounge around from morning to night or to join groups of ne'er-do-well young men in the village who roamed about looking for handouts. There had never really been a diagnosis to find out what was wrong with him.

Expecting no response to her question, she said, "I'll wait upstairs for Ifeoma. She should be here soon, I hope."

Ejituru crossed the parlor from where she had been standing near the window to the corridor and went up the steps to the top sitting room. This was her father's domain when he was alive. The sparse room in which he slept was off the parlor. It was the place where he could escape from the turmoil of everyday life. She remembered the countless discussions she'd had with him during the marriage negotiations in the room that was then his office and now expropriated by Udo as her bedroom. She remembered the time when, frustrated because Ignatius didn't appear eager to send her the application forms for universities, she'd rushed back from Enugu in agony to tell her parents that she was breaking the engagement. Her father was getting ready to go out to visit his cronies when she arrived. He was taken aback when she approached him the next morning, arguing with her about Ignatius's intentions.

She remembered the meeting at Ignatius's father's house. His family had accused her of promiscuity, which incensed her aunt especially.

Bless her heart.

In the end, it was decided that Ignatius should be informed of the termination of the engagement. It was a game on her part. She laughed now, thinking about how easily she had capitulated when Ignatius called her, promising—falsely, as it turned out—that the forms would be waiting for her upon her arrival.

Ejituru directed her thoughts back to her father, and once again felt her acute disappointment that he hadn't been buried in the house, as was the custom. It was one of those things she often thought about but couldn't bring herself to ask anyone then. For months after his funeral, she would lay awake at night worrying that her father's body was left outside to be desecrated by the elements. Why did Nkechi hate her husband so much as to allow this to happen? It was later explained to her that it was his wish that he not be buried in the house because he regarded this tradition as unchristian. But why did Nkechi not overrule him? In her own case, Nkechi's body would be forever ensconced in the room she had always called her own, the bedroom where she'd spent most of her life.

Poor man!

During her last visit when Nkechi was still lucid, Ejituru had confronted her, accusing her of sanctioning an outside burial instead of an inside burial as was the custom. It was then that she learned that it was his wish. He had mistakenly believed that the traditional burial custom was a pagan practice. At least for now, the mystery of the grave had been explained, even though she would never accept it. But what could she do? She couldn't exhume her father and rebury him. What would the villagers and his clan's kindred think?

She moved about the parlor, straightening the cushions on the chairs and puffing them up.

Finally, she sat down and looked around the room. Her brother Emeka had a room off the parlor. His bedroom door was locked, and that meant that he, too, was out and about. He couldn't have gone to work today, could he? she asked herself. She wouldn't put it past him. Did he even know that his mother was dead? She doubted he was aware of what was happening. He had always existed in his own world.

She chided herself for such thoughts. He might behave as if he was elsewhere whenever he was addressed, but he was well aware of what was happening. He must have chosen not to let it dominate his life. She recalled with gratitude his support during the church ceremony, without which she wouldn't have been able to last out the service. As a lector, he read his portion of the Bible eloquently.

She knocked and tried the door handle again. She heard a muffled sound and someone shuffling to the door.

The door opened a crack, and Emeka's muffled voice asked, "Who is it?"

When Emeka first heard a knock, he was lying in bed in his dark room. He struggled to wake up. His head ached, and his throat felt like sandpaper. He cursed himself for the evening revelry with his brothers and their friends. Reflecting on the past night, he cursed himself again for staying up late since, as it turned out, he'd been upset by Chinyere blaming every little thing that happened in their childhood on Nkechi and, by implication, characterizing Onyeka as a saint. He fully regretted having to spend his evening in such company. He did it because he'd felt obligated to stay with Udo, since she would feel lost in the midst of people she didn't know. In any case, no one ever listened to him. Eventually, he'd quietly gone to his room to be by himself.

Lying flat on his back, he tried to imagine a life without Nkechi. Even though she hadn't been physically in the house for several years now, there'd never been a week that he'd not gone to Umuahia to visit and spend time with her.

Lifting his eyes to the ceiling, he watched a gecko trying to catch a fly entangled in the spider's web in the corner. He gently coughed, trying to dislodge the irritating phlegm in his throat. Then he heard someone knock again and try to push his door open. He suspected each of his sisters for the attempt to invade his privacy. If it had been the usual suspects, Udo or Sarah, they would have shouted his name and banged on the door.

Udo would be the last person he would want to open his door to. Ever since she'd arrived for the funeral, she'd been a thorn in his flesh, sending him on little errands as soon as she saw him, asking him questions about his life that he wasn't able to answer, trying to get him to comment on the lives of his brothers, and wanting him to entertain her. She appeared stuck in the past. Those who lived in the house had their own lives and needs. She'd expected time to stand still because she deigned to visit them every few years. When she visited, she expected gratitude because she'd sent gifts at Christmas, and if none was forthcoming, she would pout the whole day. Fancy if he hadn't locked his door. The person outside would have barged in, and the next thing would have been to berate him for the state of his room.

He looked at the clock on the table beside his bed and realized that it was only eight o'clock. Could it be Chinyere at this hour? What could she possibly want from him? Prior to this funeral, the last time he saw Chinyere was at his father's funeral, when she came with her husband, who played the big man, honoring his in-law with a cow. But what he'd remembered about that time was how bitter Chinyere was and her diatribe against Nkechi. She'd waited until her husband left to say hateful things about Ejituru and Nkechi. He couldn't understand why she was so vile. To him, Nkechi was a goddess. She was the only mother he knew. She was the person who made sure there was enough food in the house for all. Even when her health was failing, her first thought was to make sure that those living at home were fed and had clean clothes. He couldn't understand why Chinyere was so vicious in her anger.

Thinking about it now, he was very proud of how the rest of his siblings who were present rallied around Nkechi and in effect, ostracized Chinyere at that time. That was why last night he'd put her down for thinking that Nkechi was responsible for the failure of Michael's first marriage. He wondered why she had come to Nkechi's funeral. Had she come to gloat at the death of her enemy? Anybody looking at her would think she was grieving for the death.

He breathed a sigh of relief when the door at first didn't open because he had locked it. Then he heard the knock again and got up, opened the door a crack and saw Ejituru standing on the other side.

"Emeka!" she exclaimed. She stared at him as he tried to wipe the sleep off his face. "I wasn't sure you were in."

"We went to bed very late. But why are you here so early in the morning? It's only eight o'clock." Trying to rub the sleep out of his eyes, he came out of his room into the parlor.

"I came to help Ifeoma with the cleanup. I didn't mean to wake you up, but I wanted to thank you for looking out for me yesterday."

"Yesterday was tough for everyone," he said as tears welled in his eyes and he was overcome with sadness. In a teary voice, he added, "Even though I was told that she had died, I never really accepted it until yesterday when I saw her lying in the bed unable to get up, so unlike her."

"I've also had difficulty accepting it. But I know that she hated the last years of her life and wanted to go as soon as possible. Let's hope she's at peace wherever she is now."

Gazing sadly at her, he said, "Sister, it's morning. Let's read the Bible together and pray for Mama." He went back to his room and came back with the Bible. He opened it to Chapter 12 of John's Gospel and read aloud. "Unless a grain of wheat falls into the earth and dies, it remains alone, but if it dies, it bears much fruit. He who loves his life in this world will keep it for eternal life. If anyone serves me, he must follow me and where I am, there shall my servant be; if anyone serves me, the Father will honor him." He stopped and turned his face to her. "I discussed this passage many times with Mama, and she often drew my attention to the writings of Paul to the Corinthians, where he states that what was sown on Earth decays, but what rises is incorruptible. I'm convinced, dear sister, that in death, Nkechi has been reborn in Christ. We must believe this because she lived an exemplary life and did a lot of good in this world. This should bring you comfort."

Clasping her hand, he prayed, "Jesus, let us be the kernel of corn sown in the earth to be harvested for you. We will follow wherever you lead. Give us fresh hope and joy in serving you all the days of our life." With that, Emeka went back into his room.

⚜

Ejituru felt comforted by the Bible reading and prayer, which reminded her of the many evenings and early mornings during her childhood that the prayer bell would ring and every member of the house would gather together in this same parlor for the reading of an appropriate verse and the offering of prayers for a good day, either by Nkechi or Nwakama.

Emeka came out of his room with his towel to announce that he was going to the stream for his bath.

"Why are you going to the stream?" she asked. "Are we short of water here?"

"No, no, we have plenty," he said on his way to the front door. "I'm a creature of habit, and I prefer the stream."

CHAPTER 15

When Emeka left, Ejituru felt grateful that she had been able to connect with him in a small way, although that hadn't been her first objective. She sat down on the nearest chair in the parlor, thinking, why didn't Emeka allow her to enter his room and sit with him? That was what she wanted when she knocked at the door. She would love to look inside his room just to see the debris that she was told existed there. She was told that for the past twenty years since it became his bedroom, it hadn't seen either a broom or daylight. The outside window had always been closed tight, and no one had been allowed in the room except him. She imagined the accumulation of dust and cobwebs inside and shuddered.

How could he live like that? That was why a year ago, she thought she would give him a present of a bed, wardrobe, and drapes, as this would nudge him to clean up.

When the presents arrived, he ordered them returned because he felt insulted. He was quite satisfied with what he had and needed nothing more. Money he would accept, because he could give it to those less fortunate than him.

Poor Ifeoma.

She had to think of how to get rid of the presents. She'd called to ask how to dispose of the gifts. In the end, it was agreed that Nwosu's room could use them. Nwosu was Nwankwo's preteen son, who was delighted to get a new bed with a good mattress, a wardrobe, and a replacement for the tattered drapes in the window.

Shaking her head, Ejituru continued to survey the parlor. She looked around and noticed the wedding photograph of her grandparents. Her grandmother wore a short, white dress and white veil and carried a bouquet of flowers. This must have been the only time she wore a short dress. She wondered who made it for her. Perhaps the missionaries had bought it for her in Calabar. She looked very fashionable in it. Ejituru couldn't remember ever having seen her grandmother in any dress other than the traditional Aro women's dress—a blouse, a wraparound cloth, and a top wraparound cloth and head tie.

Her grandfather wore an ill-fitted suit in the photograph. This she expected because as long as she could remember, he wore suits to church and school, and it was only after his retirement that he began sometimes to dress traditionally, but never to church. Suits were reserved for church.

She examined the photograph minutely, seeing no discernible background. Where had it been taken—at a church ceremony or outside the church? Perhaps this was a studio photograph. But there had never been a studio in the town, so she discounted that line of reasoning. The photograph had started fading in several places, but she could still make out the images. Both grandparents looked serious.

What were they thinking? Were they looking forward to a happy married life? Was she anticipating being the wife of a salaried person, knowing that every month, money would come in and she would never have to go to the farm or struggle to make ends meet? Did he promise her a monthly allowance? Was theirs a happy marriage? She knew in those days, all marriages were arranged, and her grandparents' marriage was no exception.

Her grandmother was the daughter of a man who had been brought into the area as a house slave of one of the minor chiefs. She had only three years of schooling, and the man she married was one of her teachers. What was the attraction? she wondered. Perhaps he wanted a girl who had some education, and there were none among his social group. In those days, Christianity was a new fad. The Amadis, the group to which he belonged, frowned on anything that would disrupt the social order, while the slave class wholeheartedly accepted Christianity. Its teaching of equality of all persons before the Almighty appealed to them.

She was one of the first girls from the slave family to go to school.

Her father, an important convert to Christianity, must have been persuaded by the missionaries to send her and her siblings to school. He wanted her to be a teacher, like the missionaries at the newly established primary school for girls. Although she never completed primary school, she did learn the rudiments of home economics, cooking, and sewing, skills that helped her land a job teaching home economics during the Second World War, when female missionaries were scarce. He, on the other hand, as a member of a prominent Amadi family and a newly minted teacher from Hope Waddle with a monthly cash income, was a catch, and many families with marriage-age daughters must have vied to have their daughters married to him.

Sitting in the parlor and looking at the photograph, Ejituru wondered what part the missionaries played in the arrangement. She must have been one of their promising students, and they wouldn't have wanted her to marry a heathen. He must have taken a shine to her, but was it reciprocated? Was she ever in love with him? Perhaps not. The decision to marry wouldn't have been hers. It was her duty to her parents. He actually stood to lose in the marriage because he was marrying beneath his social status. As an Amadi, he was demeaning himself by marrying from a slave family. Did he marry her because he needed a Christian wife in order to survive during the new era?

Thinking about it now, Ejituru felt that he truly embraced Christianity, and even though his marriage didn't advance his stature in the traditional society or within his family, he did really believe that all people were equal and that in God's eyes, there was no difference between a slave and an Amadi. His family never accepted her and did everything to punish her for marrying him. While their children were growing up, the stupid things his family did to punish her were objects of much mirth among them.

Gazing at the photograph and letting her mind dwell on her grandfather, Ejituru wondered what he would have said if he knew what she, his granddaughter, was about to do. If he were alive, would she have discussed it with him? Would she have even discussed it with her father, come to think of it?

"Hmm, let me think," she said out loud.

She couldn't remember when she had ever sat together with her father and talked about things, even mundane subjects like the weather, although she did remember discussing her marriage to Ignatius. Her relationship with him had always been that of a pupil being instructed on what to do. With him, she had no voice, no thought of her own, nothing to contribute or offer. She was just a receptacle for his instructions. When she first left home to go to secondary school, she thought her relationship with him would change. After all, she had more education than he did, and had begun interacting with children from other social groups. One would think that he would seek her views on whatever problem he had, but no, that didn't happen. She was a girl, and daughters, even the unmarried ones, had no say in the family.

Her musings were interrupted when she heard Nwankwo say, "Ma, can I get something for you to eat or drink? We have lots of leftovers from yesterday."

Startled by his voice, she turned from the photograph. "Nothing, thank you. I was just looking at the photographs of our parents and grandparents. They look so young in them."

Nwankwo came closer and glanced at the photographs. Coughing loudly, he said, "Mama said that she was only sixteen when that photo was taken. He was her teacher, you know."

Ejituru gestured for Nwankwo to have a seat. Pointing to a photo of her parents together, she said, "I wonder when this photo was taken. Do you know?"

Nwankwo screwed up his face. "It must have been before I was born, but I don't know when."

"Neither do I," she said. "I wasn't close to our dad, Nwakama. Our relationship was that of teacher and pupil, with him giving instructions to me and not prepared to listen to any objections that I might have. Perhaps it was different for you boys."

Nwankwo wrung his hands nervously before answering. "Hmm. It wasn't any different, but, Ma, in those days, fathers knew best and children dared not disobey."

Looking forlorn, Ejituru said, "You know, I thought it would be different when I visited from the US, but I'm afraid the distance between us grew even larger. We had nothing to say to each other." Lapsing into silence, Ejituru cast her eyes around and saw the new furniture Udo had recently bought and the light-green paint on the walls. She turned again to find that Nwankwo had somehow made his way downstairs. As if addressing herself, she said aloud, "Come to think of it, we never had any discussion about the land, but I was made to understand that building a house on it was what was expected from me in the same way I was expected to marry a man he chose in order to save face with his friends, who convinced him that the marriage would solve his financial problems."

Lost in thought, Ejituru didn't hear Ifeoma calling from downstairs.

Then she heard Nwankwo say loudly, "Ifeoma, you, too, are early."

Her response was lost to her because Ifeoma had moved out of the zone. Ejituru laughed mirthlessly, but rather than go downstairs to meet Ifeoma, she stared at the photographs before getting up and moving to the corridor window, where she sat and watched the women streaming onto the path leading to the house.

CHAPTER 16

Ifeoma stayed at the repast in her father's house just long enough to make sure that she was seen by those who mattered to her before making her way back to her house. She had instructed her closest friends, who had come all the way from Aba and Umuahia to support her on the occasion of her mother's death, to meet her there. She loved her house. It wasn't as grand as her father's, but it was hers, built on the spot of an earlier house that belonged to her deceased mother-in-law. Her husband was the only son of the mother and was, therefore, able to inherit the mother's house. The old house had been demolished when she was promoted to headmistress of the Umuahia secondary school, where she had been a teacher since graduating from teacher training college. The new one wasn't a big house like Ejituru's at the new extension, but it was comfortable, with enough rooms for her five children. She had installed a functioning toilet and bathroom, which set the house apart from the others in the compound.

The party in her house continued past midnight, when the last of the celebrants started drifting away, some to make the arduous journey to Umuahia, others to their village houses or hotels, and some to find a room in her house to lay down. At last, she lay in her bed, but sleep eluded her. She tossed and turned the remainder of the night, worried that the hired help and the driver she hired to collect the rented furniture would disappoint her. Unable to sleep, she rose at the sound of the cock crowing and made her way to her father's house. She was anxious to get there to see the cleanup. She always thought of it as her father's house, but in actual fact, it was Nkechi's father's house and therefore Nkechi's house. Over the years, it had been regarded as her father's house because Nkechi was a woman.

Between her house and her father's, Ifeoma must have been stopped by at least fifty people, women returning from or going to the stream or farm and men on their way to the farm or to early morning prayers or meetings, each either repeating the same thing or its variant and asking the same question.

Every step was interrupted by acquaintances who wanted to express their condolences and to offer praise to the family for the magnificence of the funeral. "There hasn't been anything like this before. What a magnificent send-off. Mama Nkechi would be pleased. You've all made her very proud. Are your sisters from abroad staying with us for some time?"

Halfway there, Ifeoma stopped to talk to an acquaintance, a young man on his way to work. A clerk at the Internal Revenue Service at the government station, he had risen early, like her. This meeting was fortuitous because it gave her the opportunity to discuss her land registration application submitted nine months ago for approval. The decision was still pending.

While preoccupied with her mother's care, she had had very little time to pursue the registration. Now she hoped to devote some time to the issue, knowing full well that nothing would be done without the usual side payment to the officer responsible.

The young man confirmed what she already knew and urged her to take the necessary action to facilitate the process. "My sister, you know how things are done here," he said.

Their discussion was cut short by a passerby who was anxious to talk about the funeral. Reluctantly, Ifeoma said goodbye and listened to this person extolling the virtues of the family and the magnificent funeral.

"Mama would be very happy at the send-off you gave her."

Ifeoma nodded and wiped an imaginary tear from her eyes with the tip of her wrapper. This funeral would be talked about until the next big funeral. She had shed tears and she would shed more, but standing there now and listening to yet another passerby saying the same thing over and over again, she wished she could just shake the woman off and step into the driveway. She spied movement in the upstairs parlor of her father's house and became distracted, halflistening to the woman who had waylaid her.

Who can that be? I didn't expect anyone to be awake at this time.

I was quite sure Udo and Chinyere would still be sleeping.

She looked at her watch: 7:00 a.m.

I'm not ready to deal with any of them at this time.

She shook her head and tightened her hand on the handle of her bag as she continued moving toward her father's house as the woman finally finished talking and walked away.

Stepping into the driveway, she was surprised to see Ejituru's hired car parked in the yard. She felt as if she'd been punched in the face by some unknown assailant. Many thoughts passed through her head. Didn't Ejituru trust her to complete the assignment? Had something happened during the night to one of the siblings, and instead of her being called, Ejituru had been summoned? Had Ejituru decided to go back to the US later in the day and come to bid farewell to everyone? Why would she do that without consulting her?

There were several unpaid bills waiting to be settled. The memorial service was to take place that Sunday, and the family was expected to make a large donation to the church. After all, Nkechi was a most prominent member of the church.

Ever since Ifeoma was a little girl, Ejituru, of all her siblings, had been her hero. She looked up to her. Ejituru was the one she felt closest to. It pained her to think that there was something that Ejituru was withholding from her.

"There is nothing I wouldn't do for her," she murmured.

She heard the sound of a car horn and turned back toward the road. A man she recognized stepped out of a vehicle with outstretched hands. He was an Aba-based doctor and was home for Nkechi's funeral. He was simply dressed in matching trousers and shirt.

Ifeoma composed her face and greeted him. "Good morning, sir. Are you on your way back?"

"No, I'll be here a few days. I'm on my way to see a friend at the barracks. But Mama Ifeoma, you are up early. You should take it easy after all the commotion of the past few days. I tell you, that was a grand ceremony. Congratulations."

With her face full of emotion, she shook his hand. Feeling that she couldn't just walk away, she said, "Thank you for coming to the funeral and for your support. How's your family? Did your son Mike get admitted to the university? Which one did he accept?"

"My sister, we decided to send him to Ghana. He's been admitted to Achimota University."

"Great," she said. "You've made a wise decision. At least he'll have textbooks and well-qualified teachers."

They talked about what was happening in Aba, where the garbage had piled up in many areas, blocking the streets, and bemoaned the fact that the contractor had absconded with the advance payment given to him in good faith with no intention of performing the work.

As they stood there talking, villagers on their way to the farm interrupted them often to pay their respects. Before the next woman could stop her to talk, Ifeoma waved at her and stepped back onto the path leading to her father's house just as the workmen were loading the last of the tables into the truck. She thanked them for their work and told them where to take the chairs, the empty bottles, and the garbage.

The driver had been sitting in a chair in the shade in the corner of the grounds. He rose and approached her. Genuflecting, he said,

"Mama Ifeoma, I've been waiting." "I know," she said.

"Sister, you know we've not been paid," he said angrily. "We're hoping that you will settle everything with us before we leave here."

"Why do you think I left my house so early to come here and meet with you?" she said with a flash of anger.

"Eh! Don't be upset," he replied in a contrite voice. "I just thought I should mention it."

"Listen, I'll be here for some time. Go and return the things and come back so I can settle with you. I can't hand over the money out here. Come back soon."

The young man grudgingly acquiesced and drove off.

When she entered the porch, she noticed that the downstairs parlor was full of visitors. She had anticipated that this would happen, since the mourning period usually lasted for at least a month, and until the memorial service, they could expect an onslaught of visitors every morning. She wondered where Ejituru and her other siblings were, and why nothing was being done. It seemed to her that everyone had abdicated their responsibility for the funeral and beyond, and without her, nothing would be done. Nobody seemed to be attending to the visitors. She could excuse Ejituru for not attending to the women in the parlor. After all, she hadn't slept there last night. But the others had no excuse whatsoever.

She glared at Nwankwo, whom she saw hovering in the courtyard looking lost. Seeing his nervousness manifested in the way he clasped and unclasped his hands, unsure what to do, she deliberately ignored him and made her way to the parlor, where normally her mother would have received her visitors. She tossed greetings to all, shaking each hand. Then she shouted for the servants, who had been working to restore order to the place, to serve the visitors with soft drinks while she arranged for the leftover food from yesterday to be warmed up and served. All the while, she wondered about the whereabouts of the other women in the family who slept in the house.

Ifeoma remembered the argument with Chinyere during the funeral over the uniforms. She hadn't intentionally decided to use a different material for hers. When the seamstress informed her that she was short by a yard of the material bought for the uniforms, rather than purchase additional yardage, she'd thought she would be saving money by using the white brocade material she had in the house. She didn't think the difference would be noticeable. It was just like Chinyere, a troublemaker, to point this out at an inopportune time.

Unfortunately, Udo had joined in reprimanding her. This didn't auger well for her relationship with Udo, given the fight she'd had with her over the money sent for Nkechi's care. She remembered that Udo wanted to be given an itemized list of how her money was spent. Ifeoma didn't mind giving her an account, but she resented the fact that Udo would predicate the gift by letting her know that her life in London had not been a bed of roses. She was a single mother and had to allocate her resources carefully. She said Ifeoma didn't fully understand what it meant to be a single mother in London with no help from anyone. A year before Nkechi's death, Ifeoma had lost it and sent the money back to Udo, saying that she needed it more, and there was no need for her to deprive herself of the necessities just to assuage her guilt over not caring for her mother. This was the first time the two had met since then.

During her fight with Udo, she had wanted to lash out and say that she, too, had a lot of responsibility, having five children to educate on her meager salary, and now with no reliable monthly income since the Abia State government was notorious for not paying its pensioners. At that date, the government was seven months in arrears. She had been able to meet her financial obligations because she had always dabbled in many things: farming, running a computer training school, trading in yard goods, running a tailoring school, to name a few. But she had held her tongue because Udo was older than her, and she had to give her some respect, even if she didn't deserve it.

She wasn't looking forward to the next meeting with Udo. Sighing, she hoped that perhaps she was making too much of the argument, and nobody would raise the issue again.

She looked around for Ejituru, who she had always felt close to even though they weren't from the same birth mother. As soon as she began her medical career, Ejituru had given Ifeoma financial and moral support. She'd never denied her anything, unlike her other sisters from the same womb. Thinking of all the good things Ejituru had done for her, she forgot her irritation on seeing the car and was anxious now to find out why Ejituru found it necessary to arrive so early.

Just then, she saw Nwankwo about to enter the house and went out to meet him.

"Ma Ife, Ejituru is upstairs," he called. "She came here just as the workmen started cleaning. She said she wanted to make sure that the place was cleaned out." Before she could say anything, he rambled on. "I haven't seen Chinyere or Udo this morning. Perhaps they've gone out. I know Michael went to the compound for a meeting. Yesterday was very tiring. I had just woken up when Ma Ejituru came."

Ignoring his chatter, Ifeoma said, "It's getting hot. I need to drink something."

"Let me see. We removed many of the leftover drinks to the room at the back, so I'm sure I can get you Coca-Cola, Sprite, or Fanta."

They joked about Udo's preference for a stout before Ifeoma said, "Fanta will do. The maids are serving soft drinks to our visitors and have also been instructed to warm up some leftovers for them. Did you save any of the ice? Would there be some in the fridge?"

"Possibly. I'll take a look," he said as he made for the storeroom.

"I'll need a paper cup, too, if there are any left. I don't want to drink from the bottle."

Ifeoma remembered that when her brother was born, Nkechi's happiness knew no bounds. Three sons who would go on and do great things! Nkechi's plan was for this new baby to be a doctor like Ejituru but in another specialty, perhaps gynecology, a highly paid profession, since women were always having babies. She'd already decided that Michael, the first son, would be an engineer, and Emeka, the second son, a lawyer. Nkechi had placed great value on education, and wanted each of her children to study for a profession.

Ifeoma scrutinized his face when he came back and saw no sign of that beautiful baby. He looked worn-out, with sunken eyes. Too much native gin had played havoc with his complexion. She saw his veined neck and his Adam's apple, and she wondered whether he was well. He looked as if he was malnourished.

She knew he had no means of livelihood, but he was highly respected in the villages because of his participation in all the rituals and could always be depended upon to help dig the graves or participate in communal activities. This was how he managed to survive. He had found schooling difficult, and had dropped out without completing his primary education, despite their mother's efforts to push him to study.

Poor Nkechi!

She had never even achieved her objective of having that second doctor in the family. When she found out that he had no interest in formal education, she'd looked at the informal sector and sent him to train as a shoe repairer. His shed would be in the front of the house, facing the main road. She cajoled Ejituru and Udo to send money for the different equipment—the lathes, the leather sewing machine, and the benches to display the finished products. In this, she was also disappointed because he lacked the discipline required to make it work. He'd had difficulty meeting deadlines, and was often found in the village drinking with his cronies. When confronted, he would complain that the machines had broken and he needed new ones, or that he had no money for inventory. In the end, she must have given up. The shed remained as evidence of a failed dream.

Ifeoma's thoughts reverted to Ejituru sitting upstairs. She felt that Ejituru must be having a rough time since she wasn't close to any of the family members. She must be wishing that she was back home with her family in the US. This probably was the longest time she'd stayed here since Nkechi became ill.

Normally, she would have left to visit friends in other places. Would this visit be her last?

Finishing her drink, Ifeoma leisurely stood up and went to talk to those who were still sitting in the room. As some left, new people arrived, and she knew that this would continue until midday. Her aunt's arrival gave her an excuse to leave the room to go upstairs. One of the bedroom doors opened, and out stepped Chinyere with her towel and toiletry bag in hand.

Startled, Ifeoma cried out, "Hey, Ma Chi, I thought you'd gone out.

Nwankwo said you were visiting friends in the compound."

"What does he know?" Chinyere muttered in a voice that brooked no response. She brushed past Ifeoma and stepped into the courtyard.

Ifeoma remembered the last time Chinyere was home, at the time of her father's death. Her husband had given a cow, and his Obowu family was there in full force. During that visit, she'd fallen out with Nkechi and had made many derogatory statements about Nkechi and Ejituru. Family members were shocked at the vehemence of her attack, since it was uncalled for. She'd accused Nkechi of disrespecting her mother and usurping her position in the family.

She'd also implied that Ejituru's absence was a slight on the memory of their father. The family had rallied against her, and she was forced to leave early for Lagos. This time, neither the husband nor her children were there. She failed to give a reason for their absence, and she didn't pledge any money, though Ifeoma believed her husband had no doubt given her some for that purpose.

When Chinyere first arrived at Ifeoma's house for the planning meeting, Ifeoma was taken aback because she hadn't been home to see Nkechi throughout her illness. Her snipes often upset Ifeoma, and since the death of their father, she'd tried to maintain a distance between them. Given her strong feeling about Nkechi, Ifeoma wondered why Chinyere even bothered to come to the funeral. Come to think of it, while everyone had been muttering about the absence of Ejituru's husband, nobody seemed to care whether Chinyere's was present. This, she felt, was very unfair.

She wondered how Chinyere was able to get away with not revealing to her husband the true nature of her relationship to Sarah. A secret like that couldn't possibly be kept for such a long time. How was she able to carry out this myth? Nkechi had tried to protect her when she became pregnant at the age of fourteen and had hidden her away in a remote area from her home until she had the baby, later on passing off the baby as Onyeka's and explaining away Chinyere's period of absence from home as a temporary stay with relatives in Kano. The story was made believable because she was a very difficult girl, always picking quarrels with Nkechi, and people believed that she had been sent away to experience the hardships other children from less affluent families were subjected to.

Unfortunately, Chinyere had failed to debunk the myth and had disavowed Sarah. This had created a problem when Sarah was listed as a daughter in the funeral brochure. Sarah objected, wanting to be listed as a granddaughter, probably because less would be expected of her. Ifeoma didn't mean to force Sarah to feel that she had to pledge as much as she did. She could have lowered her pledge. In fact, Ejituru never expected her to pledge. It was her free will to do so. Ifeoma felt that she was being unfairly blamed by Sarah. She would wait until the time when she gave the account of expenditures to raise that issue.

Ifeoma wondered how long it would take for Chinyere to put pressure on Sarah to help her children, since she was doing well in the United States. Would Sarah forgive the years of neglect? Already Chinyere had managed to ensure that both of them stayed in the same room in the house and had tried her best, albeit unsuccessfully so far, to monopolize Sarah throughout the funeral. Come to think of it, perhaps this was the reason why she came to the funeral, to grow closer to her child, whose financial help she now needed, given her husband's dire financial situation.

"Hmm, I wonder what Sarah is thinking and feeling," Ifeoma muttered under her breath. "We'll see."

Looking around, she felt slightly irritated that Ejituru, who must have heard the commotion downstairs, didn't bother to come down and greet the women who had come to mourn with her.

"This is very strange," she murmured. With her foot on the last step leading to the upstairs parlor, she called out, "Ma Ejituru, the parlor is full of people waiting to condole with you. You should come and greet them."

Met with total silence, she entered the room and found Ejituru sitting in a chair in the small corridor outside, looking out into the front yard. She must have been aware of the comings and goings. It looked as if she'd been crying.

Just as she was about to say something, the door of the room off the corridor opened, and Udo came out with her toilet bag and towel.

"Sister, Nwankwo said you went out with Chinyere early in the morning, so seeing you now is a surprise," Ifeoma said.

Udo appeared flustered at meeting Ifeoma with Ejituru. She closed the bedroom door behind her and raised her right hand in dismissal. "It's only 9:00 a.m. You know we didn't go to bed until this morning. There were so many people here drinking and shouting that it was impossible for me to get away, let alone to sleep. Then, of course, since dawn, this place has been like a train station with so much movement and noise that it's been impossible to get any rest." She turned to Ejituru, who sat there with a bemused expression. "But Ejituru, why are you here? We weren't expecting you so early."

"I thought I would come and help with the cleanup, but Ifeoma had everything under control," Ejituru whispered. "I came as the lorry pulled up to start loading the chairs and tables."

Before Udo could say something, Ifeoma forestalled her. "I was just about to tell Ejituru that the parlor is full of women who've come to sit with us for the day."

~≈◌✣◌≈~

Udo turned away from them, but Ifeoma continued to address her. "I've arranged for them to be fed and given drinks," she said. "Auntie has just arrived and will stay with them. They'll be here another two hours, I think. Ej, you should go and greet them."

Ejituru wondered why it was necessary for her to go and sit with the women. She'd heard Ifeoma talking to Chinyere and had decided to leave the parlor and sit outside, where she could see the women streaming into the living room downstairs and not be seen herself. She wanted to talk to Ifeoma, but she wasn't about to say what was on her mind in front of Chinyere, who never respected Nkechi, always arguing, always telling Nkechi how badly she treated their mother, who was the person who produced the heir for their father. Nor would she speak in front of Udo, who she knew was consumed with jealousy because she wasn't borne by Nkechi. The only redeeming factor in her mind regarding Udo was her love for Nkechi.

She debated whether she should hold back Ifeoma, who appeared flustered about the events downstairs, so she could talk with her.

Ifeoma forestalled whatever else she wanted to say by shouting at Udo, "I hope the maids have enough water for you. Chinyere just went to the bathroom!" But her words fell on deaf ears since Udo was halfway down the stairs toward the courtyard.

Apparently frustrated by Udo's indifference, Ifeoma pressed Ejituru to follow her downstairs.

CHAPTER 17

Coaxed by Ifeoma, Ejituru stood up and followed her downstairs.

When they entered the parlor, the room erupted in loud crying and moaning as the women enclosed Ejituru in their embrace, hugging her and telling her what a wonderful person her mother had been and how they all missed her. "Wellborn child, Ada Anyi! (our firstborn!)" someone cried.

"There never will be anyone like Nkechi," someone else said. "She was a person unlike others. She made sure that she paid you what you were worth."

"You are all very kind," Ejituru murmured as she clasped each person's hand. "Thank you."

"Before her, we were expected to cook and fetch water for the funerals, and nobody paid us for our labor. She began the system of payment for cooks and for seamstresses, and now look at what's happening. Those who came after her pay very little, always complaining that there's no money. Ma Nkechi, how we miss you!" they cooed in unison as tears rolled down the cheeks of the daughters present.

Teary Ifeoma, sitting among the women, tried to dismiss Udo from her thoughts. She remembered when they were growing up how they both competed for Ejituru's favor. Udo wanted to be Ejituru, and everything she did at that time was to prove to Nkechi that she was just as good a daughter, if not better. Her relationship with Ejituru was to show Nkechi what a loving sister she was compared with Chinyere, who couldn't abide Ejituru. She would make sure that when Ejituru was home from secondary school, she would sleep in the same room with her. She wanted to go to Ejituru's secondary school and follow in her footsteps. Many times she was caught using Ejituru's pomade, trying on her school uniforms, or asking her to give her some of her outgrown clothes. If she saw Ejituru talking to Ifeoma, she would insinuate herself in the middle and draw attention to herself in ways that Ifeoma, a younger sister, could not.

Growing up with Ejituru and Udo, Ifeoma felt that Ejituru was unaware of Udo's machinations and was trying in her own way to be nice and friendly to every one of the sisters. She was aware of Ejituru's contribution to Sarah's education in England, and wondered whether Sarah knew about it.

Thinking about Udo, she hoped that with Nkechi gone, Udo would now regard Ejituru as a sister rather than a competitor. She had heard Udo make snide remarks about Ejituru during the funeral and wondered how long the competition would last, and who she was trying to impress now. This competition had continued even when they both left home. Udo was always trying to show that she was the person who visited more often and brought gifts to the parents.

She shook her head in disgust, trying to focus on the din around her and the need to get Ejituru to stay put and accept the comfort of the women who had come to see her.

◄≈◉╪◉≈►

While Ejituru settled down among the women, chatting and complimenting them on their contribution to the success of the funeral, Ifeoma slipped into the room where Nkechi was buried. She saw the freshly dug grave in the middle, the broken cement pieces piled neatly in the corner, and the grimy drapes on the windows, which someone had pulled open. She tried to imagine how the room had looked when Nkechi was alive. She remembered her signature scent of Yardley's brilliantine, frequently replenished by Udo whenever she visited; her handbag, and of course, the Bible next to the bed. She envisioned the cupboard where she stored her good china and the mugs that she collected at funerals, and the trunks where her best jojis and laces were stored, taking up the whole wall next to the windows.

When the room was emptied in preparation for the grave, the trunks were no longer there. She again considered whether she should call out the brothers for their shameless action of raiding the trunks and selling off her mother's jewelry and expensive wrappers. Public shaming was what they needed, but that would serve no purpose.

Standing in the room now, her face wet with tears, she addressed the person in the grave.

Why did you have to die? I only want to remember you as you were when you were lucid, when I would sit on your bed in this room and tell you all my problems. Remember my frustration that even though I was a married woman, my children were my responsibility? I wanted very much to kick out my husband. Remember what you said? You told me that in our society, women needed the protection of the husband. You reminded me that in a polygamous household, the children were the responsibility of the wives, and this system had carried over to the present. You said that I should remember that God gave each one of us the burden he believed we could bear, and I should know that my husband gave me a measure of respectability that I wouldn't otherwise have had. You said that the children would cease to be a burden once they grew up.

Tears streamed down her face. She wiped them away with the end of her wrapper.

Mama, what you didn't tell me was that the children would grow up thinking that I emasculated their father, that they felt just as we, your children, felt about our father. The older ones would rather help their father than me, and I'm still struggling.

Looking out the window, she saw Michael entering the courtyard. She opened the door and stepped back into the room where Ejituru, now joined by Udo and Chinyere, was sitting talking to the guests.

At midday, the room was quiet. Only a few women remained. The driver who had taken away the things from the house had been to collect his debt, and Ifeoma prepared to return to her house. Concerned for Ejituru's safety, she had sent a message to Ejituru's house asking her driver to come for her. Ejituru showed no signs of leaving, though he had arrived.

～✂෴✂෴

As soon as Ejituru saw the driver, she tried to shake off her lethargy. She asked Ifeoma to come up to their father's bedroom, where they could talk undisturbed. Since Udo had converted the office to her bedroom, the desk and chairs from the office had been moved into that bedroom. They asked the maid to fix them something to eat and drink, and both ascended the stairs and sat down.

Ejituru fidgeted in her chair, trying to think of a way to bring up the subject of the will.

"We had to change the memorial service to tomorrow, by the way," Ifeoma said, taking the chair across from her. "I hope you're not planning to leave before then."

Ejituru, only half-listening, shook her head.

"I also forgot to tell you that we're expected to give a present to the church." Ifeoma took a sip of her drink and set it down. "The pastor said, given our family's social position, we should think about building and furnishing a Sunday school room in memory of Father and Mother. I've received an estimate for the work, but you know how these things go—best to plan for fifteen percent over the estimated cost."

This got Ejituru's attention. She stared at her sister, unsure of how to respond to this unanticipated expense. She should have known the pastor would use this occasion to demand more money from her. Inside she was fuming, but she decided to let it go. "You know," she said, "I thought we might all gather tonight—at my place."

"For what purpose?"

"Well, for one thing, it might be the last time we're all together in one place. We could have food and drinks and talk. And . .."

"And?"

Ejituru caught the look of worry in her sister's eyes and looked down at her lap. "Well, I could read the will. In other cultures, wills are read after funeral services conclude, and this helps to bring some closure to the family." She lifted her head. "What do you think?"

Ifeoma looked thoughtful for a moment, then shrugged. "I think this could be good, though I don't know Chinyere's and Udo's plans." Ejituru stared at her sister, biting her lip.

"I know that look, sister." Ifeoma narrowed her eyes playfully. "What do you want?"

"Would you mind being the one to let the others know.. . about the gathering?"

"But it's your idea, your home."

"Exactly." Ejituru knew that Ifeoma, being the unofficial diplomat in the family, would stand a much better chance of convincing the others to come. If her mother's death had taught Ejituru anything, it was that the deep divisions between her other siblings and herself— Nkechi's only true child— were more alive than ever.

Ifeoma stared at her for a long moment. Finally, she nodded. "Fine." Ejituru smiled. "So it's settled, then. If there's any meat and rice left, perhaps we can have that sent to my house. I'll have the maid prepare a simple meal for us. I'll also ask the driver to take over some of the leftover soft drinks and beer."

"You should go back home," Ifeoma said, giving her leg a pat. "I can take care of the food and drinks."

"No." Ejituru shook her head. "I want to stay a bit longer. More people are sure to stop in, and I want to be here to visit with them." A troubling thought popped into her mind. "Have you seen Sarah? I heard she was unhappy with me."

Ifeoma sucked in a breath and nodded. "Apparently she wasn't happy about being listed as a daughter in the program. She felt we did this to force her to pledge money to the funeral, whereas if she'd been treated as a granddaughter, she would have been under no such obligation."

Ejituru's temper flared. "Forced her? Who forced her? I saw her willingly hand over money to you."

Ifeoma tilted her head. "Come to think of it, it was Chinyere who mentioned this. I never heard any such thing from Sarah herself." She sighed. "You know Chinyere—always looking for an opportunity to sow discord."

Ejituru rolled her eyes, but this, too, she decided to let go.

On leaving Ejituru, Ifeoma's mind was busy. She'd told Ejituru that she would pass on her message, and she was wondering how best to approach her siblings. As she came down the stairs into the front yard, she saw Udo sitting on the cement bench next to their father's grave, looking pensive. How would Udo react? she wondered. Udo never wanted to go to Ejituru's house. When they first met for the pledge, Ejituru had asked Udo to stay in her house where she would be comfortable, but Udo had reacted negatively, saying that she preferred her father's house and wouldn't stay anywhere else. She never visited Ejituru during the week before the funeral, insisting that any discussion relating to the funeral should take place in their father's house.

Approaching Udo, she decided that she would tell her about the meeting after talking to Michael. "What's up, sister?" she asked in her most cheerful voice. "Why are you sitting out here looking pensive?"

Startled, Udo looked up and said distractedly, "Just sitting here thinking of the past."

Ifeoma saw the deep sadness in her face. "If it makes you sad, then you need to forget it."

"The past was what helped me most in those horrible days with Chima," Udo said in a soft voice. "I often imagined I was sitting outside here, chasing butterflies and goats, and listening to the chirps of insects and the various noises of the chickens and birds, or watching Emeka or Nwankwo shimmy up these coconut trees to bring a green one down for us to drink the milk and eat the flesh." She pointed at the trees, her face animated as if she was experiencing those events. "Remember those days, sister?"

"I remember, sister. We were young then, but those days are gone."

But Udo would have none of that. She continued reminiscing. "Sometimes, I find myself sitting on the mud bench in the anteroom of the kitchen with Mama."

Ifeoma laughed. "That place was her favorite spot. She would often sit there ordering the servants around or sharing peanuts and food with any of us who were there or with her friends."

"I could see Dad's head popping out from the upstairs window whenever he needed something or somebody. I just feel sad that those days are gone forever." Udo shook her head.

Ifeoma sat quietly next to her for a few minutes until she spied Nwankwo talking to Michael. She went up to them and said, "I'm glad I found you both. I have a message for you."

Michael and Nwankwo stopped what they were saying midway to look at her in anticipation.

"Ejituru would like a meeting tonight to wrap things up and to read Nkechi's will."

"What nonsense is this?" Michael asked. "What's a will?" Nwankwo asked.

Ifeoma rubbed her face anxiously. "I'm only a messenger. Why don't we wait until the evening to find out what it's all about?" She saw Udo rushing over from where she was sitting.

"What's happening?" she asked as she came closer to them.

"Sister, Ejituru would like us to meet tonight in her house to read Nkechi's will," Ifeoma said.

"Nkechi left a will?" Udo said incredulously. "What next? If so, why can't she read it here tonight? Why ask us to go to her house? I just find the whole thing unbelievable."

"What's a will?" Nwankwo asked again. "What is she going to read?"

Just then they were joined by Emeka returning from the stream, where he had been taking his morning bath.

"A will is a document left by a dead person stating how he or she would like what they left distributed," Udo answered.

"So Ejituru has that paper?" asked Emeka.

"Yes," Ifeoma said emphatically. "She'll read it tonight at her house."

"I never saw any such paper," Michael said, shaking his head. "If there was one, I would have seen it because I was the person who moved her from here to my house in Port Harcourt. Besides, I don't believe she would hide such a thing from me."

"Perhaps Ejituru got her to write one when she stayed with her in Dallas," Udo said nervously, wiping her face. "I wouldn't put it past her." Udo pulled Ifeoma aside to talk. "Do you really believe there's a will?"

"She was emphatic when she said it," replied Ifeoma, making a face. "Why didn't she deliver this message to us herself?" Udo asked, spitting out the words as if she was choking on a piece of fish bone stuck in her throat. "It's just like her to let you do all her dirty jobs and take the blame. I don't intend to go to her so-called house tonight."

Ifeoma patted her back. "Sister, calm down. Don't let your jealousy take control of you. Come and listen. I still need to tell Chinyere and Sarah."

Udo looked at Ifeoma with sad eyes. "Ifeoma! What gives Ejituru the right to lord it over all of us? Why should we go to her house? Whenever I think of that house, I'm angry. The land belonged to our father. That house is empty most of the time. She could ask Michael to live there temporarily until such time as she decides to live fulltime in it. This would help Michael financially. He would be able to rent out his house." She spat out each word in a loud, angry voice.

"Stop there, sister. Don't dabble in what you don't know or choose not to remember. Michael had the same educational opportunity as all of us. He's very highly qualified and could work if he chose to. Besides, our father would have lost that land if Ejituru hadn't built that house."

"I don't mean to upset you, Ejituru's lapdog, but this isn't the end of this conversation," Udo said sarcastically. "I'm sure there's no will. If there was, Nkechi would have confided in me when she visited."

"You and Michael!" spat Ifeoma. "Nkechi's favorites. Ha!" She noticed that Udo was struggling to keep calm. Udo always believed that she was Nkechi's favorite and confidant, and now this discovery of the will must have shaken her belief. I bet that's why she wanted

me to confirm that I had seen the will. She looked back and saw Udo entering the house.

CHAPTER 18

Ifeoma was the last person Chinyere expected to run into that morning as she opened the door to search for water for her bath. She ignored her for now and continued on about her business. She'd always had a love-hate relationship with her. Ifeoma was her sister, born after her birth mother, Onyeka, had fulfilled her obligation of producing a son for Nkechi. Although Ifeoma had never been disrespectful to her, she'd always felt that it was Ejituru Ifeoma loved and respected. Upset that Ifeoma never offered to organize the water for her bath, she channeled her anger at Ejituru, who'd deprived her of the love of her sister. She felt if it had been Ejituru, Ifeoma herself would have fetched the pail of water, made sure Ejituru had a towel, and she wouldn't be surprised if Ifeoma wouldn't have stopped at that. Surely, she would even have given Ejituru a bath.

Chinyere questioned why she bothered to come for the funeral of a woman she thoroughly disliked, whose very existence she despised. She'd sworn after her last visit that she would never enter this house as long as that devil was alive. Perhaps her coming was to make sure she was really dead. She knew that her siblings were wondering what her motive was. She laughed mirthlessly when she remembered that she came not really for the funeral, although that was what her husband would think, but because this funeral would enable her to get close to her daughter Sarah. She needed her American daughter's support and help for the education of her other children, and because her own health was giving her concern. She needed her daughter to agree to fund any operation she might need.

She'd stayed late the night before, hoping for the opportunity to talk to Sarah. She'd instead celebrated with the mourners, who had lingered behind to visit with her brothers. After they left, the family staying in the house had continued to drink and chat until the wee hours, so she never did get that chance. Instead, she had to listen to her siblings' refusal to admit the injustice Nkechi had done to Onyeka, their mother. It was as if that woman, even though she was dead, still had control over them.

She felt let down by Udo, who, when the conversation turned to the topic of Onyeka's treatment, dared to disagree with her by recounting how Nkechi had been an outstanding mother. Sarah's outbursts upset her and had led her to expect some difficulty in any attempt on her part to seek a reconciliation. Nonetheless, she would talk to her this morning and get her to realize that she was her mother, and she must support her.

Last night had been a waste. She'd not tried to answer any of Sarah's accusations because she needed her financial assistance. But this morning would be the beginning of good times between her and Sarah. She regretted staying up until 2:00 a.m., especially since being a light sleeper, the movements of people in the downstairs parlor and upstairs had made it impossible for her to continue to rest this morning. She'd finally dragged herself up, wishing she was in her house in Lagos instead of here for a funeral of a woman she would rather have nothing to do with. However, she was hoping for that talk this morning as soon as she'd had her bath.

She remembered her visit during her father's funeral, her pride at being married to such a rich man, and how many villagers came up to congratulate her for the honor her husband had bestowed on her father. The same could not be said of her other siblings, particularly the one who lived in the United States and didn't even show her face.

She'd never been back because during that visit, she'd had a falling out with Nkechi. Lying in bed this morning, she'd thought of that quarrel. It started when she'd accused Ejituru of insulting the memory of her father by her absence at the funeral. She'd accused Nkechi of lying about the true reason. She insisted that Ejituru's absence was not due to illness but because Ejituru had a deepseated hatred for her father and blamed him for her ill-fated marriage. This had infuriated Nkechi, who then called her to ask where she thought the money for the expenses of the funeral came from.

One thing led to another, and she capped it all by accusing Nkechi of depriving her mother of her rights as the mother of her father's sons.

She remembered saying, "You and your daughter, Ejituru, emasculated our father. Your daughter, Ejituru, disgraced him by leaving a good man who paid for her to go to America for her lover.

Your daughter is nothing but a user like you."

She could still see the horror on the faces of those present, who were stunned that one of them dared confront Nkechi, the only mother they knew. They'd rallied around Nkechi, disavowing Chinyere by turning their back on her and leaving her stranded as if on a sinking boat. She'd immediately gone to her room, packed her stuff, and thanked God that her husband had left for Obowu with his relatives before the fracas. She'd taken a taxi to the bus station to Umuahia and found a Lagos-bound bus. Since then, she'd not paid any visit home nor seen Nkechi.

She'd never regretted what she said because she knew it was the truth. She wouldn't hesitate to say it again if Nkechi was alive. She'd always resented the fact that her mother, Onyeka, was Nkechi's wife by native law and custom, married when Nkechi realized that she couldn't have any more children.

Chinyere's only concern now was to be reunited with her daughter, whose love Nkechi had stolen. She would seek an opportunity later this morning to tell her daughter her own part of the story and to seek her help with the problems she was facing.

When Chinyere came back to the main house after her bath, she heard Ifeoma talking to Udo, who was just waking up and was on her way to the bathroom. She cursed Ifeoma for always pandering to Ejituru. She remembered how, throughout their adolescent years, even Udo mooned over Ejituru. Whenever Ejituru stepped out of the taxi that brought her from the motor park, both would rush up to hold her hand and would always sit very close to her, competing to see who would be allowed to prepare a meal for her, offering her peanuts and any fruit they could lay their hands on. It was a pitiful sight.

They would follow her around the house like little dogs, accompanying her anyplace she wanted to go. Udo was the worst, always pestering Nkechi about Ejituru's movements and offering to go to the motor park to meet her.

Back in their room, Chinyere found Sarah lying in the next bed with the bedsheet drawn over her head. Though Sarah and Udo had come together, Udo had her own room in the house, while Chinyere and Sarah shared one. She sat down and watched the girl, wondering whether she was awake.

She felt that this was an opportune time to talk to her without interruption. Determined, she asked, "Sarah, are you awake? We've not had an opportunity to talk, and I have things I want to discuss with you." She waited for an answer, and not getting one, pulled the bedsheet off Sarah's face.

Startled, Sarah gazed at her with hatred in her eyes and snatched back the sheet.

Undeterred, Chinyere said, "I know you've been brought up to hate me for not acknowledging you as my daughter, but, how could I? I was only a child when I had you, and shortly after that, I was sent away. I had no time to bond with you. I blame Nkechi for that."

With blazing eyes, Sarah spat out, "Get away from me. I don't want to hear you say anything about my mother, whom I owe my life to. Just let me rest and get over my grief."

"That witch wasn't your mother!" exclaimed Chinyere, temporarily forgetting her objective. "Whether you like it or not, I'm your mother, and I want you to understand that. Your very existence came from me."

"Nonsense," retorted Sarah. "Giving birth doesn't entitle you to claim you're my mother after thirty years of neglect. What's this sudden interest in me? I bet you need something from me. You. . . you selfish idiot. Get away from me!" she shouted at her, her voice rising.

"How can you say that?" Chinyere cried, stretching out her hand to touch Sarah. "You're being very unreasonable."

Sarah shrank away from the touch. "You denied me all my life. You lied to your husband about our relationship. Isn't it too late to claim me as your child? Get away from me and let me sleep." She pushed away Chinyere's hands and withdrew toward the nearest wall.

"You have every reason to hate me, but that doesn't negate the fact that I'm your mother!" Chinyere shouted back. "I gave birth to you. That should count!"

Sarah pulled up the bed sheet and turned her face to the wall.

With the conversation going so poorly, Chinyere decided to try again at a more opportune time. Perhaps she should ask Udo, who she felt was in Sarah's good graces, to intercede. For a second, she let her thoughts scatter all over the place. Then, dwelling once again on Sarah, she reconsidered her earlier remark and thought she should perhaps concede that Nkechi had done what she thought was best for her. She could hardly look after herself then, let alone look after a child. If she'd been saddled with Sarah, she wouldn't have met her husband, who changed the trajectory of her life. She felt that Sarah should understand the reason why she didn't acknowledge her existence to her husband. If she had, he wouldn't have married her.

She was young when she came to Aba. She had no money to buy things. Her friends in the secretarial school had money and were able to buy what they needed to make themselves presentable. She was dependent on relatives for the barest necessities.

She shook her head as she rubbed her body with Yardley pomade and sprinkled her arms with the latest perfume. Her anger shifted to Udo, whom she blamed for her inability to connect with Sarah.

She fed my child with all types of falsehood simply because she was able to arrange for her to go to Britain to study. How did she do it?

Chinyere was aware of the split between Udo and Sarah, but her gloating was tempered by the knowledge that the two appeared to be reconciled and had traveled together for the funeral. She looked again at Sarah, pretending to be asleep, and marveled at how she had become a carbon copy of Udo, who talked with a fake English accent, pretending not to understand the language she had spoken from birth, and answering every question in English. Did she know how stupid she sounded? She couldn't stand her fake British accent and was troubled by it. But she couldn't afford to have Udo as an enemy, since she needed her financial support even more so now, given her husband's failing health. She couldn't afford to alienate Sarah or Udo, for that matter.

She must reconcile with Sarah. She would try again to talk to her; not immediately, but after talking to Udo. She would solicit Udo's help in convincing Sarah to help her.

She opened the door as soon as she finished dressing and went into the parlor, where Ejituru and Ifeoma were sitting with the mourners. She sat down near the door and gazed at the women, who by this time were replete with food and were being served soft drinks. One woman had demanded gin, and the young girl reputed to be the younger brother's girlfriend had gone to search for a bottle among the boxes where the leftovers from the funeral repast were stored.

She raked the room with her eyes, resting them on an elderly woman in the corner gulping down her Fanta. She thought, What if I told this old woman that she had a granddaughter sleeping next door? What would she do? She got up from her chair and approached the woman. "How are you? How's your son, Eman? I was in secondary school with him."

The old woman's eyes welled up with tears. Wiping them away, she croaked, "My daughter, he died ten years ago."

Pretending that she didn't know, Chinyere said, "I'm so sorry to hear that. I was friendly with him. What happened?"

"He died of diphtheria," the lady said, before continuing to drink.

Chinyere had never divulged Sarah's father's name, despite pressure from Nkechi and her father, who were prepared either to go to the family and insist that the boy marry her or use their influence to ruin the boy's chances of ever amounting to anything. The assumption had always been that it was one of the boys from outside the area who dared have anything to do with Nkechi's daughters. Boys from the area knew that if suspected, Nkechi would use the full weight of her position to make sure that they were properly punished, even if their sin wasn't widely known.

Looking at the woman as she sat there guzzling her drink and looking as if she, too, would drop down dead at any minute, Chinyere decided to let it go, particularly since the young man was dead. He had never amounted to anything. It was as if the incident had placed a curse on him, and he was never able to complete secondary school. He had drifted from one place to another, dabbling in all types of things but with little success. He was a burden to his mother.

Chinyere looked at her again, remembering her as a beautiful woman who traded in groundnut oil. Nkechi was one of her customers, a native midwife who helped deliver many babies in the area. She searched the face of that tired-looking, broken-down woman for any sign of the woman she had known in her youth, laughing and joking often with her customers, always well-groomed, and always full of good advice. There was none. The death of her only son must have contributed to her downfall because Chinyere had heard that after his death, she let herself go, and with no husband—her husband having abandoned her after the death of the son— she no longer had the will to live.

A thought popped into Chinyere's head. Perhaps knowing she had a grandchild would give her a reason to live. She shook her head vigorously. No way!

Just then she saw Ifeoma looking at her with her mouth wide open, as if she had heard her thoughts and was telling her to think of all the other people who would be hurt by her confession. She collected herself, and her eyes settled on a much younger woman whose head tie was covered with images of playing cards. The queen of diamonds was placed squarely on her forehead, just before the fold in the cloth.

How appropriate, she thought. She really is the queen in this place. I bet she's bought herself a title.

Chinyere had known this woman when she was a playmate of Ifeoma. She had never liked the girl because she had a habit of turning up at mealtime and sponging off the family. Like Ifeoma, she had graduated from Nsukka University. She had read medicine and was now in family practice. She'd heard that this woman married well. Her husband was a wealthy businessman from the next village, and they'd built a palatial house in the new extension.

He was my classmate, and if I had played my cards well, I would be the person he married. Nkechi was all set to arrange it because his mother was her friend. Well, it didn't happen, and I hear they have no children. What's the use of all that money and education?

Look at her. She's as dry as stock fish.

Ifeoma had introduced her the day before as Nkechi's doctor and had praised her for her help.

I probably should go and shake hands with her and thank her for her help, Chinyere thought. But then again, why should I? She was paid for her services. It's not as if they were free.

Chinyere shifted her buttocks from side to side on the hard stool and again looked around the room. Her eyes roamed the walls, decorated with various family photographs, and settled on one of Nkechi. It was the same photograph used for the announcement of her death. In the photograph, she wore a white fitted lace blouse and the traditional Omu joji. A bit of the wig she wore peeked out from under her head tie. The photograph must have been taken when she was in her prime. Her mouth was slightly parted, and Chinyere wondered what she was thinking at the time. Had she just learned that she was pregnant with Ejituru, or was she about to give instructions to Nwakama, her husband, as usual? No. Come to think of it, she looked exactly as she would have looked when she was about to command Onyeka to make sure that the backyard had been swept.

Next to Nkechi's photograph was one of Chinyere's father, Nwakama, taken when he was made an elder of the church. She wondered why there was no photograph of Nkechi and Nwakama together. Did she ever love him? From scraps of information she had gathered over the years, she knew it was an arranged marriage. Their parents were friends who wanted their children to marry as a way of cementing their friendship.

Poor souls.

Did he know his wife would keep him on a short leash and deny the woman who gave him sons her rightful place besides him? Did he ever love Nkechi, or did he stick with her because it suited him? Did he, in those early years before Onyeka, ever think of leaving her and marrying a more subservient wife? How did he feel living in the house that belonged to his wife?

Of course nowadays, nobody thought the house was his. When he married Nkechi, he got the house, people said.

She laughed mirthlessly, thinking, Poor man. At least she exhibited your photograph.

There were other photographs on the wall: Ejituru graduating from medical school, Ifeoma's graduation, Udo's two daughters aged three and two, Sarah in Trafalgar Square.

Chinyere felt that Nkechi used Onyeka and cast her off when it suited her. There wasn't even a single photograph of her. Did she ever take a photograph?

Lucky people who have records of their existence! People like Onyeka are meant to be forgotten. Even in this house, where she gave the best of her life, it's as if she never existed.

When Onyeka died, Chinyere was upset that she wasn't even informed of the death until she had been buried. The woman gave birth to six living children, and you would think that should amount to something and her contribution would be noted. Sitting there, an unwanted thought intruded, making her shake her head in shame. She remembered that even during the months when she lived with Onyeka and shared a bedroom with her in the farm village, she never called her Mama. It was Onyeka she knew her as. When someone in the village asked her about her mother, it was Nkechi she first thought of.

How did Onyeka feel having her children treat her as a servant and mock her for her outlandish beliefs in witchcraft and, come to think of it, never call her Mother? she asked herself. How did she feel about having her children not acknowledge her but fawn over Nkechi, who never carried them in her womb? Chinyere remembered that she, along with her brothers and sisters, had often mocked Onyeka, snickering when Nkechi dressed her down for a minor infraction. But then, we weren't servants but the children of the

house, she thought.

She recollected that when she lived with Onyeka during her pregnancy, she never called her Mama and regarded her as a servant. Onyeka was treated as a servant, and she accepted that treatment with dignity. The blame lay squarely on Nkechi, since children take their cue from adults. Nkechi took everything from Onyeka, even her children, who fell into the pattern of treating her as a servant. Her submissiveness was due to her lack of education and no means of support except what Nkechi gave her, if she indeed gave her anything, since she was more or less a slave bought for the purpose of producing children.

Chinyere noticed Ejituru sitting in the corner with wet eyes as the women around her talked of Nkechi. She acknowledged that of all of the children, Ejituru genuinely loved Onyeka. She'd never heard her say any bad thing about her. They must have forged a strong bond when Onyeka was her nursemaid.

Ejituru was always very protective toward her, berating the other children when they derided her, comforting her when Nkechi said harsh things about her, and of course, creeping into her bed when she had nightmares, an act forbidden by Nkechi for the other children.

However, she felt that Onyeka's love for Ejituru displaced her love for her natural children. Ejituru took the love that should have been for Onyeka's children and gave nothing in return. The money she sent occasionally from the US was just conscience money.

Chinyere stared at her now and saw nothing but a user, like her mother. Wallowing in her anger, she didn't notice that the women had started drifting away and the maids were now gathering the empty bottles of soft drinks and beer for disposal. She heard Ejituru say that she would like a word with Ifeoma. She wondered what they were planning.

As she got up to leave the parlor, she heard Ifeoma call out to her, "Sister, I want to talk to you. I hope you're not going out soon."

I don't want to talk to you, she thought, but aloud she said, "I'm going to look for Udo." She stepped out of the parlor and bumped into Michael, walking in from the courtyard.

"Have you eaten?" he asked. "I had a meeting in the compound. You all must be tired of visitors. This is how it's going to be the whole day." Words poured out of his mouth, betraying his nervousness.

She brushed him aside, intending to head to the bedroom while he entered the parlor to greet the remaining visitors. His very presence upset her. Here was the son—the head of the family who should take control and organize things. Instead, he had turned out to be a weak man unable to control his own household, a womanizer who couldn't keep a job despite the investment in his education, a disappointment compared with many men of his age group who were important members of society, holding responsible jobs in the public and private sectors. With his main support gone, she wouldn't be surprised if he were to sell off the chairs and stools in the parlor in order to support himself.

Then she remembered that when Nkechi was brought home for burial, Ifeoma had sadly remarked that the sons had left nothing of value in the trunks. Everything of any worth was gone. She'd expected a reaction from Ejituru, but when none came, she felt like slapping her for being so unfeeling. She concluded that Ejituru's only interest was self-preservation and nothing else.

She could only blame Nkechi for Michael's situation. She had pandered to him, showering him with money from the time he was in boarding school. Chinyere decided she would rather not talk to him now but would go and seek out Udo.

She called out to a servant to bring her a Fanta. It was then that she heard Ifeoma talk about meeting in the evening and about the will. She had no interest in the will, but she would go to the meeting just to satisfy her curiosity. At the moment, she would go up and talk to Udo about her concerns.

CHAPTER 19

With the house quiet, Ejituru stood on the balcony and looked out to the road. She saw Ifeoma talking to Udo, and wondered whether Udo had been informed of the meeting. Remembering Michael's kind words at Ifeoma's house, she felt that she needed to visit him. Just as she was about to leave the upstairs parlor, she ran into Ifeoma, who was coming up the stairs. Ifeoma gave her a nod indicating that she had passed on the message.

Afraid of being accosted by Udo or Chinyere demanding an explanation, Ejituru turned and retraced her steps and descended the outside stairs. She went around the house toward her father's gravesite, and seeing no one outside, she went on to Michael's house, where she found Michael.

Smiling, he welcomed her into his home. "The funeral was very well-attended. Everyone appeared to enjoy themselves."

Ejituru wondered why he was talking about the funeral instead of the will, but she nodded, deciding to keep up the charade. His next words took her by surprise.

"Sister, I have to thank you all for saving our family from shame. None of us, your brothers, would have been able to live down the humiliation of not being able to afford to bury our mother."

She looked at him and said, "Don't even think about it. You all contributed what you could. What would I have done without you all arranging everything before I arrived and handling all the visitors? Actually, I came here to thank you. I didn't expect Nwankwo and Emeka to pledge anything, but Nwankwo corralled his friends to dig the grave, and he saved us a lot of money."

Michael appeared comfortable with her words. "What are your travel plans?" he asked. "We hope you're not rushing back soon."

"I plan to leave on Monday, after the memorial service."

"So soon!"

Ejituru decided to go against Ifeoma's advice. "What happened to Mama's bank account book, jewelry, and jojis?" she asked. "I knew she kept them in a trunk in her room. Ifeoma said that when the trunks were opened, there was nothing important in them."

Michael's face registered his anxiety at being so confronted. He wrung his hands. "I know nothing of a bankbook, but I know that Nwankwo, and maybe Emeka, too, sold off some of her jojis even before her illness was diagnosed. She complained many times that she couldn't find her jojis or her expensive jewelry, but we didn't believe her because we thought she had misplaced them. By the time she came to live with me, her bank account book couldn't be found. I know I looked for it in order to pay some of the doctor's bills but couldn't find it, and she herself couldn't say where she kept it."

Ejituru looked at him skeptically. "So you think it could have been either of our two brothers who cashed out her bank account and threw it away?"

"Sister, it's possible. Emeka especially was the person she depended upon to go to the bank for her, and he's very well known by the bank manager."

"Why would he do that?" she asked, shaking her head. "He has a job. But eh, civil servants aren't being paid, and they have to survive." Ejituru sat back in the chair and stared at his animated face. Should she believe him? Perhaps the truth was that he had forced Emeka to cash out the account because of the two of them, he needed the money more. She turned to him. "Assuming what you said is true, there's still a problem. Ifeoma said she saw your wife with some of Mama's wrappers and jewelry."

Michael's face registered confusion, but he tried to cover it by saying, "Yes, what she saw were gifts from Mama when my wife gave birth to her namesake."

When she looked out the window and saw Nwankwo walking toward Michael's house, Ejituru stood up. She took her leave, greeting Nwankwo as she left, and made her way back to her father's house. There she saw Udo pacing about in the front yard.

She went up and urged her to sit with her. "I've just been asking about Mama's bankbook and other things." Udo's anger flared up.

Ejituru tried to calm her by saying, "But let's not talk about that now.

We'll never be able to find out for sure what happened."

They sat down on the cement bench of their father's grave. Ejituru looked around the yard at the chickens strutting about and the goats bleating and wondered if they were aware of what was happening around them. She wished she was one of them, carefree and only concerned with the immediacy of looking for food. She turned to Udo. Holding her hands, she stared at her warmly. "Sister, this homecoming must be hard for you, without Nkechi. She always looked forward to your visit."

"You can't imagine how bad I feel. In my head I've been reliving all my Christmases with Mama: going to church in the morning together, presenting her with the little gifts that I brought, and preparing Christmas lunch with her. I realize now that never again will I sit in the parlor on Christmas day receiving visitors with her. It's too painful to imagine." She broke down crying.

Ejituru, unsure of what to do, adjusted her posture and held Udo's hands to comfort her.

Between sobs, Udo said, "I had a taste of what was to come some years ago when I came home for Christmas and didn't realize that she would be in Umuahia."

Taken aback by the remark, Ejituru could only say, "Oh yes, I heard of that visit. I'd made it a point not to come at Christmas because of the expensive airfare. But tell me what happened."

Udo composed herself and wiped her eyes. "I arrived to see only Nwankwo at home and the house in shambles. He was very surprised to see me and immediately told me that Mama was in Umuahia. I had intended my visit to be a surprise."

"Perhaps not," said Ejituru as she tightened her hold on Udo. "Mama always expected one of us to surprise her."

"It really was to be a surprise because this time, I didn't announce it in advance."

"What happened?" asked Ejituru, raising her eyebrows. "Did Nwankwo send you away to Umuahia?"

"No, no." Udo shook her head vehemently. "He opened the door to the room I usually stay in, but . . ." She paused to watch the expression on Ejituru's face. "You can't imagine the state of the house and kitchen."

"I can well imagine it, judging from the state of the house this time," Ejituru replied. She shrugged her shoulders. By now, the road outside had become more crowded with cars and trucks, cyclists and pedestrians. Unable to concentrate, and feeling that she needed to hear out Udo, Ejituru said, "Let's move. The noise from the main road is distracting, and besides, I'm being bitten to death by the gnats. I really want to know what happened. Let's go to Dad's room. It'll be quieter. We still have to return to the parlor to sit with the latecomers."

Nodding, Udo stood up and followed Ejituru up the front steps into the parlor and into their father's room.

As she sat down on the bed, Ejituru remembered the many discussions she'd had in this room about her marriage to Ignatius. She shook her head and asked, "Should I send for something to drink?"

"No, I'd rather you didn't."

"Then tell me. You were talking about the state of the house." She raised her head and looked hopefully at Udo.

"When I took a look at the shambles, I went to the compound and hired a girl to help me, and I set about cleaning and tidying up."

"You were very lucky that you found a girl to help you. Is it the same girl helping this time?"

"No, not the current girl," Udo replied, wringing her hands. "The girl who agreed to come to stay with me was the seventeen-year-old daughter of one of the women in the compound. She immediately took a pail to fetch water from the stream and arranged for a water seller who could come the next day to fill up the tank. Between the two of us, we cleaned up the house as much as we could, and the following day, I brought someone to make new cushions for the chairs in the parlor." She scratched her head. "These were expenses I never anticipated. It was the worst Christmas I'd ever spent."

"I can well imagine," Ejituru said. "You've always spent a lot on this house. Wasn't Michael home?"

"He came on Christmas Eve. By my count, I was responsible for feeding seven people, and it wasn't cheap."

Ejituru nodded. "I can well imagine," she repeated.

Clearly upset by the memory, Udo continued. "Do you know that every market day, Michael would ask me for money to buy food for his children, and even then, they would expect to eat what I had cooked for myself. It was the saddest Christmas in that there was none of the camaraderie associated with the holidays in the house." She sighed.

"Didn't Ifeoma come back that year for Christmas?" asked Ejituru. "Because of Mama's situation, Ifeoma didn't come home, and nobody visited because the villagers knew of Nkechi's absence. I left for a few days to visit Mama in Umuahia."

"Did you stay at Ifeoma's?"

"No, I stayed at the catering rest house and visited during the day." "That explains why you stayed there this time, too," Ejituru said in a gentle voice. "What happened to the girl you hired the last time? I was told by Ifeoma that she was very good."

"I looked for her but was told that she had been sent to Lagos to stay with a relative who promised to enroll her in a trade school. However, within six months of her arrival, she became pregnant and had left to live with the father of her child. Since then, nobody has had contact with her. Apparently, the mother has a case against the relative in the village council. I asked Chinyere about her situation, since she lives in Lagos, and she just dismissed the whole thing, saying she didn't want to be involved."

"I'm sure there's more to the story than what you've been told." Ejituru waved her hand in a dismissive way.

They both sat quietly until Udo got up and said, "Let's go downstairs before we're missed."

CHAPTER 20

When Ejituru left him to meet with Udo, Michael, unsure of Ejituru's motive for raising the issue of Nkechi's bankbook, was unprepared to deal with his brother. It was just like Ifeoma to curry favor with Ejituru by badmouthing him, he felt. Should he warn his brothers of what Ejituru was thinking? He decided that they had something more important to worry about. He had deliberately said nothing to Ejituru about the will because he didn't want her to feel that he had anything to lose by revealing its contents.

Before Ifeoma gave them the news, Nwankwo was lamenting the state of the house, reminding them that during Nkechi's lifetime, she took pains to make sure that repairs were carried out in a timely manner, and during her illness, Udo had maintained the house in the hope that when Nkechi got better, she would find it in good condition.

"Did you ask Ejituru what she intended to do about the house?" Nwankwo asked.

Michael wasn't surprised that Nwankwo, seeing Ejituru leave, had evidently assumed he had discussed the maintenance of the house with her. "Don't look at Ejituru to fix anything," he replied, rolling his eyes in despair. "She won't do it. Perhaps Udo will. She cares a lot about this house."

"Udo has already done so much," Nwankwo replied. "She had the house painted, and she replaced the chairs and drapes in all the parlors."

"I don't see anything in need of fixing," Michael said. "Let the courtyard revert to a dirt floor unless you have the money for that." He turned and went out of his house and into the courtyard, yawning. He felt that the repair to the house was the least of his worries. He had to do something drastic to get money.

It occurred to him that he had an opportunity to fix his situation. Why give back all the money given to the family by well-wishers during the funeral? He had already taken the first step by giving a false account to the elders during the clothing of the dead. He'd removed 50,000 naira from the account he gave. He would keep that money and would report two-thirds of the amount he gave the elders. He would send this to Ifeoma, letting her know he had been recalled urgently to Aba.

Just then he saw Chinyere and Ifeoma stop in front of him. Chinyere, his nemesis, could tell his every move. It was then that he knew he wouldn't be able to get away with what he had planned because Ifeoma brought up the meeting in the evening for the reading of the will. Still in shock, he was at first tongue-tied. Then he croaked, "Isn't a will a paper in which dead people state what they give to their heirs? But here, the property of the dead person belongs to the sons. Therefore, the house belongs to me by customary law. So what is this rubbish about a will?" He looked at Ifeoma and Chinyere, as if challenging either one to dispute what he'd said.

"As far as I'm concerned, if there is a will, I know I won't be mentioned in it, so I don't intend to be present," said Chinyere, blowing her nose. She had previously thought she would go to satisfy her curiosity, but now she thought not. "You guys will just have to fight it out between you. I'm not interested. Has anyone seen Udo? I'm looking for her." She moved away.

Not in any way put off, Michael glared at Ifeoma again. "I have our father's box where he kept his important papers. I didn't see any will —not that he would have made one. And I don't believe Nkechi would have made one, either."

"Well, you all should come," Ifeoma said, "because apart from the will, we'll have the opportunity to discuss the expenses, as well as the intake of all the gifts received in cash and in kind." She stared at him as if daring him to say something.

He had planned to leave for Aba that evening and to hand over the amount he thought appropriate to Sarah to give to Ifeoma, but now he felt that he couldn't do so. He had to be physically present. He was angry at Ifeoma for not warning him of the will and for saying bad things about him to Ejituru. As for the latter, he hoped Ejituru believed his explanation. If there was a will, Ifeoma would have known about it. Why didn't she warn him? They'd both been together since the death of Nkechi, working side by side in making all the arrangements pertaining to the announcements and the church. It just showed where her loyalty was. Given the choice, she would throw him to the wolves to save Ejituru. He tried to discard his concern, feeling that Nkechi had loved him too much to disinherit him. He felt confident that she had provided for him.

He turned and went back to the house, followed by his brothers. Nwankwo brought with him bottles of Heineken beer and a platter of warmed-up goat meat leftover from the day before. He placed these on the side table near the window. The parlor was furnished with old upholstered chairs picked up by Nkechi when her business was flourishing.

Michael sat on an easy chair placed in a spot that enabled him to see visitors coming and going to the main house. He saw Udo prowling about in the yard, but he decided not to think of her, but to let his thoughts revert to Ejituru, who had more or less accused him of stealing from Nkechi, and the damned will.

He looked at his brothers, already attacking the food they'd brought to his house, and his anger at Ejituru boiled over. "Thinking of our big sister, I'm glad that she was verbally beaten yesterday over the absence of her husband."

"It was very unfair," said Emeka. "Chinyere's husband didn't come, nor did he send any gifts, and nobody mentioned him."

"Well, the fact is that Ignatius is one of our own," Michael said. "Immediately when he came calling, she abandoned her studies to pursue him." He stared at the rhythm of Nwankwo's Adam's apple, trying not to laugh.

Nwankwo concurred. "True. It wasn't as if she couldn't have become a doctor here in Nsukka. That had always been her ambition."

"She wanted an American degree, and who can fault her for that?" asked Emeka, who was trying desperately to control the onset of a sneeze.

"That was why she married Ignatius," Nwankwo said. "No doubt about it. If she didn't want to marry him, she would have left immediately when she arrived in the US and recognized his situation." He continued to chew his goat meat.

Michael shook his head in disgust. He wished Nwankwo would finish chewing before speaking. "How could she say that it took her some time to find what he did for a living?" he asked. He paused and looked knowingly at Nwankwo, still busy chewing his food. He saw the beer foam around his lips and smiled. "Instead, she stayed with him until she entered medical school. There must be more to it than she's telling. The fact is that once she got her wish to be a doctor, she started spreading the news that he wasn't what he said he was."

Emeka swatted a fly buzzing at his ears. "I think she was telling the truth." He raised his voice, as if to make sure his brothers understood the point he was conveying. "He didn't want to pay for her education. Even Ifeoma confirmed that. She heard it from a member of Ignatius's family." His eyes begged his brothers to stop the gossip.

"Ifeoma will say anything to exonerate Ejituru," Nwankwo said, as if trying to contradict Emeka. "How could that be true? Look at how much money he has now, a person from such a poor family." He cast his eyes downward at the accumulated dust under Michael's chair.

Michael ignored that but continued to press his case. "Even if that was true, he still was able to clothe and feed her for over four good years. He never laid hands on her at any point. If he had, her leaving him would have been justified. Look at what he's achieved since she left him. He's built a shopping center and owns several rental properties." He stood up and waved his hands around. "They say that his house in Owerri is something to behold. Look at how well he looks after his uncle and his family!"

"Brother, I agree with you totally," said Nwankwo, swiveling in his chair. "We missed out. If she'd stayed in the marriage, this family would have benefitted."

Changing the subject, Emeka said, "I felt that she gave a valid explanation for her husband's absence."

"Even so, the elders were right to fine her," Michael said emphatically. "She was lucky that, in the end, due to the intercession of Chief Ori, the fine was reduced." He sat down, his anger deflated.

"Brother, Udo was not kind to you last night," said Nwankwo out of the blue.

"Yes," Michael concurred, at first unwilling to continue this line of conversation. After a few minutes, he changed his mind. "Has anybody ever met her husband? She told us she was married, but there was no wine ceremony as far as I can tell. I suppose I could have challenged her last night, but I let it pass." He looked outside and saw Udo. He stared at her and could see the profile of his father. He turned to his brothers. "Of all of us, Udo's the one who resembles our father most physically, but I think that's where the resemblance ends."

"You're right," said Emeka, smiling. "She's a strong woman, and like Ejituru, she's determined to get what she wants. But there, too, the resemblance ends."

"She can be generous when she feels like it, but I tell you, she'll make sure you're aware of the sacrifices she's making to be able to give you any scrap," said Nwankwo, his voice betraying his irritation.

"She sends money to me at Christmas, and whenever she visits, she makes sure that we are all well-fed and are aware of how much she's depriving herself by giving us money or feeding us." Emeka's voice indicated his unwillingness to continue this discussion.

"She tries too hard to buy love," Michael said. "During our father's lifetime, she sent him shirts and money through anyone vacationing from London. But he never really warmed up to her, nor did he in his lifetime accept her marriage to the Bonny man." He kept looking outside to make sure Udo wasn't heading to his house.

"The other day, she talked of how grateful she was that she made our father's last days on Earth free of financial constraint," Nwankwo said in an aggrieved voice. "She was glad to see us wearing the expensive clothes she gave him. In the same breath, she launched into how hard she was working to put food on the table and to educate her children and grandchildren."

Michael laughed and said with a tinge of sadness, "I heard that, and I almost felt like telling her that we didn't need her help, but I remembered my predicament. I need her help with the education of my children."

"So do I, unfortunately," said Nwankwo, then added, "I need to go to the small room."

After he'd gone, Emeka turned to Michael with a sad face. "Do you remember when Udo came back after such a long time?"

"How can I forget?" Michael answered after a short pause. "Before then, our parents vowed that they wouldn't have anything to do with her if they saw her. She'd destroyed their relationship with Uche's family. Nobody knew what the problem was, and Udo never wrote to clarify the situation."

"But the next time Nkechi heard from her, it was to say that she had completed a secretarial course and was working with a small publishing firm," Emeka said, as if this was a painful memory.

"Oh yes," Michael said. "After that, nobody heard from her for a year. Then out of the blue, Nkechi got a letter telling her that she'd married a Bonny man and had a child, and that we should expect a visit from his family." Michael laughed.

"Remember how Nkechi fumed, wailing that she'd lost her daughter?" Emeka said, now convulsed with laughter. "She only got reconciled to Udo getting married to someone she'd never met when she visited Ejituru in Dallas. But then Udo came home with two daughters and loaded with gifts, and all was forgiven."

Nwankwo returned and joined the merriment. "Look at her now," he murmured, looking at Udo as she walked away. "She gave so much money for the funeral." He looked pensive. "We're unfortunate in our sisters' choice of husbands. Look at Ifeoma's. It's as if she's cursed by Nkechi."

"What do you mean?" Emeka asked, scratching his head as if to uncover the meaning of Nwankwo's words.

"Well, think about it. What does her husband do?" Nwankwo yawned. "Close your mouth when you yawn," Michael said in disgust. "I don't relish seeing your tonsils."

"Come to think of it, in many respects, he's like our father," Emeka said in a pensive voice. "Ifeoma is the main breadwinner, and her husband, like our father, depends on her handouts."

"I envy him," said Michael in between laughs. "I wish my wives held responsible jobs."

"You missed out when you divorced your first wife," Nwankwo said with a twinkle in his voice. "Isn't she a principal of a big secondary school now?" "Let's not rehash that!" Michael angrily cried. "We're talking of Ifeoma, whose fate, like Nkechi, was to be married to a socially prominent man who couldn't support her and her children. I must say, she's done very well." He stared at each one of them.

Nwankwo and Emeka turned to look at him, wondering why he was angry.

"Don't you both have something to do rather than hang around here?" Michael said, in a voice dismissing them.

Feeling they'd outstayed their welcome, both left for the main house.

Michael stood up. Talking with his brothers hadn't solved his immediate problem. He surveyed the rooms around him, wondering about the possibility of renting out his house. He lived in Aba most of the time anyway. If he rented it, he could always sleep in one of the rooms in the main house whenever he visited home. The rent should give him a small income.

Having arrived at this decision, he went outside and gazed at his father's grave. Thankfully, Udo had left and was now inside. He wondered what his father would have done if he'd outlived Nkechi. Where would he find the money for the funeral? Of course, he would be totally dependent on his children to fund it. He had no money of his own. It was Nkechi who held the purse strings and therefore made all the decisions about the children. It was Nkechi who paid for their education. His father was an impoverished great man.

Perhaps subconsciously, I wanted to be like him, he thought. I wanted my wives to support my lifestyle and look after their children. After all, not long ago, that was the tradition in a polygamous household.

He reasoned that Nwakama, his father, pretended to be monogamous, regarding his other wife as Nkechi's legal wife. Therefore, it wasn't his responsibility to support her. He behaved as he would have if he was in a polygamous relationship, putting the responsibility for his children on his wives.

Michael saw nothing wrong with his father's financial dependency on Nkechi. It was the example he'd set for Michael, and he had no other example but that. Renting out his house was a good option, and he would put out feelers as soon as possible.

CHAPTER 21

The news of the will washed over Chinyere, who felt that she had nothing to lose from it as she stood near the gate to the courtyard. Amused at the consternation she saw on the faces of her brothers, she turned her attention to a visitor who needed directions to the outhouse. She chatted with her as she led her to the backyard, where the facilities were located.

When she came back, she saw her brother Nwankwo standing in the courtyard staring at the house. She had no time for Nwankwo, regarding him as a wastrel dependent on people's largesse. "This place is looking more decrepit than before," Chinyere commented, as if reading his mind.

"You're right," he replied, wiping his face with his hands, "but it was in worse shape two weeks ago. You should have seen it before Udo's touch-ups here and there." The temperature had risen as the noon hour approached and he was sweating profusely. "The roof is also leaking in places. Udo fixed the leak in her room."

Chinyere opened her hands wide to encompass the house in front of her. "It's a shame that those whose home this is can't afford to maintain it. You all had better start looking for accommodations after tonight." She laughingly poked him in the chest.

"You're full of mischief," he said, pushing her away. "Besides, Michael has a solution for the maintenance problem."

"Is that so?" Chinyere said. "Tell me what he plans. Tell me." She poked him hard, challenging him.

"Michael intends to rent out his house and move into the main house," Nwankwo said, removing her hand. "Then he'll have to pay for repairs." He sounded hopeful.

"Does he really?" Chinyere said, blowing her snuff-filled nose loudly. "So that's your solution to the repair problems? Even if they paid him a year in advance, I doubt he'd have enough money left after paying all the school fees for his numerous children."

"Should I raise the maintenance issue this evening during the reading of the will?" Nwankwo asked. "What do you think, Ma?"

"You can do whatever you want," Chinyere answered sarcastically. "It's none of my business. I'm not interested." She made her way back to the house.

On the steps, she looked back and saw Nwankwo talking to a young girl. She heard the girl say, "My mother is looking for you. When can she come?" "Tell her this isn't the right time," Nwankwo said dismissively. He watched as the girl left.

Ifeoma breezed past. "Time for another one, eh," she commented sarcastically.

Chinyere noticed the fear this remark evoked from Nwankwo. Ever seeking something she could use against other family members, she immediately thought, Have I missed something? I'd better find out.

As both she and Ifeoma reentered the house, she turned to Ifeoma. "What was that about?"

Ifeoma said offhandedly, "If you're asking about the will, I have nothing to say. You'll find out tonight."

"I have no interest in that. It's about your comment just now. Is there something I'm missing?"

Ifeoma laughed and said, "Oh, I was referring to his little side business, which he thought nobody knew about."

"What is it? I hope it's nothing that could get him into trouble."

"He's performing a good service, his clients would say, although they would rather remain anonymous," Ifeoma said. "He helps infertile men and gets paid for it. That's all I'm prepared to say. A nice way to make money, wouldn't you agree?"

Ifeoma retraced her steps back to the courtyard and to the kitchen while Chinyere went up to her room.

Hmm! thought Chinyere. Our little brother is scattering his seeds around. She looked around the room and saw Sarah's unmade bed and open suitcase. "So the princess is finally up," she muttered under her breath.

Having failed in her objective of getting Sarah to listen to her earlier on, alone now in the room, she tried to think of other ways of getting her cooperation. Perhaps Ifeoma would help. Ifeoma, the one person who could be said to be in everyone's favor. She would talk to Ifeoma and ask her for help.

She went to the mirror in the corner of the room and scrutinized her image. Satisfied, she marched out and found Ifeoma now sitting on the mud bench in the anteroom, sipping a Coke. "Sister," she said as she grabbed a Fanta from the pail nearby, "I need your help." "What about?" Ifeoma asked, looking at her quizzically.

"I can't reach her," she said imploringly. "I've tried many times whenever I'm with her."

"Reach who? And what do you want me to do?" Ifeoma put down the Coke bottle and gave her full attention to Chinyere.

"Talk to Sarah. Tell her that I love her. Convince her to help me. I know she listens to you."

"Chinyere, you're mistaken. Sarah listens to nobody. Since she arrived, we haven't exchanged more than one word. If there's anybody she listens to, it's probably Udo." Ifeoma got up.

But before she could step out, Chinyere said, "Sister, my husband isn't well at all, and I don't know what will happen to me and my children if he dies. I'm beside myself with worry."

Ifeoma sat down and held Chinyere's hands in comfort. "You worry too much. He told me he had malaria, and it was under control. But by the way, why didn't he give you any money to pledge? I thought it was so unlike him. He was very fond of Nkechi and had such good things to say about her."

Chinyere considered confessing about not handing over the pledge money, but instead she said, "He isn't as well off as he used to be. He's owed a lot of money by the government for the contract he had. Besides, he's building a house at Obowu. You know how it is." She stopped, wringing her hands anxiously.

Ifeoma changed the subject. "How are the children? The last time I heard, the oldest was applying for college."

"He's at Lagos State. It's his first year. That's why I'm hoping Sarah will help. It's not cheap."

"Talk to Udo. She might be able to work miracles. By the way, when are you going home?"

"Possibly Sunday night if I can find a ride to Aba or Umuahia. I intend to go to the compound to see if any of the people who came to the funeral have space in their car for me."

"You know my situation," Ifeoma said as she stood up to leave the room. "I'll be here for another week."

Chinyere followed, determined to speak to Udo. When she saw Udo, she hesitated because Udo was engrossed in a conversation with one of the visitors. Instead of talking to her, Chinyere made her way to the side of the house and found Emeka leaning on a coconut tree and in a conversation with Ukpabi, the moneylender. She wondered what Ukpabi wanted. Which of the brothers was indebted to him? "What's up?" she asked Emeka.

Ukpabi answered instead. "Nothing that concerns you. I came here to visit Michael." He went off toward Michael's house.

"I remember that man," Chinyere said. "Didn't he own a carpenter shop in the village square?"

"That's him, but he also does other things," he answered, sniffling. "He's a moneylender."

"What does he have to do with Michael? Is Michael indebted to him? Tell me!"

"How would I know?" he answered, yawning. "The last time I got involved with Michael's debts, it landed me in hot water with Ifeoma."

"What happened? Tell me," she demanded again.

"Michael got Nwankwo and me to sign papers agreeing to let him sell the land at the back of the house to Ukpabi," he said, wiping his nose with the back of his hand and swaying slightly.

"What!" Chinyere exclaimed, making a fist. "How could he do that?" "He told us he was in danger of being killed by assassins for nonpayment of debt. To save him, we signed the papers." He paused and looked around. "Go on," she urged, holding his hand tightly.

"Ifeoma found out when Ukpabi started clearing the place, and she took us to the village court for selling land that belonged to the whole family without consultation. She offered to repurchase the land, and she was able to convince Ejituru to send the money at once for that purpose." He wiped his face with his free hand. "So the land is still ours, or should I say, Ejituru's, as of this evening when the will is read."

She shook her head. "Poor Onyeka! Her sons haven't amounted to anything." She threw the words at him in disgust as she marched back to the house to look for Udo. She found her in the parlor, just in time to forestall Sarah, who was also looking for Udo.

"Sister, let's go to your room," Chinyere said gently. "There's something I want to discuss with you." She guided Udo to the room.

"If it's about the will, I don't want to talk about it," Udo said as the door closed.

Breathing heavily, Chinyere said, "No, I want your advice about Sarah, since you're on good terms with each other."

Udo had no immediate response. She cleared a spot on her cluttered bed and beckoned Chinyere to sit down with her. She sighed and said, "You know how Sarah is. One day you're in and then you're out, so I can't say I'm on good terms with her."

"Nkechi poisoned her against me, and she feels I didn't want to acknowledge her as my child," Chinyere said in a contrite voice. "Please help me to correct that view."

"Let's try and be honest," Udo said, raising her voice and poking her fingers on Chinyere's chest belligerently. "Have you told your husband that Sarah is your child?"

"But, sister, you know how it is," replied Chinyere, almost in tears. "He wouldn't have married me if he knew I had a child. That was why at the beginning I kept it a secret."

"Chinyere," Udo said in an angry voice, "you've been married for how many years now? One can understand if you felt so at the beginning, but to keep up the pretext for all these years is unbelievable."

Chinyere, at a loss for what to say, simply held out her hands in supplication.

"Why do you want her to accept you as her mother now?" persisted Udo, her voice reflecting her skepticism.

"Sister, I need help with my children's education," Chinyere cried out piteously. "She can help us. My husband lost his business, and I haven't yet received my gratuity. Her brother and sister need her help. I need her help to pay for my eye surgery."

Exasperated, Udo lashed out at her. "Chinyere, you are very selfish. All the time Sarah was growing up, you never showed her any love. You never gave her anything."

"That's not true!" cried Chinyere. "I love her."

"Nonsense!" shouted an angry Udo. "She told me that when she stayed in your house in Lagos during her visa approval stage, she gave you money to buy produce. Furthermore, your children made her pay for food whenever they were out with her. If I were Sarah, I wouldn't even be seen in the same room as you. Sorry, I'm not going to plead your case with her."

"But, sister," pleaded Chinyere, "you have to help me. Please talk to her. I need her help. Please think about it." Chinyere, feeling that Udo had been very unfair, stood up, still pleading for help as Udo left.

CHAPTER 22

S arah had fumed throughout the funeral ceremonies. Her rage started when she glanced at the program listing family members and saw herself listed as a daughter. In her mind, she sought to find a reason for this final betrayal. Was it in deference to her mother, Chinyere, who had rejected her ever since she was born? Or could it be because the family wanted her to pay for Nkechi's affection all these years? Or perhaps they thought that living in America, she was loaded and therefore must bear part of the burden of the funeral. Or could there be another hidden reason?

She fretted over this during the church service, and she wouldn't let it go even during the interment and repast. Everyone assumed that the death of the woman who had brought her up and the only mother she had ever known was taking a toll on her. Those who noticed her gaunt look tried to comfort her and to tell her that they understood how hard it was for her to accept Nkechi's death.

Shortly after the interment, she cornered Udo and vented her anger on her, demanding her money back since none of the other grandchildren had given that much. One motivating factor for her being upset was that she was, in fact, strapped for funds. She'd had difficulty getting a job in the US commensurate with her qualifications, and she'd had to find a second job in order to be able to pay for her own apartment. She'd hoped she wouldn't spend the money she brought because she'd actually borrowed the amount from a friend, and she was unsure what to do about payment.

Udo didn't react the way Sarah had thought she would. As if not caring who heard her, she shouted, "Do you want your money back? Remember that Ejituru tried to stop you from pledging so much!" Without waiting for an answer, Udo heatedly added, "I have no time for your twisted thoughts now. Mama Nkechi was your mother just as she was my mother. You should be proud that you gave back something to the woman who brought you up." Udo jabbed her chest hard with her fingers.

Sarah could see that Ejituru, who was within earshot, overheard the admonition.

Stung by Udo's angry words, she ran into the house and lay on her bed, crying and worrying about Ejituru's reaction after listening to Udo's rehashing of the incident. She was certain that this would reinforce Ejituru's indifferent attitude toward her. She'd hoped that with both of them now living in the same area, she would grow closer to Ejituru. Even though Sarah tried to put aside her hurt for the rest of the repast, it festered in her mind the whole time, and it didn't help that she had to sit through the evening listening to Chinyere's diatribe about Nkechi and her relationship with Onyeka. She woke in the morning feeling extremely unhappy.

Lying in the bed next to Chinyere's, Sarah pretended to be asleep when Chinyere came back to the room that morning from her bath. With half-open eyes, she watched Chinyere rub Yardley's brilliantine on her body. Sarah noticed that she had grown rather corpulent, with rolls of fat on her middle, which she needed to suck in before putting on her wrapper and matching blouse. Without the wig she wore most of the time, she was completely bald due to years of using chemicals.

Sarah wondered what was in her mind right now. Was she thinking of her mother dearest, or of the children and husband she left in Lagos?

Sarah had stayed once at Chinyere's when she came to Lagos to obtain her green card after having won the visa lottery and again when she was on her way to visit Nkechi over a Christmas vacation. It was then that she met her half-siblings. She was introduced to them as Nkechi's daughter, who had moved from London to the US. Throughout her stay, she had been very uncomfortable. The children, one boy and one girl, expected her to buy things for them and were upset when she did not. She ended up creating a myth of a well-heeled American who would send money to them as soon as she got back and had access to her bank account. They'd each given her their bank account numbers.

At no time during her stay did Chinyere show any affection for her. On the contrary, she behaved as if it was an imposition to have her in her house, and often she demanded money from her when she needed to go to the market.

Peeping at Chinyere from beneath the bed sheet, Sarah saw a bitter woman who throughout her life had never accepted who she was, who was always craving what she did not have, who, despite being married to a man who supposedly loved her and with whom she had children, was full of jealousy. This immense jealousy had prevented her from fully accepting the love of the woman who had rescued her from poverty. She would not have all that she had today without Nkechi's love. Despite her insolence and bad behavior, Nkechi had taken her back as her daughter and brought up her outof-wedlock daughter as her own child, making it possible for Chinyere to lead the type of life she wanted, hoping that she would at some future date fulfill her obligation to her daughter. That was what Nkechi wanted and hoped for.

Sarah pulled the bed sheet over her head to avoid any conversation with Chinyere, but Chinyere now knew she was awake. Much to her chagrin, Chinyere chose that time to remind Sarah that she was her birth mother and deserved acknowledgement from her. The ensuing altercation with Chinyere upset her greatly.

Try as hard as she could, she couldn't let go of her anger at Chinyere. Why did she want to establish a mother-daughter relationship now? Why did she keep her a secret from her husband? Was she afraid that their love wasn't on solid ground and he would abandon her? If he had, she would have got what she deserved. How long would she keep the secret? Sarah couldn't summon the strength to ask these questions of Chinyere.

She was sure that Chinyere was making up to her because she was now living in the US and earning a lot of money, and selfish Chinyere wanted a part of it.

True, Chinyere had given birth to her, but Sarah had never liked her. She saw her as a shallow and selfish woman only preoccupied with what would benefit her and her immediate family, uninterested in the effect of her behavior on others. If it was possible to turn back the clock, would she have looked after her? She wondered what her life would have been like if Chinyere had acknowledged her and taken her to Lagos to live with her and her husband in that cramped house in Yaba. It would have been different for sure, as she realized three years ago when she was in Lagos for the lottery interview and had to stay in her house. She felt that most of the benefits she had enjoyed as Nkechi's child wouldn't have happened because neither Udo nor Ifeoma would have helped her. She wouldn't have attended a premier secondary school if Ifeoma hadn't been the principal, nor would she have had the opportunity to go to the UK and then on to America. She doubted that Chinyere's husband would have been prepared to educate another man's child.

⤜⤞◦⟡◦⤝⤟

When Sarah finally got out of bed, it was nearly midmorning. She hurried over to the backyard for her bath, unaware of the women in the parlor and almost tripping over Nwankwo, who was entering the main house from the courtyard. She had to search for a pail because both Udo and Chinyere had left the pails in the bathroom, and she was not about to enter there now. She had always dreaded this bathroom next to the kitchen because the walls were green with mildew formed over the years, the floor slippery with unrinsed soapy water, and she couldn't abide all the dirty, wet towels hanging on the rope strung across the room.

When Nkechi was alive, she never used this bathroom, preferring to go to the enclosed open space at the back of the house. The bathroom was constructed for Nwakama, who felt that he needed something nearer. Nkechi had also built a water closet across from it, but with no water, one had to flush it with water from a pail. Without Nkechi to ensure that the room was kept clean, the bowl was now unusable, and Sarah preferred to use the old-fashioned toilet in the backyard. Without saying a word to anybody, she quickly grabbed a pail and filled it with water from the nearest tank.

"I can't imagine how some people can sleep through the noise in the house," Nwankwo muttered loud enough for her to hear, as if trying to get a rise out of her. "It's almost eleven o'clock, and some of us are just getting out of bed."

Sarah, determined not to take the bait, just shrugged her shoulders as she carried the pail to the backyard.

But he had more to say. "Some people never grow up. Perhaps we should make them go to the stream for their bath as Emeka did this morning. Then they'll learn."

Thoroughly put off by Nwankwo, for whom she had no respect, she left his remarks hanging in the air. But after her bath, with only a wrap tied around her body, she reentered the courtyard and ran into him again. He had been loitering near the kitchen. She tried to ignore him as she hung the towel she'd used on the rope strung across the courtyard.

"We've been lucky during this funeral to have the drums filled with water thanks to Mama's friends, who made sure that there was enough water for cooking and cleaning. That's why you all could afford to have water rather than go to the stream as we mortals do." He sarcastically threw the words at her.

For a moment, it seemed as if she would rise to the bait, but instead, she stared at him with tight lips and continued with her business.

Undeterred by her silence, he shouted at her, "You all should remember to leave money for water before you depart, since at the rate it's being wasted, the drums will be empty soon! Go and dress and join your sisters in the parlor. Show respect to your mother!"

With a voice full of disdain, Sarah replied, "What are you doing here? Shouldn't you also be in the parlor? Or perhaps there isn't enough to drink there." That should put you in your place, she thought.

Fuming, she entered the bedroom to dress. She couldn't abide Nwankwo. She had hated him from the time she was a little girl. He was eight years old when she was born, and she had grown up with him and Emeka in the house. Growing up with them, she knew all their secrets. She watched Nwankwo lead a dissolute life, unbeknown to his parents, and witnessed his lack of self-control, his absences from school, his many lies and excuses to his parents, his indulgences. His hoodwinked parents finally realized that they were throwing away their money trying to educate him.

What a waste, she thought.

She had thought Emeka would amount to something. He was always quoting the Bible as justification for his actions. A pity about his accident. At least he had a reason for the way he turned out.

Michael? What a disappointment. What a wasted life.

Sarah pulled out a rumpled dress from her suitcase. Applying her makeup, she thought of Udo, who had appropriated one room in the house for herself and had decorated it to her liking, whereas she had to share this cramped room with Chinyere. Why, she asked herself, did she have to share this room with her?

Her thoughts went back to Udo. She was grateful to her for getting her into school in the UK, but nothing more. Sarah resented that Udo only gave her enough cash to cover her transportation and expected her to carry her lunch from the house. She was unhappy that she didn't have enough money to indulge her wish for beautiful clothes. Udo, in her view, had treated her as a maid instead of a sister, expecting her to do housework. That was why she moved out after she completed her studies. She resented that circumstances forced her to be beholden to Udo, and she was sure Udo was just waiting for the appropriate time to get back at her, since Udo would never forget a wrong and would never cease to remind Sarah of her generosity.

She left the room and entered the parlor, to be embraced by the women who had just finished their visit with a prayer. As they left, she stood near the window watching Ejituru and Ifeoma. She looked at Ejituru and felt nothing but resentment. She was Nkechi's only child. Why was she making the rest of them pay for her mother's funeral? It wasn't as if she couldn't afford it.

Then her resentment left her as she reminded herself that she would like to be closer to Ejituru, and she might benefit from doing so, since there'd been times that Ejituru had shown her kindness. She'd heard through the grapevine, though unconfirmed by Udo, that it was really Ejituru who paid her airfare to the UK, as well as for her initial tuition. Sarah believed that if Ejituru had done so, it was because her mother had asked her to and she wanted to please her mother.

As she cast her eyes around the place, she saw Udo watching Ifeoma. She felt that Udo resented Ifeoma because of her relationship with Ejituru, whom Udo saw as a competitor. Udo secretly wanted to be like Ejituru. She chose to go to the UK as a maid so she would be seen as having achieved what Ejituru had achieved, an overseas education. She got married to a man from a different state because she heard that Ejituru, a divorcee, had remarried. Of all of them, she felt that Ifeoma probably loved Ejituru, and that must be the reason why she felt close to her. Ifeoma appeared inseparable from Ejituru and was her confidant. Just then, Ifeoma shifted her glance and approached her. "Hi, Sarah. I'm glad you rested after your experience last night. I hear you all only went to bed this morning. I should tell you that we're all going to be at Ejituru's this evening for the reading of the will."

"What do you mean?" Sarah asked, taken aback. "Whose will? I've never heard of this."

"Well, apparently Nkechi left a will. We'll know about it tonight. We'll also finalize the expenses and decide any other outstanding issues before you all leave. Everybody has been informed." Having delivered her message, Ifeoma turned to say goodbye to the last of the women gathered there.

Sarah heard Udo shout, "Let go of me! I've had enough of your sniveling."

The door of the bedroom opened and Chinyere came out.

Sarah turned away from the door and descended the staircase into the front yard. It was there that Udo found her. Rather than let Udo know that she had overheard the argument with Chinyere, Sarah took a deep breath before saying, "Auntie, what is this I'm hearing? We're going to Ejituru's tonight for the reading of the will? Were you informed?"

Udo curtly answered, "So I heard. We'll find out what it's all about tonight." She immediately climbed the stairs.

The discussion with Chinyere must not have gone well, and Udo must need time alone, Sarah thought. Still, she didn't like being spoken to so rudely. She went back to the bedroom and picked up her handbag. She didn't want to be left with Chinyere. She didn't want Ejituru's company, either, because she didn't want to discuss her move to the US or that she had only recently obtained a job in the accounts division of an assisted living facility attached to the hospital where Nduka worked. She wasn't about to discuss the problems she was facing in the US and her difficulty finding accommodations and a good job. She would go to the compound and visit her friend.

CHAPTER 23

E jituru stood up and entered Nkechi's bedroom where her grave was as soon as the women departed. She imagined the room as it was during her mother's lifetime. She saw the bed next to the wall, the table next to the window, the trunks piled next to the inside wall, the mosquito net and the rope across where her mother hung her everyday wrappers and blouses. She saw the covered water pot in the corner, with an enamel mug on top, and the shoes, new and worn, under the bed.

Ejituru broke down and wept. She wept for her mother, whose life of achievement was erased by disease, who during her last six months couldn't even remember her. She experienced again her anguish when she visited and was a total stranger to her mother, who kept asking her to tell her who she was and where they had met, who remembered that she had a daughter in the US but couldn't associate her with that daughter. She let her tears wash over her face.

She wept for her children, who had only seen their grandmother once, and she wept for herself, who could no longer feel the love of her mother. She wept for the long-held grudge she bore against her mother for loving Onyeka's children, who she felt had replaced her in her mother's heart.

Addressing her mother, she told her that she forgave her and accepted her reason for bringing Onyeka, whom she loved, into the family.

"I understand why you brought Onyeka into the house. You needed someone to look after me while you fulfilled your dream of becoming a certified teacher."

She recalled her mother's emphasis on education, which made her work hard to fulfill her own dream of being a board-certified physician.

Kneeling at the side of the grave, she whispered, "You meant well, Mama, pushing me to get educated. I appreciate all the sacrifice you made for my education. I truly am grateful."

She told her mother of her resentment for her not supporting her point of view during the marriage negotiations with Ignatius. Even though she could understand why she didn't take her side at that time, she wished she had because it would have still been possible for her to obtain a medical education without being married to Ignatius.

"I understand why you did it," she murmured. "You wanted me to get a US education, and in your mind, that was the easiest way. I've given this a lot of thought, and I know the blame isn't yours alone. I share the blame, too. I wanted to go to the US. It was the quickest way I could think of to get my wish. I'm happy that before your disease, I did tell you this. Mama, I want you to know that I'm now in a happy place. Nduka is good for me, and he truly loves me, and our children are happy. I'm back in Maryland and am truly happy."

She pulled her small notebook out of her purse and opened it to where she had copied a prayer she wanted to read during her mother's interment but couldn't because of all the confusion. She had searched the Internet for a suitable prayer and had come across a text written by Barthold Brockes (1680–1747) and translated by Denys Darlow.

She read from it out loud. "Lord, I trust thee, I adore thee. Ah! Thou friend of man, restore me! On thy loving grace relying, for the bread of life I'm sighing. Quench my thirst and let my hunger cease. Fill my heart with joy and endless peace. When the breath of life has left me, may my soul be blended with thee." She continued to kneel for a while.

"Mummy," she said, "I hope that your soul is blended with the Lord. I will never forget you. You are in my heart forever." She wept again for her mother, Nkechi.

It was there that Ifeoma found her. She lifted her up, and sharing their grief, they left the room and climbed the stairs to enter the upstairs parlor.

Ifeoma and Ejituru walked into the parlor and sat down.

When Ejituru was calmer, she turned to Ifeoma and said, "My mother's death brought back to me all that I've lost. I'm so sad I wasn't here when Onyeka died." Clasping Ifeoma's hand, she continued. "I should have been here, but nobody informed me until after the funeral. I loved her very much."

"I understand. It happened suddenly, and nobody knew she was sick." Ifeoma squeezed her hands. "The burial was quick, and in fact, only Nwankwo and Emeka were here. Don't dwell on that now."

"I have to. Onyeka was a mother to me, and I loved her. For two years when Nkechi was at Nsukka, she looked after me. She would put me on her back and take me everywhere she went. I loved her to the extent that when Nkechi came back, I thought Onyeka was my mother, even though I knew she was too young to have been. I know she loved me, too." Ejituru's eyes shone as she remembered those happy times.

Ifeoma, transfixed, looked at her with parted lips.

"Did you know she was the first person I told about Nduka, my husband?" Ejituru asked. It was a rhetorical question, and without waiting for an answer, she continued. "I had come back before my residency intending to discuss my divorce from Ignatius and my attachment to Nduka, but Nkechi was very busy. I could never get her alone without any interruptions." She paused, looking for confirmation from Ifeoma, before continuing. "The only person who had time for me was Onyeka. She would come early in the morning to the room where I was sleeping and sit by my side and ask about my life in the US. I told her things that I wouldn't tell my mother.

Sometimes in telling the story, I would break down, and she would hold me." By this time, she was openly weeping.

"Sister, you don't have to tell me any more. I understand."

"No, I have to get it off my chest," Ejituru said in between sobs. "I told her about my life with Ignatius, the people who helped me get into college, how I met Nduka again, and what precipitated my separation from Ignatius. I told her how it had been impossible to find time to talk to my mother. Onyeka was very understanding, and advised me to go to my mother's room before the morning prayer to talk to her. That was what finally happened after the visit of my college friend. I truly loved and appreciated Onyeka. I was sad when she had a misunderstanding with Nkechi and had to leave the house. You can't imagine how glad I was that they reconciled and she came back."

Ifeoma couldn't believe what she was hearing. She knew vaguely that Ejituru had a strong attachment to Onyeka, but this was the first time she'd heard her openly confess it. She sat quietly, processing what Ejituru was saying. She thought of her own feelings about Onyeka. She was never close to her and didn't see her as a mother. To her, she was just one of the maids. She'd never at any time confided in her. Nkechi had been the repository of all her doubts and ambitions. Nkechi was the person she ran to whenever she had personal problems. How ironic that Ejituru, who was not the child of Onyeka, should feel so close to her, and Ifeoma, who was the child of Onyeka, preferred Nkechi, who was Ejituru's mother.

Ifeoma was aware that Ejituru had never joined in when Onyeka was being ridiculed by the other children, but she never in her wildest dreams thought the bond between the two was so strong that Onyeka would be the first person Ejituru would share her confidences with. What had she missed? she wondered. Were they both talking about the same subservient woman that she knew, who couldn't do anything right?

To each his own. She wouldn't dare to disabuse Ejituru of what she felt. So instead, Ifeoma said, "Sister, I know that Onyeka loved you, and both of you shared a bond. I remember whenever she heard that you were back from school and college, she would come all the way from the plantation to see you and would bring pears and corn when in season and groundnuts for you. Sometimes, she would bring your favorite soup, just for you." Freeing her hands from Ejituru's clasp, she stood up and embraced her. Then she sat down and faced her. "We used to wonder why you were so solicitous of such a person. I never really cared for her or loved her. I always regarded her as being illiterate and uncouth. Funny, the only mother I knew has just been buried. Nkechi was very good to me and I loved her." Overcome with emotion, she wept.

It was Ejituru's turn to hold and comfort her.

"Do you know," Ifeoma said when she calmed down, "that when I was growing up, I would creep into Nkechi's bed whenever I had a nightmare? She would comfort me. She was truly a mother to all of us, even though we weren't from her womb. Udo can tell you the same."

"I know, and I've spent a lifetime being jealous of her love for you all," Ejituru said in a contrite voice.

But Ifeoma, feeling she had to unburden her soul, said, "Chinyere could understand, too, if she wasn't full of bitterness. Look at how Nkechi struggled to make sure that Michael would turn a new leaf.

She spoiled him, covering his debts and manufacturing excuses for his failures."

"I presume her blindness toward Michael's failures was because Michael's birth saved her marriage," Ejituru said as she burst into fresh tears. Moving her chair closer to Ejituru's and holding her hands, Ifeoma said, between gulps of weeping, "Chai, sister, she tried her best with Nwankwo and Emeka. No one can say it was her fault that they didn't succeed. Look at Sarah! What would have become of her if Nkechi hadn't brought her up?

Chinyere totally forgot that she had a child out of wedlock."

"I often wonder about that," Ejituru said, looking up to Ifeoma. "One would think since her marriage is secure, she would tell her husband about Sarah."

"Sister, I will tell you a secret," Ifeoma murmured. "Chinyere's husband knows about Sarah. He knew about her when he came for Dad's funeral. He chose to pretend to her that he didn't know."

"No way!" Ejituru said, freeing her hand from Ifeoma's and wiping her face. "How could he keep up the charade? I just can't believe this."

"Do you know that he has a mistress who also has children by him?" Ifeoma calmly said. "All this will be clear when he dies and Chinyere has to face his people."

Ejituru shook her head and tearfully said, "I don't wish anybody ill. I hope that with Nkechi's death, everybody will try and lead their own lives."

Changing the subject, Ifeoma asked, "Have you considered the advice I gave when I visited?"

"What advice?" Ejituru asked, looking baffled. "We talked about so many things then."

"Remember when I asked you to help our brothers, and you said you would have to consult Nduka because you couldn't do anything without his knowledge, since you have joint accounts?" Ifeoma's voice reflected her anxiety at raising this subject.

Ejituru laughed and said, "You're still at that? I'll never do that. I can never do anything without Nduka's agreement."

But Ifeoma persisted. "You're making a big mistake. You should keep your money separate. Our mother drummed that into our heads. Remember?"

"That may be so—if you don't trust your husband. But I implicitly trust Nduka, and we discuss everything openly. We have nothing to hide from each other. Our marriage is secure." Ejituru changed the trajectory of the discussion. "I understand Sarah resides in the US now. She's never contacted me, so I wonder where she's living."

"The address she gave me was in a place called Bowie, in Maryland," replied Ifeoma.

"Really! I also live in Maryland now, but in Silver Spring. Maybe she doesn't want me to know, so let's pretend that I don't."

"Sister, I have to warn you. Be careful of Sarah. She's a green snake in green grass. You don't know when she'll strike. Don't forget this warning. You have to take care of yourself. Look at you." With a surge of emotion, she added, "You must be tired. Go home and rest. I should also go home and get things ready for tonight." She grabbed her bag and stood up.

"Wait," said Ejituru. "Why don't I drop you?"

They descended the steps and bade goodbye to Nwankwo, who was standing outside talking to one of the visitors looking for Michael.

CHAPTER 24

When the car arrived at Ifeoma's house, Ifeoma turned to Ejituru and said, "Come inside for a little while and have some tea or coffee with me. It's been a rough time."

Ejituru hesitated for a minute before getting out of the car, then followed Ifeoma to her parlor. She looked around the room with its heavy furniture and gazed at the photographs of Ifeoma's children.

Ifeoma ushered her to a sofa placed near a wall and called out for hot water and tea.

"I think I'll have a Fanta instead," Ejituru said, "since it's a hot day." She relaxed for a moment. "Where is your husband? I was hoping to visit with him and to thank him for his help."

"At a village meeting today," Ifeoma replied. "But, it should have ended. Perhaps he's gone to visit some friends. You know how it is in the village."

"How are things between you?" Ejituru asked. "It must be hard being the sole provider in the family." She gazed tenderly at Ifeoma who feeling overwhelmed said,

"Well, as Mama would say, God gives each one of us the burden he thinks we can bear. Hmm, my sister, I'm managing.

What makes it difficult sometimes is another woman taking your hard-earned money—not that that's the situation here."

"I sincerely hope not," Ejituru said. "If it was, would you tell me?"

Ifeoma stared lovingly at Ejituru, thinking, of all my siblings, I truly love her and would do anything for her. Aloud, she said, "Sister, I can never lie to you. There was a woman between us, and I caught him with her. The matter has been dealt with."

"What are you saying?" Ejituru replied angrily. "You know our mother wouldn't hesitate to leave our father if she caught him with another woman."

"You're right. I thought about it, but decided against it. We've come to a compromise. I lead my life, and he leads his, as long as he doesn't spend my money on other women. Just now, he's a born-

again Christian. You know what that means." Both burst out laughing.

"If he ever strays again, you will let me know, won't you?" Ejituru said, smiling.

"Of course," replied Ifeoma firmly. "Who else can I confide in?"

The two sisters sat chatting companionably about their children, and inevitably the talk turned to their siblings. Ifeoma wanted to know whether Ejituru had ever met Udo's ex-husband.

"No, I haven't," replied Ejituru.

Ifeoma screwed up her face and pursed her lips, wondering whether to share a secret she was privy to. Having decided, she said, "I understand one of her daughters recently made contact with the father."

"I bet Udo was very unhappy about that." Ejituru shook her head. "That's true," Ifeoma said.

"Did she find him?" Ejituru inquired, looking sharply at Ifeoma. "And is she now in a relationship with him?"

"She did find him, but it didn't turn out well," Ifeoma replied, smiling. "What happened?" Ejituru asked. "I'm really curious because I know of similar cases."

"The father only wanted a relationship that would benefit his Nigerian-born children. He demanded money from his British child. You know how Nigerians are." Ejituru shook her head. "I'd hoped it would end differently. I'd recently read an article about a famous artist with a Nigerian father and a black American mother who was abandoned by his father at a very tender age. He went to Nigeria in search of the father, only with the knowledge of where he lived and the school he attended while in the US."

"With so little facts, I bet he never found him," Ifeoma said.

"He did find him, but sadly, his father didn't want to have anything to do with him, because he didn't want his Nigerian family to know he'd married and fathered a child while in the US. He did eventually manage to be on good terms with his Nigerian siblings. In this case, the outcome was different," Ejituru said. "I feel awful for Udo's daughter to be so disappointed when she hoped very much for a different outcome."

"Sister, please don't mention this to Udo," pleaded Ifeoma. "It would end our relationship."

"I hear you, and I promise I won't." Ejituru stood up and walked over to scrutinize the wedding photograph of Ifeoma on the wall. "By the way, did Mama ever talk to you about her parents' marriage? I thought of them this morning when I was in the upstairs parlor looking at wedding photographs. It shaped her whole attitude toward husband-and-wife relationships." She walked back and sat on the carpet with crossed legs, leaning forward over the coffee table.

Ifeoma followed suit and sat opposite her with the table between them. "She did, and she drummed it into me that I should be financially independent of my husband. It was her mantra. Eh, come to think of it, we all abide by that. Wasn't he a principal of a primary school, one of the few salaried positions in the community?" Ifeoma adjusted her seat on the carpet.

"So he was," Ejituru said, "but he gave her a pittance for the family budget, and out of that, he expected her to feed and clothe the family, pay school fees for those in secondary school, and maintain the household. He expected her to augment what she was given with the meager income she got from her petty trading and her small plot of farmland."

"Yes, I remember Mama laughing when she told me that and remarking that in that regard, her mother was lucky."

Ifeoma laughed, too. "In Mama's case, she got nothing from her husband."

Both sisters laughed so much that tears ran down their cheeks. Recovering, Ejituru said, "I can understand how this could cause friction."

"Mama told me that she tried to get her parents to communicate with each other," Ifeoma said, "but she failed because her mother firmly believed that her husband had more money than he was letting on, even when she tried to convince her to the contrary, having from her own research found out her father's monthly income."

"She told me the same thing," Ejituru said thoughtfully, "but she added that the problem was that her mother couldn't reconcile his spending on his brothers and sisters with the notion that he had no spare cash for his own family. She felt that he placed the needs of his extended family before that of his immediate family."

"I actually sympathize with him." Ifeoma stood up and stretched her arms before resuming her seat on the sofa. She scratched her head and looked at Ejituru. "Mama said that he never really tried to defend himself but just sat there and listened. He was that kind of a man. On that day, she vowed that she would not be dependent on any man for support, and if she ever got married, it would be to someone who could support her if necessary. In this, she failed."

"My sister, she failed miserably," Ejituru said in a voice reflecting her frustration. "She married a man who wasn't able to support her financially. I pointed out to her that at least her father had a good job and was able to support his extended family and to build this grand house where we're living. It was only as a pensioner that he failed his wife. Whereas, our father never held a job, nor earned any money, and as far as we know, was totally dependent on Nkechi." Ejituru lifted herself from the floor and smoothed her skirt.

Ifeoma swallowed a lump in her throat and coughed. In a skeptical voice, she said, "I bet she blamed the civil war for his unrealized dreams. She'd given me that excuse, saying that it interrupted his education, and that after the war, he was unable to cope with changes in society."

Ejituru turned toward the door as if to leave.

"Besides," Ifeoma added, "marrying him put her in a higher social group.

To her that was enough."

CHAPTER 25

After Ejituru had gone, Ifeoma lay on the couch trying to process everything that had happened. She called a maid to bring her a bottle of Coca-Cola. Since her husband had an important event that day and the children were all occupied with their friends, she was all alone in the house. She needed to get the accounts ready for the evening meeting, but that could wait. She knew that Nkechi had left no will, but she wasn't about to tell the others.

She thought of her siblings. Were they worrying about the contents of the will? Michael must be wondering why he had missed it. After all, Nkechi lived in his house, and it was he who removed her from this home. If there was a will, why didn't he find it when he emptied the trunks and allowed his brothers to sell Nkechi's wrappers and jewelry, which by right should belong to the daughters of the house?

He must be cursing himself for not being as vigilant as he should have been.

Emeka didn't give a hoot about anything. He lived in his dream world, where he listened to the BBC or Al Jazeera and dreamt of being in the places mentioned in the news.

Nwankwo, she was sure, didn't know what a will was. He was probably thinking of the next funeral or the next infertile man who would demand his services. He thought his activities in this regard weren't widely known, but in this town, nothing was ever hidden. Ifeoma had often worried about what would happen if the children he fathered discovered the truth. She herself had been trying to find out which children were his, but even her informant had refused to divulge this information.

Lost in thought, she heard a taxi stop outside her house, and she wondered who could be visiting at that time. Visits were usually expected in the morning or evening, not during the day.

To her shock, Udo walked in. "Sister, I was visiting Mazi Ukwu at the new extension, and rather than go home to deal with the hoopla about the will, I thought I should drop in to visit you." Udo dropped her handbag on the sofa and sat down.

Ifeoma, who couldn't believe that Udo was finally in the house, tried to cover her shock by giving Udo an embrace. Udo normally expected Ifeoma to visit her and had never, as far as she could remember, deigned to come to her house. Her thoughts ran through a whole gamut of reasons for the visit. Perhaps she came to talk about the will. Too bad. She'll get nothing from me.

After having asked the maid to bring some snacks for Udo, Ifeoma, looking pensive, asked, "How is Mazi Ukwu? You know that his first wife died, and he's remarried."

"Losing his first wife was a big blow to him because it was her brother that brought him to London," Udo said. She munched on the roasted peanuts the maid had brought. "They'd both planned for this retirement."

"I heard that it wasn't long after he arrived that his brother-in-law died in a tragic accident," Ifeoma said as she got up to get a soft drink from the fridge in her dining room. Coming back, she said, "I met his sister once. She trained as a nurse in the UK and worked there for a long time. She died four years ago."

"That's correct. Mazi Ukwu is an example of someone who made use of all the opportunities available to him. He was mailman for the post office until his retirement. He lived modestly, taking advantage of all that the state offered to educate his children, and he was a most faithful member of the indigene association. He never missed a meeting. We were sad when he decided to retire and live here."

"He's very highly respected," Ifeoma said. "I heard that he was handling various projects of the London indigene association here."

"That's right, and that was part of the reason why I went to see him." "His house here is something to behold," Ifeoma exclaimed. "It must have cost millions!"

"It was such a huge shock to see it," Udo said. "It explains why he didn't take advantage of the government offer to buy his council house. We couldn't understand why he never made any improvements to it or moved. The house here explains it all."

"I bet his house was swarming with visitors this weekend," Ifeoma said as she covered a yawn with her hand.

"You're right there," said Udo. "I couldn't have any useful discussion there, and it was frustrating, since I won't have another opportunity before I leave." She started to cry, as if she had suddenly removed the wall holding the water in the dam in place.

Taken by surprise, Ifeoma looked imploringly at her. "Did something happen while you were at Ukwu's house? Tell me!"

"I didn't expect Nkechi to die. I knew she was ill, but I thought she was getting good medical care. I had planned to come at Christmas to stay with her. Oh, God, I can't think of my mother dead!" She beat her thighs in despair as tears rolled down her face. "Before her illness, we were planning that she would visit me in London. I really wanted her to come again. Her last visit after visiting Ejituru in Texas was too short."

Ifeoma got up and embraced her, trying to comfort her. "It happened suddenly. She was feeling a lot better the night before. She was very lucid, and even remembered who I was. She ate well. It was a shock when the maid came and woke me up to say that she was very agitated. I rushed to the room, only to find that she had died. Sister, I'm still in shock. You should take comfort that you did your best, sending money for her care."

The sisters sat together, each weeping softly.

Then Ifeoma said, "You can imagine how Ejituru must be feeling now. She tried to hold her grief in, but just before she left, she broke down. I didn't want to leave her alone, but she insisted on going to her house. She's going to call her husband. She's been worried about her family."

Udo replied offhandedly, "It must be hard on her, but the loss is not hers alone."

"She's grateful that we all tried to contribute toward the funeral. She was going to go it alone. She appreciates the love we have for Nkechi."

Udo bristled, showing her irritation. "Why shouldn't we? Nkechi was the only mother I knew. I felt nothing when Onyeka died because I never thought of her as my mother. She did nothing for me."

Ifeoma clasped her hands and unclasped them. She was dumbfounded to hear Udo express similar views as herself. She breathed heavily, pausing to collect her thoughts as she watched Udo's anguished face. Then she exclaimed, "Wow! I feel the same, but you know Ejituru feels differently. She told me that she misses Onyeka more now that Nkechi is no more. She longs for Onyeka's comforting embrace and love." She looked at Udo and saw disbelief on her face. "Believe me, she had such good things to say about her. She felt really close to her, and Onyeka knew more about her life than Nkechi did. I was touched by what she said about Onyeka. She regretted missing Onyeka's funeral. She said if she had known about it, she would have come for it, but I told her it was sudden and quick, and except for Nwankwo and Emeka, none of us attended."

Udo shook her head, as if in disbelief. "But she didn't come home for Dad's funeral, although I understand her reason for not coming. Something to do with illness, I think. In a way, I'm happy she didn't come, given the horrible things Chinyere said."

At the mention of Chinyere, Ifeoma's face clouded. She breathed a sigh before saying, "Why did she come? I bet people are thinking that she contributed to the funeral expenses."

"That was my biggest surprise," replied Udo, wiping her tears. "It's so unlike her husband not to give her money to contribute, because I know he thought highly of Nkechi."

"She more or less almost confessed to me that he did. I wouldn't put it past Chinyere to hide the fact." Ifeoma shook her head. "I can't understand that woman. I know she's our elder, but she's full of hate and bitterness. I only hope Sarah won't end up like her." They sat silently together for a while.

The silence was broken by Udo. "Do you know that she hasn't even bought any food since she came?" she complained angrily. "She's eating the food I bought, and so is Sarah. Neither of them has thought of buying food. But of course, for these few days, they're eating leftovers from the funeral."

"Poor you," said Ifeoma, laughing. "What can you do? I can't imagine you allowing them to watch you eat and not offering them any."

"What is it with Sarah and her complaint?" Udo asked. "Ejituru said she would refund her the money."

"She's being silly," Ifeoma said, banging the table. "Wasn't she treated by Mama as her daughter? Let her raise it tonight to her shame."

"Chinyere is telling everybody that she hasn't received her gratuity and pension from the federal government, and she's short of cash," Udo said.

To this, Ifeoma angrily retorted, "How can she say so? Weren't we told that her husband is rich? I remember how she boasted about his wealth when our dad died. She's the most ungrateful person I know. I can't believe that we're related. Mama loved her and brought her up as her child, but she feels nothing but hate toward her. Remember how hard Nkechi was on you because Sarah told her you treated her as a servant?"

"I know," replied Udo. "Believe me, she's no different from Chinyere.

They're cut from the same cloth."

"Sister, thank you for your support of your brothers." Ifeoma extended her hand to shake Udo's. "Without that support, I don't know what would become of them."

"Nonsense!" cried Udo. "I give only out of duty and nothing else. I know there's no real love between us."

"Chai, don't say that," Ifeoma said forcefully. "They love you and are grateful."

"Are you kidding?" said Udo. "I don't desire gratitude. I only wish they would show respect for what I've tried to do for them."

"Sister, I'm sure they do appreciate your help," Ifeoma said, pleading for understanding with her eyes. "Michael was very grateful that you paid for the secondary education for one of his sons."

"That may be so, but I was all set to pay for his university education, too," said Udo.

"What happened?" Ifeoma asked. "I actually expected you to do so but never understood why you stopped."

"Well, I realized that the money I had sent for him to pay for the exams wasn't used for its intended purpose," Udo replied after a pause. "He frittered it away with the excuse that he couldn't stand to see his siblings destitute without helping them."

"What?" exclaimed Ifeoma. "This is the first time I've heard of this." Udo stared at Ifeoma before replying. In a voice full of concern, she said,

"I honestly couldn't understand that type of attitude because ultimately, he would be more helpful to his siblings with a college education. When I heard this, I withdrew my support."

Ifeoma abruptly changed the subject. "Sister, I've been meaning to ask you. Are you in contact with your ex?"

"Why should I be?" Udo responded, annoyed. "Knowing him was the worst experience of my life."

"Papa, when he was alive, often wondered why his people never came to do the ceremony and claim you as a wife, especially since you gave them children. He felt it wasn't normal. Please don't be annoyed that I ask. I also wondered why you haven't remarried."

Udo laughed a hollow laugh. "I presume if I had given him a boy, it would have made a difference, but my two children were girls. I had this conversation with Mama in my house, and she knew everything. It wasn't a good marriage, and he treated me very badly. I'm glad I don't have him in my life, and for my sake, you should be happy for me, too." Udo screwed up her face in disgust. "Regarding your other question, I'm not as lucky as Ejituru. I haven't met a man who would take me plus my children." Udo stood up to leave. "Look, the taxi's waiting for me. You have to prepare for this evening. I'll see you then." She headed to the door, then added, almost as an afterthought, "Why did you decide to give Michael the task of recording the gifts? He's so untrustworthy with money. We all knew what would happen."

"I'm tired of being asked that question," Ifeoma said angrily. "He felt excluded from the arrangements, and he complained that he was left out. I couldn't think of any other task for him. He may still surprise us."

"Let's hope so," Udo said. "Perhaps Sarah's oversight provided a check, but I doubt it." She made for the door.

CHAPTER 26

C hinyere, angry and unhappy with the outcome of her conversation with Udo, left the house with Lucy, one of the mourners, intending to accompany her to the ancestral compound where she had relatives whose sons and daughters in Lagos were her acquaintances. Lucy had been a close friend and confidant of Nkechi, their having both been young brides in the compound before Nkechi went on to train as a primary schoolteacher.

It was a busy road, crowded with carts, cyclists, and pedestrians taking advantage of the sunshine after an early morning drizzle to conduct their various business. Women on their way to the farm or market greeted Lucy warmly, and also expressed their condolences to Chinyere. Approaching the public primary school on the right side of the road, the two stopped to watch the children playing soccer in the school compound.

Lucy, who by this time was sweating profusely, wiped her brow with the tail end of her top wrapper. "I remember when your brothers played football here. Michael would be the last person to quit the game. Nkechi sometimes would send a servant to get him. His younger brothers were even worse. Those boys! Nkechi's pain!" She shook her head vehemently.

Chinyere looked at the school building in disgust. She turned and said, "I vaguely remember Michael and all his truancies, but Ma Lucy, this school looks different from what I remember. It looks rather dilapidated. I wonder when it was last painted."

Lucy glanced at her. "Blame Abia State government. Those who govern aren't interested in our town."

As they walked, the pedestrians they encountered continued to express their condolences to Chinyere, repeating over and over again the same phrases: "Our daughter, the loss is not only yours. We all lost a wonderful woman who contributed a lot to this town. She will be missed."

After the tenth repetition, Chinyere began to lose control of her irritation, so she turned to her companion. In a voice dripping with anger, she said, "This is getting on my nerves. I don't want to hear any more talk of the funeral or of losing Nkechi. I have nothing good to say about her. In fact, I hate her, and I'm glad she's gone."

In no uncertain terms, Lucy exclaimed, "Hate! What did she ever do to make you hate her? You should be grateful to her." She turned toward Chinyere and slapped her on the cheek, pushing her toward the edge of the road. As if that weren't enough, she spat on her.

Shaken by such unexpected behavior from Lucy, Chinyere could only stammer, "Grateful for what?"

As if not caring who heard her, Lucy shouted, "You've forgotten what you were when you were growing up—a harlot, always chasing men! You think because Nkechi pretended that you had gone abroad, nobody knew that you had a child out of wedlock. Look at you!" She used her fingers to emphasize the point she was making. "You're no saint. I will make sure everybody knows what you said. Do you know that many mourners were disgusted when they saw you pretending that you were mourning her death? Thank God you're not from her womb."

Dumbfounded and aghast at such vitriol, Chinyere was unable to retaliate. She stood on the roadside trying to restore her composure as she watched Lucy walk away. She pretended not to be aware of onlookers who were wondering what was happening.

Collecting herself and shaking off her dismay, she considered going back to the house but felt that she could face neither her sisters nor her brothers. She wouldn't know how to describe what had just happened or to speculate about what was in the will because she knew that both Nwankwo and Michael would be knocking themselves for not being aware of it. What did she care? She had nothing to offer them. Pretending to be unfazed by Lucy's action, she walked on to the village square where the few stalls open were crowded with shoppers buying fresh produce. Several groups of people were discussing the events of the day. Recognized by some, she accepted their greetings, and moving on, she spied Ejituru's rented car approaching. She quickly entered the nearest shop, posing as an admirer of the fabrics displayed.

The shop owner, a seamstress who introduced herself as Ivuatu, greeted her warmly and asked if she was interested in a purchase.

"No, no, I'm just browsing," she said.

Ivuatu went back to her machine, but on second thought, looked up and said, "You're Ejituru's sister. I saw you at the funeral."

Oh no, Chinyere thought. This can't be happening. If she says any vile thing to me, I'm sure I'll hit her on the head. I don't want a reprise of Lucy.

Before she could frame an answer, Ivuatu said, "Ejituru was my friend from primary school. We used to see a lot of each other when she came back on holidays from Ibiaku and Nsukka."

"Were you also at Nsukka?" asked Chinyere, who now had moved nearer to a table with a display of different types of zippers and buttons.

"Our paths deviated after primary school," Ivuatu said. "I went to teacher training college and became a primary schoolteacher at the school down the road." She concentrated on her sewing.

"I'm sorry you haven't been in touch. But tell me, why are you now a seamstress?"

Ivuatu looked up. "This used to be my mother's shop. When my mother died, I decided to leave teaching and take over the shop." She removed the thimble from her finger. "The funeral was the first time I've seen Ejituru since she left to go to America. I'm hoping to go over to her house in the new extension tomorrow to visit. Do you know when she'll be traveling?" She stared expectantly at Chinyere, who had moved toward the display of materials and was now fingering a light-blue lace, pretending she was thinking of buying it.

"We have the memorial service tomorrow," Chinyere said, "so she'll still be here."

"Then I'll definitely go to her house after the service. Please tell her to expect me."

As Chinyere moved toward the door, Ivuatu offered her a Coke, which she accepted. She sat down in the chair meant for clients, and they discussed the grandeur of the funeral.

Moving about the shop and rearranging the displays, Ivuatu suddenly said, "The last time I saw Ejituru was during her traditional wedding to Ignatius. She looked so beautiful, but I heard later on that the marriage didn't last. I wasn't surprised, because I knew she had doubts."

Chinyere, quietly sipping the Coke, refrained from commenting, letting the seamstress prattle while she thought, the silly girl used Ignatius to achieve her objective, and once there, she left him. She is a user, like her mother.

"I hear she married her college sweetheart," Ivuatu said. "That's the way it should be. Arranged marriages are fast becoming a thing of the past, even though some of our elders swear by it."

"Amen," Chinyere said. "I'm not in an arranged marriage, so I have no such experience. What about you? Are you in an arranged marriage?"

"Yes, but we grew up together, and I knew everything about him," Ivuatu said in a voice that brooked no disagreement.

"I picked my husband myself," replied Chinyere cheerfully.

"Perhaps that's why it's lasted so long."

"Do you have children?" asked Ivuatu, seeming to be genuinely interested.

"Of course. I have one boy and two girls. They didn't come because you know how expensive travel is, and when you have three children in college and secondary school, the bills mount." By this time, Chinyere was tiring of the conversation and looking for an out.

"I understand, although at the funeral, many people were saying that Ejituru should have brought her children. I defended her, saying that I can understand, given the high cost of airfare."

Composing her face, Chinyere said, "I totally agree with you. I have to go. I want to drop in on some people in the compound." Leaving the shop, she was angry with herself. *I should have left when she first mentioned that paragon of goodness. I'll go bonkers if I hear her name again.*

Rather than proceed to the compound, she decided to head home to join Michael and Nwankwo, who by now had several visitors. Halfway home, she turned back, and with her head held high, oblivious of the people going about their business or calling out her name, she walked across the square to a path leading to her father's ancestral compound. It had been ten years since she was there. When she came back for her father's funeral, she had her husband and children with her, and her movement was restricted to the family house. It was there that the ceremony for the clothing of the dead was carried out, and besides, she had to make sure her family was fed. After the departure of her husband and children, she left a day after her big quarrel with Nkechi, so there had been no time to socialize with her friends in the compound.

The first person she ran into as she walked along the narrow path to the entrance of the compound was Lizzy a girl she had gone to primary school with and who was now married to one of her cousins.

"Ndewo," Ifeoma cooed. "Welcome. What brings you here? You should all be resting after yesterday. That was a fabulous funeral. It's the talk of the town. Da Nkechi deserves it. Truly, you all must be tired. Besides, you still have the memorial service tomorrow." "That's true," Chinyere said sadly.

"I hope you and your sisters will be staying with us for some time."

"We decided to carry out the memorial service immediately after, since most of us live overseas, and you know how expensive airline tickets are."

"I understand," Ifeoma said. "Tomorrow's entertainment will just be for church people."

"Yes, but you know how it is," replied Chinyere, who was not privy to the arrangements. "We'll be expecting many uninvited guests, too."

Leaving Ifeoma, whose house was in the opposite direction, she walked on, greeting passersby until she came to her destination. The compound looked seedier than it had the last time she was here. Some of the houses had their roofs upgraded to corrugated iron sheets, but the paths remained unkempt and overgrown with weeds. The house she went into was the one house that had been rebuilt with cement blocks and a zinc roof. This was the house of one of the young men she grew up with who traded between Aba and the town where they both came from. Although he lived in Aba, he had come home for the funeral and would remain until the memorial service. Chinyere had come to visit in the hope that he would give her a lift to Aba, where she hoped to get transportation to Lagos. She had high hopes that the visit would produce the desired outcome.

Her knock was answered by the man himself. Light-complexioned with a round, fleshy face, a stubby beard, and cropped, gray hair, he exuded confidence, as befitted a self-made man. Chinyere knew that Kanu had started life as an assistant to a wholesale trader in Aba, running errands for him, and had progressed from there to have his own shop, where with his two assistants, he sold assorted manufactured goods. He'd returned home for this funeral because he had extreme respect for Nkechi, who had been his confidant when she was alive and had, in fact, found a suitable wife for him. It was a good choice, and he was happy with her. His wife hadn't come home for the funeral because she was recuperating from childbirth.

Greeting Chinyere, he called out to an unseen maid to bring some glasses and a bottle of Fanta and a bottle of Coca-Cola. A chair was produced and both sat down to talk. He appeared happy to see her and congratulated her on the success of the funeral. He asked her when she intended to travel. "I'd like to leave for Aba or Umuahia on Monday if I can arrange for transport," Chinyere said quietly, clasping and unclasping her hands nervously. "I understand it's easier to get transport to Lagos from Aba."

Kanu scratched his head and looked pensive. "I wish I could offer you a ride, but that isn't possible. I have several business meetings here. But I'd suggest that you consider the Aba option."

With a sinking heart, Chinyere said, "I'm concerned about where to stay in Aba, given the time most people travel out from here on Sunday, the day I intend to leave." Kanu remained silent.

Chinyere felt that she couldn't lower herself by suggesting that he put her up in Aba, so she sheepishly said, "My brother, thank you for the information. If you know of anybody leaving early on Monday with space in their car, let me know. I had considered taking the late Sunday bus to Umuahia and spending the night at Ifeoma's, but she told me she wouldn't be traveling for another week." She paused to sip the last drop of her drink. "But tell me, how is the new baby? I hear it's a boy. Congratulations. You now have three boys."

Kanu offered her a weak smile and said, "Well, Enyidie was hoping for a girl, but you know these things depend on God, and one has to take what you're given."

"True," she said as she got up to leave. "While I'm here, I might as well say hello to other relatives. Everybody has been so helpful during this funeral."

Leaving Kanu's home, she decided not to waste any more time but to go back to her father's house. She told herself that she wouldn't think of the so-called meeting tonight or of the will. She would go back to her room and rest.

CHAPTER 27

S arah, rebuffed after her attempt to connect with Udo, who was enraged by Chinyere's request, felt betrayed by Udo for ignoring her. Collecting her handbag from the room, she walked briskly to the main road. She would go to the ancestral compound and socialize with the girls she had grown up with, some of whom had come from other cities for the funeral.

Once on the main road, she ran into an acquaintance. She'd been quite friendly with this man when she first went to the UK. They'd grown up together, and had gone to the same secondary school. When they met in London, she'd hoped that by being thrown together in a strange land, something stronger than sisterly love would develop between them. During those days, they'd shared many confidences, and he was privy to her frustrations about Udo and her living situation. When she decided to decamp from Udo's home, he was the first person to know her plans. He'd offered to help, and had arranged for and paid for the cab that moved her to her new surroundings away from Udo.

However, the relationship had soured when she heard that he had entered into an arranged marriage with the daughter of his father's friend. Enraged, she had accused him of lacking the moral fiber to make independent decisions without incurring the ire of his parents, and he on his part had accused her of being too materialistic to fit into his lifestyle.

His visit to Nigeria had coincided with Nkechi's funeral. Since his mother had been very close to Nkechi, he'd postponed his departure in order to honor her. Given the throng of people at the funeral, Sarah had been unaware of his presence. Seeing him walking on the opposite side of the road was a big surprise.

She knew she couldn't avoid acknowledging his presence, so she crossed the street and decided to be civil. "Jacob, I didn't know you were visiting. When did you arrive?"

"I've been here for three weeks," he said, shaking her hand warmly. "Someone said that you're building a house in the new extension." "That's correct. I try to come several times a year to supervise the construction. I extended my stay to be present at Mama Nkechi's funeral." "Her death was a great loss," Sarah murmured. "I know how close she was to your mother."

"How are you? I hear you won the lottery, and you're now in the US."

Sarah turned to greet a passerby before replying, "I moved to the US two years ago. It took a while to secure employment, but I'm settled now. I must go. This is my last chance to visit friends, since I'll be going back immediately after the memorial service tomorrow. It's been nice seeing you. Bye." Leaving him, she thought, I wonder where he got the money to build a house. He's probably selling drugs on the side. I hear his senior brother has been laundering money overseas for one of the ministers. They're all thieves. At the compound, Sarah went straight to the home of her best friend, Rebecca. Inseparable in primary and secondary school, they'd tried to keep in touch through letters during their years of separation, but it wasn't quite the same as when they could see each other in person. They'd met the night before, during the wake. Anxious to spend time together, they had agreed to meet privately before Sarah's departure in order to share some confidences, which was impossible during the funeral celebration.

On hearing Sarah's knock, Rebecca opened the door and welcomed her effusively. They hugged and expressed their delight at this opportunity to be with each other again.

"I've missed you!" Sarah said, wiping her eyes. "Come in. I want to hear everything."

"Me, too," murmured Sara. "Look at you. What a beautiful outfit! I wish I had time to go to Aba to look for material."

Unlike Sarah, Rebecca was a tall woman for the area and quite slim. She wore a beautiful, long batik skirt and matching blouse with colorful patterns of crowns. Her hair, which was quite long, was in braids.

"I'll get it for you," she said, "since I know you like it. I'll take your measurements and have an outfit made for you. But come, let's go to my room where we can talk."

Once inside the bedroom, they hugged each other again. "I can't believe it's you!" they said in unison.

"Where are the rest of the family?" asked Sarah once she calmed down. "They're out somewhere. I stayed back because I was expecting you. Tell me, are you married? If not, do you have an American boyfriend?" Sarah laughed and said, "I wish. But what about you?"

Her friend shrugged. "It's a long story. Remember when we were young, how we read all those romances in English magazines and wished one day we would find our prince who would carry us far away from here?"

Sarah nodded. "I remember, but we were only hoping it would be a politician with lots of money and a big house in Enugu or Abuja, nothing further."

They burst out laughing.

Rebecca abruptly stopped. "It almost came true for me. Not the love part, because it was just a financial arrangement."

"Hey!" Sarah said sharply. "Your parents didn't sell you?"

"No, it wasn't quite like that," explained Rebecca. "My parents found a man for me who lived in the US. You probably know him. He's the son of Phillip Okoro from the Atani village. His name is Frank. He'd been in Texas for several years."

"This sounds like my aunt Ejituru's story," Sarah laughed.

"Not quite. He was here four years ago, and that was when my parents were approached to give consent to our marriage. They liked him, and arranged for me to meet him before he left for the US."

"Did you like him?" asked Sarah, wondering where this story was leading.

"That, as you well know, is immaterial. His family completed the marriage arrangements and paid the necessary bride price. He promised to arrange for me to join him, but I haven't been able to get a visa, and we're not quite certain that he did actually apply for it."

"Sadly, the approval process can take a long time," Sarah admitted.

"My parents wanted me to resign from my post because they thought the whole process would take at most six months, but it's been four years and I'm still waiting. Luckily, I didn't listen to them and kept my job. If I hadn't kept it, where would I be? I'm tired of waiting, and now it's become complicated." Rebecca wrung her hands nervously.

The first thing that crossed Sarah's mind was the thought that Phillip might be in jail. She had heard that Texas had quite a number of Nigerians incarcerated, and Phillip might be one of them. Rather than voice her suspicions, she said, "First, Rebecca, are you sure he's filed the papers? Have you ever been called for an interview?"

"We can only take his word for it that his lawyers helped him to file the papers four years ago when he went back," replied Rebecca in a distraught voice.

"Have you heard from him recently?" Sarah asked.

"No. It's been a year since I personally had a phone call from him telling me that he was working on making sure I could join him soon. His parents often complain that they've not heard from him."

Sarah took her friend's hand and quietly said, "Perhaps he ran into problems in the US. Life isn't easy for our people, especially those living in Texas. Do you have access to the Internet in Aba?"

"I know there are Internet cafes there, but I've never been."

"When you go back, go to one and search the Internet for his name. If you don't find it, then you can assume that he's not in jail or in trouble and that there must be another reason why it's taking so long. But have you considered that he may be married? Many of our men marry citizens in order to legalize their stay in the US. He may be one of those, and he may be having problems divorcing his wife." Having said this, Sarah noticed that her friend now appeared even more agitated than when they started the conversation, so she said in a gentle voice, "None of the reasons I've given may apply in this case. It may really be that the US visa office is overwhelmed with applications, and you may still hear from them."

Instead of being calmed, Rebecca burst into tears. "Let's talk about other things," Sarah said.

But in between crying, Rebecca said, "Sarah, my dear friend, it's complicated. I wish I didn't have to say this. I'm in love with a fellow teacher from Umuahia, and I'm expecting his child."

"What!" exclaimed Sarah with disbelief. "You aren't serious!"

Rebecca had been staring at the floor. She raised her head and looked at Sarah. "I wish it wasn't true, but it is. I feel so guilty. It's too early to show, and I don't know how to tell my parents. I'm not in love with Frank, but I'm traditionally married to him since my family accepted the bride price. I agreed to the marriage because I wanted very much to go to America and was getting tired of playing the lottery. I really am in love with my boyfriend here. I don't want to have an abortion because I do love my friend and he loves me, and we're both staunch Catholics. We want to get married before it shows." Words poured from Rebecca's mouth without giving Sarah a chance to interrupt.

When Rebecca finally stopped, Sarah, feeling numb, was unable to respond.

Both friends clasped each other.

After some minutes, Sarah said thoughtfully, "I know you're close to your mother, unlike some others here. This, then, is my suggestion. Find a time when your mother is alone and tell her about your predicament. Your parents, as Catholics, won't let you have an abortion, even if they want you to keep your commitment to Phillip."

Rebecca had no immediate response.

"Eventually, everyone will understand that the situation you are in isn't fair," Sarah said. "Your parents will be angry for a few weeks, but they'll understand."

Recovering somewhat, Rebecca said, "My parents will lose face in the community."

"Nonsense," Sarah said. "The bride price isn't much, and you can give it to them to return to the Okoro family. They'll go to the family and tell them that you're no longer willing to wait, and they should free you from the obligation to marry their son. I urge you to go to your parents before you start to show."

Rebecca, now openly crying, said, "In any case, my boyfriend and I have already decided against abortion."

"Good," Sarah said with misty eyes. "I wouldn't advise you to have an abortion. Take it from one who foolishly did. The psychological impact is too much, and it tends to stay with you forever."

"My dear Sarah, what happened?" asked Rebecca, looking genuinely shocked. She moved near Sarah on the sofa and held her hand. "Did the father refuse to acknowledge his responsibility? Tell me."

"He didn't know, and I never told him because I was afraid he would blame me." Sarah paused. "I had to swallow my pride and ask Udo for help. That was the hardest thing I had to do, and I bet she's just waiting for a time to bring it up."

"Did she help you without asking questions? You've mentioned that she has difficulty parting with cash."

"That was the most surprising thing about it. I told her what I intended to do because I was afraid I might die. Her only comment before sending the money was that I should make sure that I was in no way in danger of losing my life. Perhaps she's waiting for an opportune time to hit me. You never can tell." Sarah looked around the room, which hadn't changed much from how she remembered it when she was growing up except that the table where Rebecca's textbooks used to be was now used for storing piles of dress materials waiting to be cut up, since Rebecca's mother was a seamstress.

"Perhaps not," Rebecca replied. "I'm sure she had your interest at heart, and you may need her now that Mama Nkechi is gone. What is going to happen to you? Will you ever come home to visit?"

Overcome with emotion, Sarah searched for a hankie in her purse and wiped her face. In between gulps of air, she said, "I promise to be in touch with you, and maybe one day I'll come and visit you."

"What's your relationship with Ejituru?" Rebecca asked. "She seems like a nice person."

"But you know I'm not close to any of my relatives, and I don't think Udo's attempts at kindness will endear me to her," Sarah said firmly. "I want to be freed from the family, especially Chinyere."

"I was hoping Chinyere would acknowledge you now, given the death of Nkechi," replied Rebecca, seemingly genuinely concerned.

"Let's not talk about that," Sarah said dismissively. "She only needs money from me for her other children."

"I know you said you wished you were married or had a boyfriend.

Isn't there anyone in sight?"

"I'm not married, and doubt that I ever will be," Sarah answered.

"Were you able to get a good job in the US?"

"I'm trying to settle in the US. I work two jobs, and I'm a Mary Kay beauty consultant. I'm doing everything I can to survive. I'm not like you, who have a loving mother and father, so I urge you to talk to your mother. Both of you can find a solution to your dilemma."

There was a brief silence, during which Rebecca held tight to Sarah's hand. Then she said, her voice full of anguish, "I miss talking to you, and this could be the last time we get to speak so intimately. I'll take your advice. My father is going to Calabar in the morning. I'll talk to my mother then. She, too, has been worried because of the time it's taking to get the visa. She's always hinting that I'm not young, and she wants grandchildren now. She may be my ally."

Abruptly, Sarah changed the subject. "I saw Jacob as I was coming here. Remember him?"

"Yes, you were a little in love with him when we were in school," answered Rebecca.

In a faraway voice, Sarah said, "Did you know that I met him again by chance in London? He was very helpful to me. At that time, I was dealing with a lot of problems with my aunt Udo, who as I mentioned, treated me as if I was her servant. He helped me find a different place to live, and at first he was very supportive, but then I found out he was being sent a girl from home."

"I'm so sorry," Rebecca said. "I know that hurts. I remember now that he did mention some time ago that you two were friendly in London. You know he comes home frequently because he's building a house in the new extension. I, too, was surprised when I heard he married a cousin of his, a semiliterate girl."

"My dear friend," replied Sarah, "his marriage was the reason I stopped having anything to do with him. I had a lot of personal problems afterward, and I was just lucky that my number came up in the lottery draw and I could leave the UK for the US."

"You are very lucky, my friend," Rebecca said with a tinge of envy in her voice. "I, too, entered the lottery many times, but I wasn't successful. I hear that some successful people were never able to go because they didn't qualify."

Hearing noises indicating that the rest of the family had returned, they left the room to join Rebecca's parents, who were glad to see Sarah. They offered her food, which she graciously accepted. They asked about her life in the US and talked about the difficulty Nigerians faced trying to get immigration visas. It was obvious from the oblique way they spoke that they had Rebecca's situation in mind.

CHAPTER 28

S hortly after Sarah left the compound to make her way home from Rebecca's house, she came to the village square, which by now was full of people. Groups of people danced to the beating of the drum, and others talked animatedly to each other. She wandered from group to group, looking for any acquaintances of hers and dodging petty traders determined to sell every item that could be sold—small packets of peanuts, akara balls massed together in enamel containers, hairpins, bundles of chewing sticks, shoelaces, candies and chewing gums, oranges, underwear, ready-made shirts, singlets and T-shirts, to name a few. Every now and then, a car horn would sound to warn people to get out of the way, since the main road passed through the square.

CHAPTER 29

When Ejituru left Ifeoma's house, she intended to go straight home and call her family in Silver Spring. But as the driver was about to pass the junction leading to her maternal village, she redirected him to her aunt Esther's house. Esther, her mother's only living sister, was a sprightly, eighty-year-old divorced woman. She lived in the original home of Nkechi's father before he moved to the house Nkechi had inherited. It was in this house that Esther brought up her only daughter, Dora, now a divorcee with three grown children. The one-story house, which had been added to over the years, now consisted of three small bedrooms, a little parlor, and a kitchen at the back adjoining a tiny yard where she kept a big jar for collecting water. The yard also contained an outhouse.

Today's visit, Ejituru felt, would give her the opportunity to socialize with this branch of the family. Growing up, she was close to Esther and had always, on each visit home, given her gifts of money. She could remember countless stories of her escapades with Esther.

One such episode stood out in Ejituru's mind. It happened during her first year of medical school at the Enugu campus of Nsukka University. This was one of those times when Esther had left home without telling anyone of her whereabouts. Ejituru ran into Esther at the market in Enugu, and Esther was so pleased to see her that she immediately asked her to follow her to her abode, which wasn't far from the market, but was situated on a very busy street. Esther rented one room in the house but was allowed to use the veranda facing the street for her sewing workshop. Finished dresses and blouses hung on the rope strung across two poles on the veranda where several women were waiting for Esther. Her apprentice was busy finishing a blouse on a hand-run Singer sewing machine. Ejituru found a spot to sit while Esther conducted her business.

Later on in the afternoon, Esther took her to a dive where highlife was playing and palm wine and beer flowed freely. The room was dimly lit and unsavory. Ejituru recoiled, knowing the effect her presence there would have on her mother, who on being told would instantly have had a heart attack. There were very few women, and those who were present were either serving the customers or sitting on their laps. Esther evidently felt quite at ease eating and joking with the men, who all seemed to know her.

Ejituru remembered the plate of goat entrails. Esther shared it with her, urging her to let go of her inhibitions and enjoy herself. Although the visit lasted for less than an hour, to her then, it felt like ages. When they left, Esther begged her not to tell Nkechi about having seen her or about the visit. She wanted this part of her life to be separate from the life she led in the village.

In the car to Esther's house, Ejituru recalled that Esther's relationship with her mother hadn't always been smooth. Esther represented the black sheep of the family, always contradicting tradition. In her youth, she was a rebellious young girl who found the family atmosphere constricting. At sixteen, she ran away from home to the North, where she worked in a hospital and acquired a rudimentary medical knowledge, which she never failed to espouse whenever the need arose. She got married to a man from Uzuakoli, with whom she had one child, a daughter. On his insistence, she came back home to regularize the marriage, but the marriage didn't last.

With her father's help, she became a trained seamstress, but she lacked the discipline that would lead to success, since she was very unreliable, always restless, never able to remain in one place for a long time, always looking for new pastures. It was these traits that Nkechi found most disconcerting, and for this reason, she refused to do any business with her. However, despite their differences, Nkechi and Esther loved and respected each other.

On arriving at Esther's village square, Ejituru made her way to the little house. Esther was busy in her kitchen assembling lunch. Ejituru found Dora and one of her sons in the parlor watching a Nollywood film. They greeted her effusively and called out to Esther to tell her Ejituru was visiting.

"Ej, come into the kitchen!" Esther called. "I'm frying plantain." When Ejituru entered, she pointed at the stool. "Sit down. You look happy. You're just in time to eat with us. I know you're tired of jollof rice, but unfortunately, that's what I have with fried plantain. We can make salad for you if you want, or do you prefer some bread?"

Ejituru looked around the little room and said in an amused voice, "Auntie, I'm actually hungry, so I can use some jollof rice, and the plantain looks scrumptious. Can I take one? Mmm! I love them hot."

Esther called out to her grandson, "Umez, go and get some bottles of water and Fanta from Okoro next door!"

The discussion during lunch centered on the educational performance and activities of the grandchildren, and of course, the funeral. As the table was cleared and Ejituru was left with only Esther, the conversation became more personal.

"Tell me, how are you getting on with your sisters?" Esther asked. "Is Chinyere behaving?"

Ejituru hesitated before answering. "Honestly, Auntie, I haven't interacted much with her. We met, as you know, in Ifeoma's house in Umuahia for the budget, and she didn't contribute anything." She took a deep breath. "She wasn't alone. The boys didn't help, either, but I can understand. They have no money. I've been wondering why Chinyere came, knowing how much she hated my mother." She stopped to refresh her glass with water.

Lost in thought for a while, Esther finally said, "You're not alone. Nobody can understand why she came. I'm surprised that her husband, who's reputed to be loaded, didn't send a gift. He was on good terms with your mother."

Ejituru shook her head. "It's all water under the bridge, and whether or not he gave her instructions about what to contribute is immaterial. I can afford to bury my mother."

Esther stared hard at Ejituru. "Dear, that's not the point. They're all her children, regardless. But speaking of Chinyere, I hope she hasn't created problems for you."

"So far, none. Unlike my one and only visit to her place in Lagos, when she used that visit to castigate me for all the wrongs done to her." Ejituru placed her elbows on the table and stared sadly into space, as if the memory was still painful. "Seriously, Auntie! I felt ambushed during that visit."

"Surely, her husband would have said something." Esther patted Ejituru's hands.

"Oh yes, his kindness and her children's solicitous attitude toward me were mitigating factors," Ejituru replied. "I ended up giving each of the children an envelope with a thousand naira, for which they were grateful, although I understand that Chinyere felt it was a paltry sum."

"I hear the elders were very hard on you for Nduka's absence." Esther stood up to get some more snacks from the pantry.

When Esther came back, Ejituru said, "Yes. In the end, the elders imposed a fine; but seriously, Auntie, with Nduka's new job and the associated expenses of our move, it wasn't possible. I was lucky to hire a housekeeper from Honduras to come in and help while I'm away. If it works out, she'll be a great help, since she can help Nneka improve her Spanish." She sat reflecting for a moment. "I don't expect people to believe that, since they all think I'm swimming in money; but

I wonder why they spared Chinyere. We both are married to outsiders."

"The unequal treatment is probably because you've defied tradition by divorcing a man chosen for you by your father and the elders," Esther, looking pensive, replied. "You slapped them on the wrist and, in the process, felt no guilt."

"That may be so," Ejituru retorted, "but why did they berate me for not bringing my children but say nothing to Chinyere?"

"I can only speculate, Ej, that it was because you're Nkechi's natural daughter," said Esther. She looked lovingly at Ejituru.

"Maybe so," agreed Ejituru, dropping the subject.

Esther leaned over and gently scratched her right knee. "You know, Ej, I'm really disappointed with Michael. He hasn't been able to live up to the promise expected of him. He can't keep a wife, and he can't keep a job. Now that Nkechi is gone, I wonder what will happen to him." Esther shook her head and wrung her hands in despair.

"Auntie, of all my brothers, he's the one I can't forgive for wasting his life," Ejituru said sadly. "Here's a man who was given the best education, with an engineering degree from Nsukka, a good job at the beginning of his career, and further training in France. Or was it England? I can't remember. Whatever, he just frittered away his life." Esther nodded. "I agree with you, but I mostly blame your mother, Nkechi," she said in a challenging voice. "She excused all his frailties and subsidized his way of life, and with her now gone, what will happen to him?" Ejituru laughed vacuously before saying, "He's expecting his sisters with good jobs and good incomes to support him. As far as I'm concerned, that will never happen. I don't give a hoot what the others will do, but I will never subsidize him."

"What will happen to your other brothers? Emeka sometimes comes here to eat." Esther wiggled her butt to the left and to the right, then cracked her fingers, which tended to be stiff with arthritis.

Ejituru wondered whether she was tiring of the conversation, but she was determined to have her say on the subject at hand. "Auntie, I've made it clear that from time to time, I'll send small sums to Emeka, but it won't be regular. Udo is free to do what she wants, but I feel that they should be able to take care of themselves." She banged her hands on the table for emphasis. "I'm glad Udo has been a lifeline for my brothers, and I don't begrudge her their love, but I feel that her unconditional financial assistance has created an unhealthy dependency. I've often said that to her."

"However, she really does take care of the house whenever she comes," Esther murmured. "Udo genuinely loved your mother, and everything she did was to cement that love for her."

"There's no doubt about that, and though I'm aware of her jealousy and competition, I've never allowed that to affect my relationship with her. My only complaint is that she never forgets any slight, imagined or real, and brings these up at unexpected times as examples of injustices done to her by family members. A case in point relates to Sarah." Her voice tinged with sadness, Ejituru wagged her right hand for emphasis.

"What is that about?" asked Esther. "Didn't Udo send her to England?" "Well, on the surface that's true," Ejituru said, her tone serious.

"Whatever I tell you now should remain between us, okay?"

"Okay, I give you my word." Esther looked around to make sure no family member was listening.

"When Udo made the decision that Sarah should join her in the UK, it was assumed that she would bear the expenses involved. When Udo approached me to help defray the cost, I said that I would if Sarah was bound for the US. Udo, irritated, felt that I was trying to take credit for her idea and snapped back, accusing me of wanting Sarah to become my maid. So I pulled back."

"My sister did mention that Udo was trying to convince you to help," said Esther, her eyes misting.

"Oh yes, she wore me out," Ejituru said with a smile on her face for the first time. "At her urging, I relented and paid the airfare and associated costs. But, Auntie, in retelling this story,

Udo tried to show that my interest in the family wasn't to help them grow but to put them down." Ejituru wiped her face with both hands as if to clear away all evil thoughts.

Both paused, lost in thought. Esther offered Ejituru another soft drink which she declined.

"Honestly, Auntie, I don't care. I've made it clear to Ifeoma that nobody should expect anything from me after this funeral. My biggest problem is my house. It will be difficult to sell. Nduka suggested that I should give it to my favorite niece, Ifeoma's daughter. I think perhaps that's what I'll do."

Esther let this sink in before saying, "But you know that Michael won't be happy about that decision. He'll challenge it, since he's the first son, and the land is your father's."

"Let him try. I really don't care. He won't be successful, and besides, where will he get the money to hire a lawyer? The fight will

be between him and Ifeoma, and you know who will win."

"What of Sarah?" Esther asked. "How is she?"

"I haven't seen much of her, either. I understand she's moved to the US, but I'm pretending that I don't know, since she hasn't said anything to me. She appears to be lovey-dovey with Udo just now, but who knows how long that will last?" Ejituru stood up to help clear the table.

Esther embraced her. "I'm glad we had this time together. Are you seeing any of them before the memorial service?"

"We're meeting tonight to close the books and decide what to give the church in remembrance of my mother and father," replied Ejituru. "Auntie, I have to go. I want to call Nduka before he goes to bed and tell him when to expect me. I'm sure he'll be wondering how I'm surviving."

"When will we see you again?" asked Esther.

"I'll see you before I depart on Monday." Ejituru embraced her aunt, who clutched at her. She called out greetings to her cousins and went in search of her car.

~❦~

When the driver dropped her at the gate leading to her aunt's place, he had sought a shady part of the village square to park the car. She couldn't immediately locate him and had to cast her eyes around the square; a gathering place for villagers. It had started filling up with people socializing or trying to buy small items from the lock-up stores lining both sides of the place.

Approaching the car, which was parked at the far side of the square, Ejituru ran into the elderly son of Nkechi's favorite relative in the compound. Obed's father had been very important to Nkechi, to the extent that she wouldn't make any important decisions without asking for his advice. Ejituru knew that if it hadn't been taboo by customary law, the two would have been married. His death was a big loss for Nkechi, and she had mourned him for years. Ejituru knew that it was his funeral that gave Nkechi the idea of starting her catering business.

Holding her hand, Obed said, "Ej, how are you bearing up? This is a great loss. Your mother was like a mother to me. My father was very close to her, and our relationship continued even after he died. I visited your mother many times in Umuahia, and I was there just a week before she died. You should be proud of how everything was handled. It was great. Everyone is very happy about it. Are you staying long?"

"Dede," said Ejituru, "I just came to see Auntie Esther for a short time.

We still have the memorial service tomorrow to prepare for, and I hope you'll come to the house afterward. I'll be going back on Monday, but as I said to Auntie Esther, I'll come to the compound on Monday to say goodbye to everyone."

Still holding her hand and staring into her eyes, Obed said in an earnest voice, "Okay then, we'll talk on Monday. I understand that you've moved to Maryland. You may not know that my son Frank and his wife live in a place called Takoma Park. He works in Washington at Howard University. I'll give you his address when I see you on Monday. I'll call him today to tell him that you live in Maryland. If you aren't too far away, perhaps you both can meet. He was sorry he couldn't be present at the funeral. Nkechi meant a lot to him. He'll be glad to get in touch."

Ejituru thanked him for the information. "That'll be great." She gave him her cell phone number. "I'm sure Nduka would like to meet him, too."

Just as she opened the car door to get in, she heard someone call, "Ejituru, is that you? Ewoh, it was impossible to get near you yesterday. Do you remember me? We were in primary school together, and as I recall, we were very good friends. Have you forgotten?"

Ejituru let go of the door handle and searched the woman's face and her own memory, hoping to recall who the woman was, but she couldn't. In order to not give offense, she feigned knowledge. "Of course I remember you. It's been a long time." They embraced warmly.

"I'm one of those people who remember faces but not names," Ejituru said. "So, my dear friend, tell me your name again."

The woman laughed and said, "I know you don't remember. I'm Sybil Oji. My family used to live off the road to the barracks not far from Mama Nkechi's house. I married Peter Onu from this village immediately after primary school. One of our children lives in a place in the US called Baltimore. He's a medical assistant at a big hospital there called John something. I visited the place last year when his wife had a baby. I was there for three months."

"How are your parents? I remember them. Your mother was a primary schoolteacher at Slessor. You see, I haven't forgotten everything altogether. I live not too far from Baltimore now, and I do hope when you come next, you'll let me know so we can visit each other." Ejituru, sweating profusely and anxious to get home, wiped her brow. Not wanting to give offence, she wondered how to end this conversation.

"When are you going back?" Sybil asked. "My husband said to ask you if we could give you a letter for our son. It would get to him quicker than if we mailed it."

"I'll definitely be going back on Monday," Ejituru said, a little flustered. "I have to get back to work."

"I hear God blessed you with three children. I hope Mama Nkechi was able to see them before she became ill."

"Thank you for asking. She visited us when we were in Texas. We only just moved to Maryland. Sybil, my sister, it's good to see you, but I'm meeting the family in a few hours and I need to head home to prepare. Send someone to bring the letter tomorrow, or you can give it to me after the service."

Ejituru quickly got into the car, but before the car could move, it was stopped by another person who also wanted to compliment her and to ask for financial help. "Our firstborn, do you have anything to spare? I need a few pennies to buy food to eat."

She rummaged in her purse and pulled out a rumpled twenty-naira note, which she gave to the woman. She cursed herself for being such a pushover. Shouldn't they have pity on her, considering the enormous cost of the funeral? But then, they saw her as a moneybag and nothing else, and of course, the elaborate funeral had reinforced that idea.

On her way to her house, she tried to remember her time at the primary school and the friends she'd made there. She could only remember one girl that she was close to. They were in the same age group, and her mother, a seamstress, had her shop in the village square. She had heard that this friend had recently left teaching to take over her mother's shop. She would like to see her before going back to the US. Apart from her, she couldn't remember any of them, but they all remembered her.

On the other hand, she could remember all her friends in secondary school and university, and had kept in touch with some of them. Her eyes welled up as she thought of her best friend, Stella, who had just visited. What would she do without her? What a gem she was. The week with her had eased the loneliness she felt without her mother. She only left her side on the Thursday before the wake because of her own family emergency.

On the drive to her house, Ejituru thought of the evening event. She wanted it to end well. She wanted to have a good memory of the family to carry to the US, since she currently had no intention of coming back to Nigeria. But would it end well? she wondered. Would Chinyere, who had spent her whole life hating Nkechi—and by extension, her—try to disrupt the meeting by dredging up all the supposed slights that she had harbored within her all these years?

Anticipating the phone call she was about to make, she felt that her primary objective from now on was to ensure the welfare of her family. She had the unconditional love of her husband, and he had hers. She didn't expect to be loved by her Nigerian family, since that love was dependent on the amount of money they received from her. She was well aware of the situation, and she didn't need anyone to spell it out for her. Her mother, the only person who had united them, was gone.

Of all of them, Ifeoma deserved her love, and this she would reciprocate. As she thought of Ifeoma, she felt enveloped by a warm feeling, and she thanked God that Ifeoma would always watch her back, and she would do the same for her.

When she arrived at her house, she made her call. Satisfied, she sent the driver to collect the food from Ifeoma's house, then changed gears and started to pull out whatever dishes she required.

She noticed that she didn't have complete sets of anything. Never having thought of living here full-time, she hadn't really furnished the house. She'd brought spare plates, bowls, and cutlery whenever she came to visit. The glasses were mason jars that had contained jams or other relishes, the plates were leftover pieces from when she was in her first apartment before her marriage, the cutlery was plastic she'd brought over when Nkechi first became ill. For napkins, she used the paper towels she had brought during this visit. There were water bottles in the fridge, which she placed on the table.

By the time she finished and had instructed the maid to reheat the food, it was almost time for her family to arrive. She decided to use the hour left for a little rest and to arrange her thoughts.

CHAPTER 30

S arah, entering the path leading up to the main house, saw Michael standing outside his house looking lonesome. She wondered where the others were. Nwankwo especially liked to hang out with Michael, and it was rare not to find him in Michael's house lounging around, drinking, and welcoming occasional villagers who came by to socialize with them.

As she watched, she saw him enter his house. Feeling that this was an opportune time to visit him, and perhaps learn some more about the will and the meeting that evening, she walked to his doorstep and entered his parlor. She expected Michael to express surprise at this intrusion, but he didn't. He just stared at her as she made herself comfortable on the chair nearest to where he was standing and looking outside.

Returning his stare, she said without any preamble, "Have you heard from Daisy, your first wife, recently?"

"What brought about that question?" he fired back. "Why should I hear from her? She has her own life, and I have mine." He coughed.

She lashed out at him. "Ha! She should've been here or sent her children. She's better off without you, I must say. You never really appreciated her when she was with you." Sarah looked into his eyes. I must have hit a raw nerve.

Michael left the window and stood opposite her. "What makes you think I didn't appreciate her?"

"Because if you did, you wouldn't have allowed Mama to poison your mind about her," Sarah said frankly. "Everybody knows that

Mama wanted you to be dependent on her." Michael didn't immediately answer.

"It doesn't auger well to say bad things about a dead person, especially one as loved as Mama, but let's face it, Daisy was a stumbling block, and she worked hard to separate you from her."

Recovering his tongue, Michael said, "You're wrong. I know she wanted to handpick my wife because she was suspicious of strangers. But once she got over her initial objection, she worked to make my marriage successful." "Maybe so." She paused, thinking. "Okay, maybe it's not her fault entirely. You're also to be blamed."

"Ha!" exclaimed Michael, his face clouded. "I wish you would just stop this line of discussion and mind your own business. Daisy was no saint, but she never owned up to any wrong. I know that after four kids, Nkechi had reconciled herself to the marriage."

"I presume she did. But then you slept with your maid. That was the nail that ended the marriage."

Michael went back to the window and looked out just as Nwankwo came into the house with soft drinks in a pail of ice. He ceremoniously placed the pail near the table and offered a drink to Sarah, which she accepted. Nwankwo sprawled on a chair next to her.

"We've been talking about my uncle's first wife," Sarah said, "and the reason why she left."

Michael, who by now had left the window and rejoined her, said, "Cut that out, Sarah. Let's talk about you."

"No!" said Sarah. "You're the most interesting topic, my uncle. Do you admit that Rose was your worst mistake? I know she produced sons for you. How many? I can never remember."

Nwankwo stared at Michael's face, as if to discern what was going on in his mind.

Michael flinched and wet his lips.

Having started this line of discussion, Sarah wanted to pursue it to the end, so she said, "Daisy always blamed herself for bringing Rose into the household. She said it was out of necessity. She'd just been promoted and had too much to do and needed help with the kids."

"Sarah, cut it out," Michael said, sounding frustrated. "What's the point of hashing over the past? Yes, I admit that I was unfaithful."

"Why did you have to marry her? You could have sent her away." Sarah, like a dog with a bone, wouldn't let it go.

Michael looked hard at Sarah. "She was pregnant with my child, that's why. I wasn't happy that it ended with Daisy. Mama tried to get her to forgive me and stay in the marriage, but she wanted me to abandon Rose. I couldn't do that. After all, she was expecting my child."

Sarah sat upright, put down the glass she was holding, and as if an inquisitor, persisted with another question. "Why didn't you stay with Rose?"

Michael scratched his head and thought for a moment. "What is this sudden interest in my marriages, Sarah? Are you thinking of getting married yourself? Who's the lucky guy?"

"Nothing like that, but I've always wanted to know why you're unable to keep a wife."

"Since you're interested, the failure of that marriage was because of Rose's ambition. Rose thought I was very rich and didn't realize that my lifestyle was because of two incomes. She nagged me for not having enough money, and after five years and four children, I could no longer take it. I knew it had to end."

"Was that why you pounced on your next victim, your maid?" Sarah howled with laughter and was joined by Nwankwo.

"Rose was a lazy woman," Nwankwo said when he finally stopped laughing.

Sarah directed a murderous glance at him. "I didn't see her like that." "Mama felt that in order to sustain our lifestyle, Rose needed to pull her weight," Michael said. "In her attempt to do so, Rose brought in a young girl, Liza, who was more intelligent and knew precisely what was required of her."

"By this time, you'd lost your job and had to move to Port Harcourt," Nwankwo murmured quietly.

"Yes. It wasn't a good time," Michael recalled. "There was constant fighting over money and expenses with Rose, and the new girl found her niche. Liza was more resourceful. She was able to take advantage of the vacuum left in the household when Rose abandoned me saying she could no longer live with a man who couldn't provide for his household."

"Uncle!" exclaimed Sarah. "She left you with the children. At least Daisy took her own children with her when she left."

"Sarah, what do you know?" said Michael, sounding exasperated. "You want to dredge up my life today. That's why you started this whole conversation, isn't it?"

"Actually, I liked Liza, and I remember she started small, sewing for neighbors and then trading in yard goods," said Sarah, latching onto the one good crumb she could toss to him.

"Yes, that's true," Michael said. "It was from these activities that she was able to keep the household afloat until I was able to secure another job. I appreciated her for this, and out of gratitude, I married her, and in time, loved her. It was unfortunate that I was unable to keep the job, and Liza became the sole provider of the family." He sounded desperate.

"Where is she now?" Sarah asked. "And why didn't she come to the funeral?" This was her main reason for raising the issue of his wives.

"She's currently living with her brother. I can't blame her for leaving me. It was entirely my fault. But what can I do? I have no money to go to Abuja to convince her to come back, and I'd have to prove to her that I could maintain her before asking her to do that."

Nwankwo blew his nose and yawned. "Didn't you tell her of Mama's death? She should be here with you."

Michael looked at him in disgust and shuddered. "You all seem to forget how badly Ejituru treated her, accusing her of not caring for Mama when she lived with us, and unceremoniously removing Mama from our house. Please, Sarah, halt this conversation. Get on with your own life and let me be."

Sarah stood up, indicating that she was ready to go back to the main house, but before leaving, she said, "Even though I liked Liza, I heard she was very mean to Mama when she came to stay with you."

Michael bristled. "Who told you that?"

"Auntie Udo," she said truthfully. "I heard her say that she was glad Liza didn't come to the funeral because she was going to complain about her to the elders."

"I heard her say that," Nwankwo murmured. "I tried to defend Liza, but Udo wouldn't listen. I fault Ifeoma for that gossip."

"Uncle, are you working now?"

"I've had . . . a spell of bad times," Michael stammered. "It's been years since I worked. I tutor students taking the examination for the West African School Certificate."

Sarah remembered that Nkechi, when she was alive, complained that his inability to hold a job was due to witchcraft practiced on him by her enemies who didn't want him to succeed. They hated his father and would do anything to see that the male members of the family remained worthless. Nkechi, bless her heart, had always stood by him and had supported him without apportioning blame, unlike his sisters, who wanted to see him twisting in the wind.

※❦❧

Sarah went into the courtyard of Michael's house to wash her hands and face because it had been a hot day and she was sweating. Then she went through the downstairs parlor and came out to the front of the house. She looked across the yard past the road and saw knots of people gathered outside the house of one of their neighbors. She wondered what was happening, but rather than dwell on it, she turned toward the main house and saw her uncle Emeka talking to one of his cronies. Just as she reached the front steps, Emeka's visitor emerged and greeted her.

Emeka called out to her, "Your mother is at Michael's, and I was thinking of going there now myself. I wanted to find out when we should leave for Ejituru's!"

She looked at his flushed face for a moment before saying, "You seem to be having a lot of visitors today."

"Maybe I needed a lot of company today," he replied in a forlorn voice. "Ha-ha. Indeed! How can that be? You've always been selfsufficient, and you don't need anyone to keep you company.

Anyway, I'd better just go to the bedroom and lie down."

"Stay for a bit," he implored. "I've hardly seen you to talk to."

Sarah sat in the easy chair next to the wall and looked at him lovingly. She remembered the many battles he had fought for her when she was growing up. "By the way, I hear salaries are in arears. How do you manage?" "What can I say?" He raised his head toward the coconut trees outside. "Look at those birds flitting around without a care in the world. They sow not, neither do they reap, nor gather into the barns, and yet the heavenly Father feeds them. That's why I don't worry."

"That's all very true, but, Uncle, you should worry," Sarah said, smiling at his use of the Bible to address every problem.

"Oh, but didn't Christ say that life is more than food and clothing?" Emeka said cheerfully, drawing from his Bible knowledge. "And even though I'm not paid on time and have no other visible means of livelihood, the Lord has made sure that I'm not hungry or thirsty or naked. I've always been able to survive. Didn't he also say one shouldn't be anxious about tomorrow, because tomorrow will take care of itself?"

"You may feel like that because manna descends on you often via Udo, Ejituru, and Ifeoma, but you need to think of what you will do once the manna stops flowing." She cackled as she got up from the chair. "I'm tired."

Emeka looked at her before saying, "The house has been very quiet since you all left. Where did you go?"

"I went to the compound to see my friends and acquaintances. Have you been home all this time?"

"Yes. Udo is also out, I think. There hasn't been a sound from her room." He nodded toward the room.

"I saw her taxi moving from the direction of Ifeoma's house," Sarah said. "Have you been able to find out more about the will?"

"No, and Ifeoma didn't have anything more to say before she left with Ejituru."

"Didn't you talk to Ejituru or Udo about it?" Sarah asked.

"I talked to Ejituru earlier today, but she never mentioned the will. In fact, I tried to comfort her. And by the way, you, too, can benefit from that parable."

"What parable?" she asked, brightening up.

"Remember the parable about how new life is produced by the dead seed sown into the earth? It was drummed into us many times in catechism when we talked of death."

Sarah nodded, wondering where this was leading to.

Animated, Emeka said, "I told Ejituru how it should be interpreted. Christ was saying that when we die in the flesh, we rise to new life in him. I'm convinced that Mama only died in the flesh. Because she did so many good deeds while alive, she had already been reborn in Christ, and this should give us comfort."

"I also believe that she's up there watching over us," Sarah said, nodding in agreement.

"I believe Ejituru was comforted when we prayed together this morning," he said, beaming.

"You prayed together?" Sarah exclaimed. She laughed out loud. "Perhaps that prayer will save you if you're disowned by the will." She got up from the chair.

"Wait, I hear you are now living in the US. Are you living near sister Ejituru?"

"Why? From what I heard, we are in the same state but not near each other," Sarah replied as she returned to her seat.

"Well, Ejituru needs her family, especially now, with Mama gone. I hope you will make an effort to visit her often, or even better, move nearer to her," Emeka murmured.

Sarah laughed out loudly before replying, "Ejituru does not need family.

She has her husband and children."

"Why do you say that? Is it from experience? Did she treat you badly?" Emeka rapidly shot back.

"Nothing specific. I really do not know her at all."

Sarah's sad voice made Emeka look sharply at her before saying, "Don't let others poison your mind. She is a nice person. I've never heard her say any harsh thing about anybody. She's always given to both Nwankwo and me freely and had never expected to be thanked for her gifts. Even Michael has benefited from her generosity."

Sarah looked at his earnest face. Wiping her face with both hands, she stood up and turning to Emeka said, "I'll leave you now. Go to Uncle Michael as you intended. I've had enough of people. I'm sure Chinyere will let me know when it's time to go to Auntie Ejituru's."

At the mention of Chinyere, Emeka wondered what Sarah's relationship with Chinyere was. Had Chinyere accepted her as her child? This had always been a moot issue in the family since she was born. Perhaps she had, now that Sarah was living and working in the US. He wouldn't put it past Chinyere to try and ingratiate herself to Sarah now.

He stood up and walked to Michael's.

CHAPTER 31

When Chinyere returned to the main house, she saw Sarah leaving Michael's house and wondered what she was doing there. Eager to rehash her experience with Kanu, whom she'd just visited, she walked over to Michael's house and entered the parlor, snatching a beer from the pail of ice brought by Nwankwo.

After wetting her lips with the liquid, she moaned, "I've just been in the compound, and I saw trader Kanu. Can you believe it? He didn't even offer me a seat in his car to Umuahia, even though he's also traveling back early Monday morning or Sunday afternoon and could easily have offered me a space." She swallowed a mouthful of beer before resuming her grousing. "I bet his only other companion is his sister, and his car is a big Peugeot that can take at least four people. If he's leaving late on Sunday, he could have offered to let me stay in his house so I could catch the early bus to Lagos in the morning. He knew what I wanted, but he kept silent. The ingrate! Nkechi spent the money she should have used for her family educating him and helping to educate his brothers. Remember, one of them lived with us." Nwankwo let what she had said sink in before daring to make a comment. Raising his eyebrows, he said, "Ma Chinyere, what do you expect? If

Nkechi was alive, you can be sure he'd be fawning over you and offering his services."

Michael, his thoughts interrupted, jerked himself up straight and impatiently exclaimed, "Trader Kanu! Hmm. He's now a big shot, you know. Besides the Peugeot, didn't you see how he's expanded his father's house, making it one of the largest in the compound? What do you expect?"

"Well," said Nwankwo, "with our mother gone, everybody will be showing their true colors."

It seemed as if they'd exhausted the topic of Kanu.

Chinyere turned to Michael. "Bro Mike, what's the latest about Liza? I was surprised that neither she nor her family members came for the funeral. I was also surprised that only two of your children came, and none were Daisy's. Didn't you tell them? Why did the elders let you off, whereas they were very hard on Ejituru?"

Losing his cool, Michael lashed out at her. "What of you? Did you bring your children or your husband? This is like the pot calling the kettle black." Adjusting his wrapper, which was slipping and exposing his briefs, he shouted, "Your husband not only didn't come, he didn't send any gift! That is most unusual." He moved toward her and lifted his right arm as if to slap her, but he stopped just as his hand was almost on her face. "In fact, during the same clothing of the dead, which you wisely absented yourself from, the issue was raised. I tried to cover for you by saying the he had been ill, and we were just glad that you could spare a few days away from your very sick husband, whose death may be imminent." With his anger spent, he sat down in the nearest chair and spoke more calmly. "So, my dear sister, did your husband give you the money to buy a cow and other things, and you kept it? Tell me. I promise I won't tell the others. It'll be a secret between us. After all, you left Onyeka's milk for me."

Chinyere didn't know what to say at this unexpected outburst. Nwankwo had been sitting there quietly, drinking. She noted the bemused smile on his face.

Finally, Chinyere angrily retorted, "Even if he did, why should I contribute to the funeral of a woman I never cared for? Nkechi wasn't my mother, and you all know my history with her. She is Ejituru's mother, and she alone should have paid for the funeral." She stopped and loudly blew her nose. "We, the children of Onyeka, should give if we feel like it. I wasn't happy during the budgeting process to be asked to contribute as if I was obligated to do so." She lifted the beer bottle and drank a mouthful. Before Nwankwo could say a word, she stopped him with a motion of her hand. "Let me have my say. I don't even see the purpose of going to Ejituru's house tonight. She should have taken care of her mother's funeral.

As for the will, I don't want to know what's in it because I know I won't be mentioned."

As if aghast at what Chinyere was saying, Nwankwo retorted angrily in a raised voice, "Hey, Ma Chinyere, you're carrying your grudge too far! What has Ejituru done to you? I have never heard her bad-mouth you."

"It is not what she did, but who she is that I hate. She is that woman's child who drank her milk and therefore inherited her evil ways."

"You are too much. I cannot believe you are hating someone who did you no harm for the simple reason that she was born by someone you hate," Nwankwo said, shaking his head vigorously.

Michael, dismayed, stood up from his perch in the room, went up to where Chinyere was sitting and said, "Ejituru has contributed more to this family than you have ever done. She does not deserve what you have just said. I don't want to hear you bad-mouthing our mother."

Blowing his nose, he said, "Ejituru, whom you say you hate, never to my knowledge ill-treated Onyeka. She loved her more than we, her children, did. So please, keep your hatred and evil thoughts to yourself." He pointed his finger at her for emphasis. "If you don't want to come this evening, you don't have to. Nobody is forcing you to do anything. Perhaps after tonight, we may not see each other again. You can carry your hatred back to your family in Lagos or Obowu, or wherever they may be."

Chinyere noticed the protruding veins on Nwankwo's neck and wondered if he would have a heart attack.

Nwankwo interjected, "Chinyere, I bet Kanu's refusal to help you is because he knows your relationship with our mother. If you hated her so much, why did you come to the funeral? You said you came to pay your respects, but here you are, bad-mouthing the dead woman."

"I need to get out of here for a while," Michael said. "I'm going to go to our father's grave to cool down."

～✥✥✥～

When Michael came back, he found Emeka present, and the new topic of discussion was the will. All three had been speculating on the contents.

"If the house becomes Ejituru's," Emeka said, "I wonder what will become of me."

In a voice dripping with bile, Chinyere answered, "If Ejituru is given the house, I'm sure she'll want to rent it out. I hear she even rented the chalet on her place. She won't let you stay here for free."

Shaking his head, Michael retorted, "Sister Chinyere, you always think the worst of Ejituru. I feel certain that she won't turn anybody out. The worst that can happen is that she'll require that we foot the bill for the upkeep of the house."

"We'll find out tonight," she said, laughing.

He changed the subject. "Has anybody seen Udo? Ejituru said she would send her driver, but I doubt we can all fit into her car."

Emeka, who was quietly listening, shifted his body and stood up. "I'm going to take an Okada. Okoro Nta will pick me up. He'll be passing by here at 6:00 p.m. on his way home.

He lives near sister Ejituru's house." He turned to Nwankwo. "I think three people can fit comfortably on the motorbike."

"I'm going to walk," Nwankwo said. "It's now four thirty. If I start walking at about five thirty, I should be there in time." He cast a murderous look at Emeka for his suggestion.

"Nonsense, Nwankwo," Michael said. "You will come with me. What of you, sister Chinyere? You, Udo, Nwankwo, and Sarah will come with me in the car. We'll leave at six. I still have to gather the information for my report."

Chinyere looked at him, stood up, and left without answering.

Michael left the parlor for his bedroom while the others sat and gossiped some more, waiting for the time of the meeting.

He had avoided thinking about the will or talking about it. Given his precarious financial situation, he'd been thinking of renting his own house out and moving into the main house and perhaps taking up the two rooms his father had used while he was alive. The contents of the will might change his plans, and he would rather not think about it. Just now, he had other things on his mind.

CHAPTER 32

C hinyere entered the courtyard, grabbed a pail, and put enough water in it to wash her face and hands. She scrubbed as if she wanted to get rid of her brothers' words still swirling around her ears.

Satisfied, she looked around for a towel, but not finding a clean one, she wiped her face and hands with her wrapper. She started for the main house but changed her mind. Instead, she went into the anteroom of the kitchen and sat down on the mud bench, on the spot where Nkechi had often sat. From there, she surveyed the courtyard with eyes filled with unintended tears.

She wept for her birth mother, whom she'd treated badly while alive. She remembered all the times she'd ridiculed her for being subservient to Nkechi and for not fighting for her rightful place in the house. She remembered how badly she'd behaved when she was sent to live with her during the time of her pregnancy with Sarah. She had never at any time called her Mama. She was always Onyeka and nothing else.

When Onyeka lived in the house, she never thought of her as her birth mother, even though she breastfed her and looked after her. It was natural that Nkechi should have a maid to care for the children, since she was busy with work and business. Besides, Onyeka hadn't been treated any differently from the other servants in the house. True, in those days, she was on equal footing with Ejituru. She was never denied anything, nor treated differently. Ejituru was her big sister, whom she followed around and looked up to.

When did things change? she asked herself.

Back then, Ejituru was always loving toward her, and she never seemed to do anything wrong. She was too well-behaved, unlike her, who was always getting into scrapes. She resented her for that. She'd been glad to see Ejituru off to boarding school because then no one could compare them.

She looked across the courtyard toward the main house. In her mind's eye, she could see her father looking out the upstairs window, calling one of the servants to prepare his bath or bring him something, or, as was often the case, telling Nkechi that some visitor had come and her presence was required.

Sitting there with her memories, she was joined by Nwankwo. He sat down opposite her on the bench with a worried look on his face.

"Do you remember when Ignatius first came to ask for Ejituru's hand?" she asked. "It was so unexpected. We were all thrilled that a 'been-to' was interested in our big sister."

"I vaguely remember it," he said, shooing away a fly. "I wasn't yet of school age. We tossed so many questions at Ejituru, but she showed no interest whatever in the event."

"Look at how the marriage turned out." She shook her head.

"Perhaps she wasn't interested because she wanted to finish her education," Nwankwo said reflectively. "Remember, in those days, she showed no interest in boys."

Shaking with laughter, she said, "How would you know? You were only about three or four years old. Those of us who were older thought that Ejituru, the princess, had at last found a prince. Little did we know that the prince would turn into a frog. She wanted to be treated as a princess, and when told she needed to act as a wife, she rebelled, looked for a real prince to commit adultery with, and she ran." She laughed some more, slapping her thigh.

Nwankwo laughed, too. "Sister, you're funny. You are back to your evil thoughts. You like to think the worst of Ejituru. I'm sure it didn't happen like that. Perhaps from the beginning she didn't see a prince but a toad, and her vision was correct."

"Nonsense," she said heatedly. "She's a user. My analysis is the correct one. Our mother, Onyeka, devoted her whole life to her, loving her, caring for her. Did she ever think of her?"

Nwankwo stood up from the bench and angrily stomped his feet on the floor. "Of all of us, Ejituru for sure loved Onyeka, no doubt about that. You do not have to believe it, but it is the truth."

She wouldn't let it go. She grabbed his hand and pulled him down. "Listen to me," she said in an urgent voice. "Ejituru lives in the lap of luxury in the US. You would think she would consider sending money to the woman who devoted her life to her. She and her mother used Onyeka for their own good. I will never forgive them."

"You're deranged!" Nwankwo shouted. "I know Ejituru sent money to Onyeka from time to time. You're just grasping at the wind. I can't stay here listening to your foolishness." He pushed her away and left, walking across the courtyard into the main house.

As she sat there, oblivious of everything else, she thought of Nkechi and again asked herself why she had come to the funeral of someone she hated so much. As if in a trance, she answered herself, saying, "I hated her because she usurped the position of my mother, Onyeka. By rights, Nkechi should have been my mother's wife, not the other way around. After all, she gave my father what he wanted —a male child. I wanted to make sure she was really dead." Her hate began when she was nine and inadvertently learned that Nkechi wasn't her mother. Before then, she had always felt loved as Nkechi's second daughter and Ejituru's loving sister, whose nanny was Onyeka, who helped Nkechi with her chores. Unlike Ejituru, Chinyere was sent to the local primary school as a day student, where she had to socialize with children of different social classes. Unlike adults, children had no compunction about divulging secrets, especially when they wanted to hurt those who looked down on them. When she was nine, she got in a fight at school and had to appear before the principal, who threatened to inform Nkechi of her bad behavior.

"Chinyere," he'd said, "this isn't what I expect of Da Nkechi's child." Her opponent laughed and repeated what she had heard in her home.

"She isn't Da Nkechi's child. She is the child of her maid. Ha-ha!"

The principal hushed her. "Stop your nonsense. She is Da Nkechi's child."

Stung by what she had heard, Chinyere rushed out of the room, vowing to find out the truth. Afraid to confront Nkechi, and fearing she wouldn't tell her the truth anyway, she sought her aunt and begged her to tell her if what she'd heard was true.

It was Da Erima who tried to explain to her that by native law and custom, she was Nkechi's daughter because Nkechi married Onyeka to give her children. Da Erima asked her never to doubt that she was Nkechi's child, nor to discuss the matter with Nkechi because she would feel hurt.

Chinyere wanted so much to be Nkechi's child, to belong to the same social class as Nkechi, to be on an equal level with Ejituru, and it pained her that only Ejituru had that position. If she couldn't be Nkechi's child, she vowed to make Nkechi's life a misery, to disobey her, to ridicule her in every way possible, and that was what she had done.

She was still sitting on the bench in the anteroom of the kitchen when Emeka came to scrounge some food. "What did you do to Nwankwo?" he asked, as if ready for a fight. "I saw him just now coming out of here looking angry."

She rubbed her face with her hand as if she was just waking up and stared at him. "I told him some uncomfortable truths."

Emeka gave a hollow laugh. "You mean your truth. Let me tell you the truth. Even though you treated Nkechi badly, she was never unkind to you." "Her so-called kindness was to preserve her situation in the society and not for my benefit." Overcome with grief, she started weeping.

"Stop making yourself sick wallowing in your nonsense," Emeka said in a firm voice. "You're wrong, and the sooner you realize it, the better."

"Listen to me!" she exclaimed. "Michael is what he is because of her. She spoiled him. She never pushed Nwankwo to get an education. And look at you!" She wagged her finger at him. "You are what you are now because she never gave you the medical attention you needed. She hated our father. Nkechi was the witch who didn't want our father's sons to succeed. You may not realize it now, but you will eventually."

Emeka, dumbfounded by what he was hearing, stomped the floor with his feet, angrily raking his hair with his fingers as he walked away toward the main house.

~∽◦⊹◦∼~

Filled with anger and hatred, Chinyere wiped away the tears that poured down her cheeks, got up from the mud bench, and made her way across the courtyard. She entered the main house, oblivious of the greetings from the young helpers loitering around. She looked at her watch and decided she would rest a little before making her way to Ejituru's house—if she were to decide to go.

When Chinyere entered the bedroom, she found Sarah, who had emptied the contents of her suitcase on her bed and was frantically searching for something. Before she could say anything, Sarah left the room without giving her the opportunity to say a word.

Left alone, Chinyere gathered her things together, determined to depart shortly after the memorial service. She would get the last taxi to Umuahia, and she might just get the last bus to Lagos from there. She was glad that Sarah wasn't in the room because she was in no mood to talk to her or to anyone else. She thought of her husband, whom she had left in Lagos.

"Maybe I should have given them the money he gave for the funeral; but then, why should I?" she muttered.

Then she remembered that when Onyeka died, her funeral was quiet, and she had only heard about it after the burial.

Unable to stop herself, she marched into the room where Nkechi was buried and closed the door.

She stared at the pile of dirt and said out loud, "I'm here to tell you one other thing I have against you, witch. You didn't even send a message to tell me that my mother was dead. Neither Udo nor I were present. You stopped me from paying my last respects to my mother. Who knows what you did to her? She should have survived you. Perhaps after our dad's death, you poisoned her because you no longer needed her."

Having said her piece, she reopened the door and marched out. Back in the room alone, she tried to still her mind by focusing on her husband and children. She wondered what they were doing. Her husband's business had, over time, faltered, and he currently didn't have the income he'd had before. It had been difficult for him to scrape up the fees for their son at the university and their daughter in boarding school. With her government pension and her gratuity in arears, she'd had to resort to petty trading to make ends meet. She had hoped during this period with Sarah to make her understand that she had to help her because she was her mother. Sarah hadn't given her that opportunity, but would rather talk and laugh with Udo and with the boys than spend any time with her.

She sighed and looked at the mess on Sarah's bed. She thought of tidying up for her but refrained for fear that Sarah would misunderstand her effort. She wondered how she could convince Sarah to help. After all, judging by her contribution to the funeral, she must have money.

She heard someone knocking, and lifting her eyes toward the sound, she saw her brother Nwankwo open the door to announce that she had a visitor. She came out of the room and went to the downstairs parlor, where the women had gathered during the morning.

Her visitor was Ngozi, one of Aunt Da Erima's children, who had come for the funeral. "Ma Chinyere, we've not seen each other for a long time, so I wanted to see you before departing for Owerri."

Chinyere looked at Ngozi, a much younger image of Da Erima, and commented on her resemblance to her mother. "Ewoh, you're the

spitting image of Da Erima. How are you?" The women embraced.

"What are you doing in Owerri?" Chinyere asked.

"My husband works for the government," Ngozi said. "You know I married someone from there. In fact, he was at the funeral. Mama Nkechi meant so much to us that we couldn't stay away and not pay our respects. I often visited her when she was in Umuahia, and actually, I was with her just before her death. She was in good spirits, and I was surprised to hear she died that night. What a loss."

Chinyere made appropriate noises before saying, "Are you coming to the memorial service?"

"Of course," replied Ngozi. "We'll be going back to Owerri on Monday. I've just been to Ejituru's because someone said that she was leaving shortly after the memorial service, and I wanted to tell her that Ogechi, my daughter, will be joining her husband in the US in about a week. She'll be in Washington. I was so happy when Ejituru told me that she now lives near Washington. She promised to help her make the most of this fortunate event."

Chinyere listened while wishing that Ejituru's name hadn't been mentioned. She didn't want to hear another encomium about how great Nkechi was. Composing her face to show how happy she was at the good fortune that had befallen her relative, she said, "I'm so glad for you. That's what we want— that our children should marry well. What does Ogechi's husband do?"

"He's with the embassy, a foreign affairs officer," Ngozi gushed. "But, Mama Chinyere, when are you going back?"

"I hope to catch the last taxi to Umuahia tomorrow and the first bus to Lagos. I thought I would get a ride from here to Umuahia, but so far, that hasn't been possible." Chinyere hoped to force an offer from Ngozi.

But Ngozi clasped and unclasped her hands, betraying nervousness, her face looking as if it was carved in stone.

Finally, she plucked up the courage to say, "I wish we could give you a ride to Umuahia, but our car is full and we have no room. But, sister, since we don't know anybody in Lagos, and I'm told my daughter's plane to the US takes off from there, would it be possible for Ogechi to spend the night in your place if needed? She's a bit nervous about the journey."

"Of course," replied Chinyere, hiding her disappointment. "Which airline is she taking?"

"United Airlines. It flies direct to the US. She'll be departing Port Harcourt on the first flight."

"In that case, it may not be necessary for her to spend a night in Lagos," replied Chinyere, visibly relieved. "That flight leaves by noon."

"Is that so? When she mentioned Lagos, I told her not to worry about where to stay since you live there."

"Not to worry, Ngozi. If she needs somewhere to stay, she can spend the night in our house. Tell her that."

Ngozi stood up, thanked her for the drinks, called out to Nwankwo, and left.

Chinyere sat in the parlor, lost in thought. Sarah must be prevailed upon to help me. I'm her flesh and blood! I deserve help from her.

Nwankwo came in and spoke to her, interrupting her thoughts.

She reluctantly turned her attention to him. "Ngozi's daughter is going to America to join her husband. Did you know?"

"Which one?" he replied, watching her face. "You know she has four daughters and no son."

Chinyere wanted to say that Ngozi was lucky not to have had a son, since sons in this family were all useless, but she bit her tongue and said instead, "The one married to an Owerri man."

"She's her second daughter," he said. "Her marriage ceremony was three years ago. Her husband is in the foreign service. They've been living in Abuja, so it must mean that he's been transferred to America. I'm glad she's going to join him. He's a very nice young man. Ngozi must be very happy. I bet she, too, will soon be going to America to look after her when she becomes pregnant."

She kept quiet. After a short time, she said, "You know, I didn't even know that Ngozi was married and had children."

"Well, how could you know?" he said, smiling. "You don't live here, and they don't live in Lagos."

For a while, they chatted and discussed the happenings in the extended family. Nwankwo, who had no ill will toward anybody, was glad that Da Erima's family was doing well. His only regret was that Da Erima wasn't alive to enjoy her family's good fortune.

Back in her room, Chinyere thought of Ejituru. She wondered whether to attend the meeting at her house. I bet they think I won't go, but I'll surprise them, she thought. I will go, and I'll be the devil they will never forget.

She returned to Michael's house, ostensibly to find out when to expect the car. She lingered, making small talk.

Looking out toward their father's grave, she said, "Compared to our father's funeral, this funeral is very different."

"The difference is that your husband gave a cow in honor of our father," Michael said, sounding irritated, "whereas for this one, he didn't see fit to contribute even a kobo."

For a few minutes, Chinyere had nothing to say. Then she found her tongue. "Maybe so, but I think there were many more people at this one, and many more cows from the grandchildren."

Michael shook his head and said angrily, "Your children, not counting Sarah, gave nothing. But then, Sarah has never been your child." Perhaps feeling that he had overstepped the boundaries of propriety, he asked her in a mollified voice if she intended to attend the meeting that night.

Chinyere sullenly replied, "I wouldn't miss it for all the world. It promises to be interesting. When will the car come?"

"Chinyere," Michael said, "if you have some ulterior motive for wanting to attend, perhaps you should consider not going."

Chinyere looked at him hard. □ Perhaps.□ She said nothing else before making her way back to the main house.

CHAPTER 33

After seeing Udo off, Ifeoma reflected on the events of the day. She thought of the family. The glue that held it together was gone. Her siblings seemed to wallow in jealousy and hatred. She needed to avoid falling into that trap. She got up and peered through the window, looking at the houses across. The village meeting this morning should have ended by now. The meeting was at the chief's house, directly across from hers. She saw the chief getting into his car, surrounded by his children, who were bidding him a safe journey. Seeing the suitcase loaded into the car, she waved at him and remembered that there was a planned meeting of Abia State titled chiefs in Umuahia on Monday, and this man was invited to attend.

Where is Nkem, then? she wondered.

She reasoned that he must have gone to visit friends and acquaintances in the area. On one level, she was glad he wasn't home because if he were, she would have had to talk about her siblings, whom, except for Ejituru, he didn't think much of. She knew that with Udo, the feeling was mutual. Udo despised him and considered him a sponger. Udo never understood why she married a man who couldn't provide for her or his children. To Udo, it was reminiscent of Nkechi's marriage.

Not wanting to dwell particularly on her marriage, she decided to have a short rest.

Just then, she heard the clapping of hands indicating that someone had come. As if on cue, the maid came to announce a visitor. She shrugged on her shift dress and came out with only a loosely tied head tie on her head. The visitor was Peace, a close friend and confidant of hers. "You must be tired of all the visitors so I will not stay long. I just thought I would come to see if you needed any help with the memorial service tomorrow."

"Eh, Enyim, I have not had any time yet to think of that. We plan to serve just drinks and snacks, and Mrs. Ume is making the akara and moi moi. We are having a meeting tonight at my sister Ejituru's house."

"Don't worry, I will stop on my way home to remind her."

Just as she was walking towards the door, Ifeoma stopped her and said, "Visit a while. I have so many things to talk to you about. Have a drink at least."

As they settled down on the sofa, drinking, Ifeoma said, "You'll never guess who came to visit me."

Peace raised her eyebrow, knowing that Ifeoma could not resist telling her and said, "I cannot think of anybody but the governor, since I didn't see him during the funeral."

"No! No, it was my sister Udo. I've often complained to you that she had never been to my house. It is just as well that Nkem was not here when she came because she would have voiced her contempt of him to precipitate a crisis."

"What did he do to her to make her hate him so much? I often wonder." "It's because he reminds her of our father. When we were growing up, we often talked disparagingly of him for his dependence on Nkechi for his financial needs. We often joked that our very existence was due to Nkechi, who procured our mother for him. Both Udo and I vowed that we would never marry a man who couldn't support us financially. Yet here am I in the same situation that I never wanted to be. I can understand Udo's dislike of Nkem."

"We've often talked about this, but you know that money is not everything. You have also benefitted from the marriage in other ways. Besides, isn't Udo divorced? That should tell you something," Peace said reflectively.

"I know that I have only respect and no love for Nkem; but I often wonder whether Udo, at the beginning, loved her husband, and perhaps that love turned to ashes. Maybe that is why she is extremely frustrated and lonely. You know we never met him."

"Isn't Ejituru also divorced and remarried?"

"Yes, but I envy Ejituru for having the strength to leave a loveless marriage to Ignatius for someone she truly loves and who also loves her."

Peace, watching her face, saw a face full of deep emotion. "I remember you met her new husband when you went to Dallas."

"Yes, when I visited, I was struck by the relationship between the two. It was obvious that they loved each other deeply. They hid nothing from each other. I even, judging from my experience, tried gently to tell her that she did not have to be so trusting. But she dismissed my suggestion, saying that if either of them hid anything from each other, it would be the end of their marriage," Ifeoma said as she wiped her face over and over again with her hands.

"My friend, we cannot be like her. If we put such trust in our husbands, we will be done for. Is her husband not a Nigerian man? You cannot trust them with your finances." Peace shook her head vehemently.

"I just hope she will not live to regret such trust." Then, again wiping her face, she said, "What I can say about my marriage is that after living together for such a long time and producing so many children, I am comfortable with him. We are good friends. I did not marry for love. My marriage, like Ejituru's first marriage, was arranged between our parents. I agreed to it because I wanted Mama to have one daughter suitably married, since she'd had to face the shame of Chinyere's pregnancy and Ejituru's divorce. I did tell Mama of my misgivings but she assured me that both parents would ensure that the marriage would last."

"Stop regurgitating the past. As you know, I am in the same boat. You are lucky that Nkechi gave you a lot of emotional support. Some of us cannot say that."

"Yes, she did, especially when it became clear that Nkem could not support the family. I was very angry, and thought I should leave the marriage."

"That must have shocked her." Peace shook her head.

"True. I can never forget that she sat me down and said that I should, like generations of women before me, take responsibility for my children by working hard and pursuing possible incomegenerating efforts that I could find."

Before she could continue, Peace interrupted, saying, "Come to think of it, Ifeoma, she was right. From time to time in our society, women have been responsible for their children. That's the norm in a polygamous society, and even though polygamy is less prevalent now, nothing has really changed. That is probably why every working woman in our society controls her own income."

Peace stood up, retied her wrapper, and hugged Ifeoma, saying, "I must go and run errands for you. Rest before your next meeting, my dear."

Ifeoma, seeing her friend off, again recalled Nkechi's advice. True, Nkem wasn't a graduate or a trained professional, but he was very intelligent and astute. He understood people and the rules of society to which both of them belonged. He had enriched her life by introducing her to high-ranking people.

Of course, her success wasn't entirely due to him but to her own ability to maneuver her way through the state bureaucracy, she reasoned. Her position as principal of several secondary schools for girls helped in that the daughters of most of those in positions of authority and of businessmen in the state had passed through the schools. She got to know the parents and helped to solve any problems their children had in the school. Because of this, she had become the most influential person in the state. People came to her to ask her to intervene on their behalf with state officials.

If she'd wanted to, she could have obtained a political appointment within the state government, but she'd refused many such offers because she preferred her anonymity and independence. The villagers had marveled at the number of influential state officials who had come all the way from Umuahia for Nkechi's funeral. They came, not because they knew Nkechi, but because they wanted to support her in her hour of need.

She thought of her own family. She'd, that morning, made sure that those children returning to boarding school had everything they need. The funeral had provided them a rare opportunity to socialize with friends they only met during school holidays. Those in the university that had exam preparation did not come. Since she had not seen her nine-year-old around, she called, "Ezinne, where is Ifeatu?"

"She is next door. Should I get her?"

"No, no. It is just as well. She'd be bored sitting here alone."

In her bedroom, she desultorily tried to organize the receipts and papers that she needed for her report, but her attempt was interrupted by a knock. Eunice, her sister-in-law, burst into the room like a hurricane. She remembered that she'd promised to intercede on behalf of her sister-in-law with Ejituru. Eunice's daughter needed a job. Since graduating from high school, she hadn't been able to find employment, and her scores didn't qualify her for entrance into any of the local universities. The idea was for Ifeoma to persuade Ejituru to help her enroll in a US college. Ifeoma hadn't raised the issue with Ejituru because she knew how difficult it was to obtain even a student visa to study in the US, and she knew that this was something Ejituru wouldn't consider, anyway. She'd been hesitant to tell Eunice the truth because it would seem as if Ifeoma wasn't interested in the success of members of her husband's family. Instead, she planned to use her local contacts to get the girl into a local training institute. She preempted Eunice by saying, "I have not had the chance to talk to Ejituru yet, but I think she will not be able to help because of the tightening of the visa award by the US government. But I have a solution. I did talk to the principal of Aba Practical Training Institute and he promised to get back to me. As soon as things settle, I will go back to him. Don't worry."

"Thank you, ma. I also wanted to tell you that the produce you wanted me to prepare for Da Ejituru is ready. I've put them in different cellophane bags for you. They are in the kitchen. But I really need your advice on a very important issue but since you are busy, it can wait. I will talk to you later." Ifeoma breathed a sigh of relief. She didn't feel like giving advice right then, so she tried to deflect her by asking about the funeral in the next village, which she couldn't attend because of her family situation. Why, she asked herself, had she become the one to come to regarding many of the illicit and ugly things happening in the village? People came to ask her for advice on everything imaginable—fights with husbands, with in-laws, and with neighbors, or monetary matters—just to name a few. She shook her head and wondered what they thought of her own life. She also had issues for which she would like someone's advice, but whose?

Alone in her bedroom at last, Ifeoma looked at her watch and realized that she had very little time before the driver's arrival. She gathered the papers she was working on just as she heard the sound of a car door closing and Ejituru's driver came in to collect her.

"I was told to pick you up," he said. "Should I wait for you to get ready?"

"No. I have a few things to do yet before coming. I'll take a taxi to Ejituru's. You should go for the others. I'll ask the maid to give you a few things to take with you now. I will bring whatever is left."

Just then Nkem, her husband, walked toward the house. A stocky, light-brown man, he always enjoyed his freedom. He'd spent the day doing what he enjoyed most, wandering from funeral site to funeral site, talking to his friends, and eating a stew of goat entrails. He expected his wife to be engaged with her siblings and had been surprised when he saw the driver outside talking to her.

He looked at her and saw the tired lines in her face and shook his head.

Poor Ifeoma, he thought. This funeral has been hard on her.

Aloud, he said, "Are you going to Ejituru's? Perhaps I should come with you. How is she bearing up? It must be hard on her, away from her children and husband. Has Chinyere been acting up as usual?"

"I was looking for you earlier to tell you the latest. No, I have nothing to say about Chinyere. So far, she's behaving. But guess what? Ejituru has called a meeting to read the will."

"Did Nkechi leave a will?" he replied, aghast. "I bet all your siblings are afraid of the contents. Nwankwo and Emeka will be wondering if they'll have to leave the house. After all, it belonged to Nkechi. Am I invited?"

Ifeoma laughed. "You are not invited. We're also going to give an account of the expenses and the gifts."

"Ha! Ha! I wonder how much Michael pocketed." He paused and watched her face. "Nkechi must be turning in her grave at the thought of them." He sighed and sat heavily on the sofa. Ifeoma burst out crying. It was as if the dam had broken and all the sadness she had been holding had to come out. He stood up and held her, letting her cry on his shoulder. She heard him say, "Poor Nkechi!"

In between her sobs she cried, "The only reason for her to bring another woman into her household was to have a son."

He held her tightly as he said in a calm voice, "A pity they've not turned out the way she wanted." He gently led her to the sofa and sat her down. Wiping her face, he said, "If she had depended on her sons to bury her, her body would still be languishing in the mortuary. You, all her daughters, have made her proud. Stop crying. Her funeral is the talk of the town and you especially should be proud of the fact that because of you, many big shots came from Aba, Umuahia, and beyond to pay respect to our mother Nkechi." After she had calmed down, he said, "I'm tired. I think I'll go lay down and rest. I'll find something to eat later on. Why did you send the driver back?"

"I still have a few things to do. I need to fix food for the children because I don't know how long I'll be at Ejituru's. I'll probably be the last person the driver will take home tonight. I'll call you if I need you."

Just then, her youngest daughter entered the house, hugged her, and turned on the television. Later, the taxi arrived, and Ifeoma and the rest of the food left for Ejituru's house.

CHAPTER 34

When Chinyere entered and sat on the bed, Sarah stood up and left the room. She wouldn't spend even a minute alone in Chinyere's company. Determined, she went in search of Udo. She climbed the stairs and entered the upstairs parlor, hoping to see Udo sitting there reading. Not finding her, she proceeded to Udo's room, but just as she was about to knock on the door, she looked outside and saw Udo descending the outside staircase. She noticed that Udo had changed into a long batik shift dress with matching scarf tied over her wig and low-heeled leather sandals with a matching handbag.

She rushed to the top of the staircase and called out as she descended, "Auntie Udo, wait! I've been looking for you."

Udo, who by this time was halfway up the path leading to the main road, hesitated and turned just as Sarah came abreast of her. "Why are you looking for me?"

"We haven't talked since we heard about the will, and I thought perhaps you have some more information on it."

"Why are you worried about the will?" Udo asked impatiently. "The boys who have no means of livelihood should be worried, not you."

"All the same, aren't you curious that there was a will and only Ejituru knew about it?"

"Sarah! I'm just as ignorant as you, and even though I was at Ifeoma's house, we avoided talking about it." Udo looked at her watch. "Unless you have something else to talk about, I'm in a hurry."

"Auntie, where are you off to now? The car will come for us in about an hour."

"I've decided to take the shortcut to Ejituru's rather than wait for the car. It was impossible to rest this afternoon because of all the noise made by the young boys playing their music and horsing around."

Sarah noticed the sweat trickling down her face. "I'll see you later," Udo said as she turned and left.

Sarah herself was sweating profusely. She hadn't anticipated the heat. At that hour, the sun smote the earth like a woman's nagging tongue. She had expected it to cool off by this time when the sun had begun its western journey, but no. Now at five o'clock, it was still as hot as if it were two o'clock in the afternoon. There was no breeze, and the air was heavier than a cook's breath. The atmosphere was stagnant. Nothing stirred in the humid air. She wondered how Udo could decide to walk to Ejituru's in that heat. Could it be that Udo knew more about the will and wanted to discuss its contents privately with Ejituru? She turned to reenter the house and get away from the burning heat.

Once inside, she sat in the upstairs parlor and listened to the whirling of the ceiling fan pushing the hot air around. She thought of Ifeoma, who she felt had been able to educate her children with Ejituru's support, ostensibly meant for Nkechi's upkeep. She wondered whether that support would continue now that Nkechi was dead.

She thought of Michael, whom she knew was the person most hit by the death of Nkechi, who had been his lifeline since he lost his job, and the source of that support had been Ejituru. She hoped the contents of the will wouldn't be a huge disappointment to him.

She thought of the younger uncles and decided that whatever was in the will wouldn't be disastrous for them, since they had nothing much to lose. Even if the house was willed to Ejituru, and in the worst-case scenario, she put them out, Michael would be obliged to house them.

She closed her eyes, hoping she could empty her mind of all the thoughts crowding it. In her thoughts, she was in Nkechi's room going over things she should do before her departure to England. She felt Nkechi's joy that Udo was helping to get her away from Nigeria and thankful to Udo for taking her in until she could support herself.

Just then Emeka's door opened and he came out, bringing her back to reality.

"The driver hasn't arrived yet," Sarah said.

"I know, but I've decided to use an Okada. In fact, I asked one of my friends who has one to come for me, and he should be waiting on the road outside." He made for the door.

He must be really worried about the will, she thought. She wondered what it felt like to have a full-time job and not be paid for it for six months.

It must be hard for him. Would Ejituru or Udo consider helping him?

She remembered that, privately, Nkechi lamented that her husband never supported her efforts to discipline the boys. She often attributed this to his desire that they should see her as the enemy. This might be so, but Sarah doubted it, feeling that the boys' failure could easily be attributed to lack of a strong male authority within the family. She shook her head. Miffed that Emeka wasn't even willing to engage in more conversation, she stood up and moved to the corridor.

Soon she saw the car arrive and Nwankwo walking up to talk to the driver. Michael opened the trunk and put a small suitcase inside. He looked angry. She heard him shout at Nwankwo, "Go tell Sarah and her mother to come out. We can't keep the driver waiting!"

Sarah decided to come down on her own. "I'm here," she said. "What about Chinyere?" Michael asked. "Is she coming?"

She could see him seething, anger gnawing at him like a toothache. She answered back in a voice devoid of emotion, "How do I know? I haven't seen her."

Just then, the maid rushed out to inform them that Chinyere said to wait for her.

Sarah looked at Michael pacing up and down and occasionally looking at his watch and wondered why he was so angry. Standing there in the heat, she thought of going back inside the house, where at least the fan gave the semblance of providing cool air.

Just as she made up her mind to do so, Chinyere finally came out, a good one hour after the driver had arrived. By this time, Sarah had taken a seat next to the driver. Chinyere asked her to change places with her, and a one-sided squabble ensued, with Sarah totally ignoring whatever Chinyere had to say.

Nwankwo, scowling at both of them, pleaded, "Sister Chinyere, please get in. It's a short drive, but we have to get going."

In the end, Chinyere was forced to get into the backseat with her brothers. Sitting next to the driver as he drove off, Sarah tried to ignore Chinyere, who had tussled with her about the seating arrangement. It made her remember Nkechi's caution that living with Udo wouldn't be easy, but she should remember that Udo had a good heart and would always do the right thing by her, unlike Chinyere.

True, she thought.

Chinyere was a snake and should be avoided. However, Nkechi, she felt, had totally misjudged Udo, who never forgot a slight. Her grudges lasted forever, and she would recount them when one least expected to hear about them. On the other hand, she really could be quite generous. She did come through for her when she needed help, but who knew when she would strike? She recalled telling Nkechi, hoping for sympathy, the hardship she suffered with Udo, being treated as a maid. Nkechi had caustically replied that she didn't consider helping with chores within the family setting as a hardship, and if she'd wanted to be treated as a daughter, she should have opted to go and stay with Chinyere, her mother. She wondered why Nkechi had never faulted Chinyere in her presence. She felt that it was probably because she wanted her to have a good opinion of her birth mother, even though she knew that Chinyere was evil. She shuddered at the thought of having to spend another day in Chinyere's presence.

Out of the corner of her eye, she could see Michael sitting next to the rear window staring in disgust at Chinyere, who was squinting and holding her mouth in a tight line. Thinking about Nkechi, Sarah remembered feeling betrayed by her when she heard later on that Nkechi, the one person she thought would be on her side, had mentioned her complaint to Udo. Udo had felt hurt by her ingratitude and had then vowed that no other family member would ever live with her. Michael had let it slip that her behavior had blocked the chances her children had to go overseas.

Preoccupied by these thoughts, Sarah was unaware of the discomfort felt by those in the backseat, who never said a word to each other throughout the ride.

※⚛◆⚛※

Michael, at that point in the ride, shifted his gaze from Chinyere and closed his eyes. He remembered the purpose of the visit. What would become of his brothers if the will really existed, and the house was given to Ejituru? Would she expel them from the house? She couldn't be faulted for doing so, since the house never belonged to their father, who had never contributed anything to its maintenance. Nkechi handled everything. Since her illness, all the repairs had fallen to Udo. Perhaps Ejituru needed to be reminded of that fact tonight.

As the car approached the turnoff to Ejituru's road, a Peugeot appeared and slowed down. Michael asked the driver to stop, since he recognized the owner. He got out and greeted the man who was sitting in the backseat. "George!" he exclaimed. "How are you? I recognized your car. Why are you out at this time of the night?"

George, whose clean-shaved head glistened with brilliantine and drops of sweat, got out of the car and greeted the ladies, who looked glum. He turned to Michael. "I had some business in the village. Are you all going to Ejituru's?"

"Oh yes," Michael replied, smiling broadly. "She invited the whole family to dinner."

"Give her my best, and tell her I hope to see her after the memorial service," George said, his face animated as he looked at Michael. "I spent a very nice time with her and Nduka in Dallas. What a nice man! I was looking forward to his company during this time, but Ejituru said he was starting a new job and couldn't make it." He got back in his car and drove off.

When Michael returned to the car, Chinyere burst out, "Nice man, huh? But wicked wife!"

Sarah opened her mouth to lash out at Chinyere but was forestalled by Nwankwo, who adjusted his buttocks, squeezed Chinyere further into the corner, and nudged her vigorously. "Keep your nonsense to yourself," he said.

Sarah was relieved to see Chinyere being put in her place. Shortly afterward, they arrived at their destination. Nwankwo was freed of discomfort when Michael quickly got out of the car.

CHAPTER 35

Ejituru's rest was interrupted by the maid, who told her that there was a woman at the gate arguing with the gateman. She got up to take a look. Leaning over the balcony, she saw Udo and heard part of the exchange between her and the gatekeeper. She instructed the girl to let the man know that Udo was expected, settled herself in a chair, and picked up her unfinished novel. She could hear the slap, slap of the servant girl's slippers on the stairs and a harder sound from Udo's sandals.

She reluctantly put away the novel, went to the top of the stairs, and called out a welcome to Udo. "Where are the others?" she asked.

Udo, breathing heavily from the strain of the heat and from climbing the stairs, said, "They'll be coming. I left early so that I could visit with you before everyone comes."

"In this heat!" Ejituru exclaimed. "I hope the car dropped you off or that you took a taxi."

Udo shook her head. "Oh no, I walked, but I didn't anticipate the heat. I was saved from heatstroke by Vincent Oji, who saw me resting under the tree at the junction and gave me a ride to your house. You know, I've never been here. I didn't expect such a big edifice."

Ejituru laughed. She remembered the one time her visit had coincided with Udo's, and she had invited Udo to come and stay in this house because she felt she would be more comfortable here than in the family home. Udo had bristled at the suggestion, saying, "I prefer to stay in my father's house when I visit." Besides, one of Ejituru's brothers—she couldn't remember which—had told her that during one of her Nigerian visits, Udo had expressed a wish to see the house, and he had brought her here to look around. It looked as if Udo was suffering from amnesia. But she wouldn't remind her of that invitation, nor of the numerous invitations she had proffered to Udo to come and visit her in Dallas when she heard that Udo was vacationing in Florida with her children.

So, with a straight face, Ejituru said, "I agree it's big, but as you can see, it looks unoccupied. I, too, was surprised at the size. When the architect sent the plan, I thought I was getting a small, twostory building. When I saw the finished product, I was in shock. There was nothing I could do about it but to grin and bear it, as the saying goes."

"What do you do about water? I noticed that you collect water from the tank outside."

"Last year I put in a borehole, and now I have a constant water supply. The generator often doesn't work, so perhaps I should think of getting a better one. I haven't been able to furnish the house properly, and I doubt that I will do so. I'm not sure of my plans just now. I may decide to sell it, since the upkeep is a drain on my pocketbook." She directed Udo to a sofa and asked the maid for a bottle of water for her.

"Sell it? You may be lucky, because I heard it is difficult to sell a village house," Udo replied as she sat heavily on the sofa.

Udo chose a beer from the selection of drinks presented by the maid. She felt no sympathy for Ejituru. She thought she was fabricating a burden that never really existed. Why did she incur the expense of building a house in the first place? She wanted to show off her wealth, and now she thought it was a burden. Give me a break. You like having a big house like your mother's house here to show that you've arrived, as they say.

As they both settled down, waiting for the others to come, Ejituru, choosing a safe subject, inquired, "Have you been able to talk to your kids since you arrived?" She could not think of anything else to say.

"No," Udo replied. "If I call them, they'll think I'm going to give them some bad news, so I always refrain from calling from Nigeria.

As a rule, I have no cell phone here."

"I've been able to talk to my family today. The children had so much to tell me that Nduka could barely get a word in. I'm actually feeling homesick now." Ejituru's voice reflected her sadness.

"I hope this coming year to visit so I can meet your children," Udo said. She sounded surprised at herself. "Have you spoken to Sarah?

You know she's emigrated to the US."

Ejituru wondered why Udo had raised the topic. She had to be careful what she said because it could easily be twisted when relayed to Sarah. "We haven't had the opportunity to talk. About your possible visit, we'll be very glad to have you. Ifeoma visited us in Texas many times. My family has just relocated to Maryland. We'd only just moved into a rented apartment when the news of Mom's death came. I'd just hired a housekeeper from Honduras before coming here."

"Sarah is also living in Maryland," said Udo. "She has a job at a hospital there."

"I'm so glad for her. I just learned that Ngozi's daughter will also be in the Washington area. Her husband is with the embassy. I've told Ngozi that she should give her my telephone number, and I can arrange to meet with her when she comes and offer any help she may require, although I doubt she'll need help, since the embassy will take care of all their needs."

"Sister, be careful of those people," said Udo. "I try not to have anything to do with them."

"What do you mean? Da Erima was very kind to me when I was growing up, and she always gave me good advice," replied Ejituru politely. "I'll be happy to help Ngozi's child."

Udo let it slide and moved on. "I just can't get over the size of these houses around here. Earlier today, I visited a friend from London who is now living here. My apartment can easily fit into his parlor. I can't imagine living in such a big house."

Ejituru laughed. "I don't see myself actually living here, either. I've spent, mmm, let's see, perhaps a total of six weeks here since it was built. In any case, it's a monument to my father. You know, Nkechi never set foot in this place while it was being built."

"Really? I wonder why," Udo said, her face showing her surprise. "One would think she would have been eager to supervise the construction."

"I really don't know why," Ejituru said. "She never divulged her reason.

But before then, she used the land to cultivate cassava."

Lost in thought, neither said anything. Then the conversation moved on to the event of the night. Udo wanted to know if there was anything she could do to help, and Ejituru said that the maid had taken care of everything. "I hope Ifeoma and Michael will present a good report," Udo remarked. "I'm sure Michael is trying to profit from the funeral. You know he's totally broke. I've been feeding all of them since I came."

"I don't expect him to give a total account of the gifts," Ejituru said. "And there's no way we can know if he fudged the books except if Sarah, who was with him, challenges his account."

Udo laughed. Cocking her head, she said, "Sarah wasn't with him all the time. Michael doesn't deserve any sympathy. The tendency has been to shift the blame to Nkechi for holding him back. This, of course, is what Chinyere harps upon every time Michael's ineptitude is mentioned."

Ejituru sat with closed eyes, letting what Udo had said sink in before opening her eyes and staring at Udo. "I agree that Nkechi should have been forceful with him instead of secretly giving him financial help whenever he floundered. She prevented him from growing up."

"With her death, I wonder how he'll be able to survive," Udo said. "I bet Ifeoma, the mother hen, will take on the responsibility."

Ejituru laughed at the thought of Ifeoma as the mother hen. Then, looking hard at Udo, she said, "I despise my brothers for their dependency." Udo quickly tossed back, "I know you've often blamed me for fostering that dependency and have urged me to help them grow up. If I withdrew my financial support, would they be forced to learn how to survive?"

Ejituru had heard that Udo thought she was very selfish and only concerned about her own welfare, but Udo didn't say so. For the moment, she kept quiet, watching Udo's face for any sign of deceit. "Although Emeka is employed," Udo said, "his salary is uncertain, and is often several months in arears. Nwankwo has no skills and barely supports himself from his voluntary efforts within the community and from what he can get from Ifeoma." She stared back at Ejituru as if daring her to disagree.

Ejituru kept silent.

"You're lucky that Ignatius took you to America," Udo said. "Whatever you'd say about him, he made it possible for you to work and study. You should thank God you aren't a Nigerian-trained doctor earning a pittance. We're both lucky to live abroad."

Taken aback by Udo's reasoning and assured of Udo's real thoughts, Ejituru's first instinct was to attack Udo for her remarks because she firmly believed her achievements could not be attributed to Ignatius, who never wanted her to continue her education. What would arguing with her achieve? she reasoned.

Changing the subject, she said, "I wonder whether Sarah will raise her concern tonight. Remember how she went off in a huff because of the placing of her name in the brochure?"

Udo laughed. "Silly girl. All of a sudden, she wanted to be Nkechi's granddaughter instead of daughter, when all her life, she never wanted to be her mother's child. I'm sure the motive is money. As a daughter, she had to contribute to the funeral, whereas as a granddaughter, very little would be expected of her."

Ejituru silently sipped the Coca-Cola she was holding and watched Udo's agitated face. She wondered what the cause was. She saw that Udo was fidgeting in her seat, as if something was worrying her. "Sister, is there something else you want to say?" she asked.

Udo, as if plucking up courage, said, "Sister, I'm also worried about the expenses. I hope Ifeoma will account for everything." Udo's voice rose. "I asked her for the cost of the liquor, and you would think she would know this outright, but she had a long story of how she couldn't be sure, since it was her husband who made the arrangements. I also asked her how much she paid for the hearse, and she couldn't give me even a ballpark figure. I'm saying this because I hate to be taken advantage of. We've both worked for our money, and I hope Ifeoma will give us a good account."

Ejituru was saved from answering by the arrival of Emeka, who had come on foot. They heard him asking the maid to give him a big glass of cold water to help him cool off, since his friend with the Okada had at the last minute failed to turn up.

When Emeka reached the top of the stairs, Udo immediately complained of her treatment by the gateman as opposed to his.

"I'm not a stranger," Emeka said jokingly, louder than he had intended. "I'm a familiar face, even when Ejituru isn't here." He wondered why Udo had come early and what she had to discuss.

Ejituru welcomed him and asked him to sit down.

Frowning, Emeka tried to rearrange his composure and adjust to having to share this moment with Udo. "You can't imagine how hot it is outside, even though the sun is now setting. The cold water was delicious." Declining any offer of soft drinks, he settled himself on a chair and took a handful of roasted peanuts from a bowl placed on a stool close by.

For a brief moment, no one spoke.

Then Emeka broke the silence by saying, "Ma Ejituru, do you have any photographs of your children? They must be quite big now."

"Bless you for asking about my family in the States," Ejituru said. She pulled out her wallet and passed him a photo of her with her husband and three kids.

He admired the photo, remarking on the likeness between her and her first daughter.

"A lot of people say we look alike, but I don't see the resemblance myself," she said. She then told him a little about the children, their academic achievements, and the sports they were interested in. "Of course, things will change since we're now in Maryland. Before this, they were enrolled in Catholic schools in Dallas because we both wanted them to have a good Christian background."

"Isn't religion taught in schools in the US?" he asked, sounding surprised.

"Not in public schools, because of the separation of church and state rule. That's why, now that we're in Maryland where the public schools are very good, we're torn."

"But public schools are private, aren't they?" Udo asked.

"Public schools, unlike in the UK, are state-run schools," Ejituru explained. "We do have private schools, some of which are run by religious institutions. We'll have to make a decision soon."

"My children went to schools in the neighborhood, and they thrived and did well," Udo said loudly.

"I'm not saying that US public schools are bad," Ejituru angrily responded. "But I remember when I first went to the US, how surprised I was that my friend Esther—a hairdresser—sent her children to a Catholic school in Silver Spring. At that time, it reminded me of schools in Nigeria, with students in uniform. I can tell you that those kids had very good educations and have all gone on to universities. The daughter, whom I knew quite well, is now doing her residency in adult medicine at George Washington University Hospital."

"In the UK, all kids wear uniforms," Udo said. "My kids did not go to private schools, but I never allowed them to slide. I made sure they studied and took advantage of all the opportunities available to them."

"Sister," Ejituru said dismissively, "we were brought up to value education, and it's only natural that we try to pass that on to our children." She changed the subject. "Someone said that your first daughter is due any moment now. Is that true?"

"Oh yes," replied Udo smugly. "I hope I'll get back in time. She has a month to go."

"So you'll be a grandmother again," Ejituru said. "How nice. Congratulations." Udo got up and excused herself.

Ejituru turned to Emeka and said, "How have you been? You look well, at least. It must be hard not having your salary on time." She pulled an envelope from her handbag containing some naira and gave it to him.

Taken aback, he didn't know what to say as he gazed at her with eyes brimming with tears.

In response, she could only say, "I know," and left it at that.

Both were silent when Udo returned and the maid announced the arrival of Ifeoma.

Even before the gate was opened for the taxi carrying her to enter into the compound, Ifeoma was loudly calling everyone around to help unload and carry the packages she brought into the kitchen. Those sitting upstairs couldn't help but be aware that she had arrived, so the announcement of her arrival was superfluous. It was as if a whirlwind had blown into the house, but rather than pass through, it had stayed swirling around. She continued to discharge instructions on what needed to be done as she mounted the steps leading to the parlor, where her siblings were sitting. She paused briefly to acknowledge their presence, then continued to the kitchen to await the arrival of the maid and the gateman with the bags and bowls she had brought.

Satisfied that everything was in order, she called out to Ejituru, "Sister, we've been very lucky. Today's sunshine was good for the drying of the bitter leaf, so you needn't worry. I've left also the packages of egusi and crayfish on top of the counter. I think they can fit into your suitcase. I brought them now because I don't want you to leave them behind." Not waiting for an answer, she went to the fridge and pulled out a bottle of Coca-Cola, then returned to the parlor and sat down heavily, casting her eyes around. Settling on Udo, she cried out "Hey, sister Udo, you're early. I saw the car in front of the house as my taxi passed. I was expecting you to come with Chinyere and Sarah. Were you able to get a regular taxi, or did you and Emeka both take an Okada?"

Udo couldn't seem to find her tongue.

It was Emeka who replied. "Sister Udo was here before me. I was surprised to see her here when I arrived."

"I can't believe how Ifeoma can just breeze into this house and start throwing her weight around," Udo muttered under her breath, too low to be understood by the others.

It fell to Ejituru to keep the conversation going, so she thanked Ifeoma for the gifts of ground crayfish, egusi, and the dried bitter leaf. "I totally forgot to place orders for them and am glad you remembered that I always take them back. Thank you. Tell me how much I owe you."

Ifeoma would hear nothing of this. She waved her hand and shook her head before saying, "These few days have been hectic, and nobody expected you to remember to order them. In fact, I asked my sister-in-law to get them together just before you came. But you know how it is. You can never trust people to act without prodding. I, too, only remembered to ask for them the day before the funeral, but can you believe it? She only started drying the bitter leaf yesterday."

Ejituru smiled. Fidgeting in her seat, she looked around and saw Udo sitting there stone-faced. To defuse the stifled atmosphere, she said, "I'm very grateful. We'll settle everything tomorrow evening after the memorial service." She turned to Udo. "Sister Udo, do you usually take egusi and other foodstuffs from here to the UK? Are you allowed to bring them in?"

Hearing her name, Udo came back to the moment and took some time before responding. "I normally do, but I prefer getting them from Lagos on my way back. How are you traveling, sister?"

"I came through France by way of Port Harcourt, so I have to leave here early on Monday," Ejituru said wistfully. "I'll get the Air France flight to Paris, where I'll connect to a flight home."

They heard the car horn outside the gate and the arrival of the rest of the family.

CHAPTER 36

When the maid came to announce the arrival of the rest of the family, Ejituru quickly left the parlor, ostensibly for the powder room. Instead, she sat on the bed in the master bedroom with her elbows on her thighs and her head between her hands. She needed to still herself for what she envisaged would be a difficult evening. As she sat transfixed in her room, she could hear the loud chatter of family members. She tried to get herself ready to face Chinyere, whom she had never expected to see in her house. She could hear Michael's booming voice asking for her, and Ifeoma's shrill voice saying she was in the bathroom. The ten minutes she sat in the bedroom seemed to last forever.

Finally, she got up, sought the mirror, and rubbed her face with her hands in an effort to remove any sign of fatigue. She smoothed her skirt and blouse, opened the door, and walked along the corridor to the parlor. She greeted everybody there, glad that Ifeoma had already made sure that the drinks had been served and everyone had what they desired. She saw Nwankwo and Michael, each holding a tumbler of native gin. She couldn't remember having bought it. Then it dawned on her that Ifeoma, who knew the tastes of each family member, must have brought that in an attempt to make everyone feel at home. Udo still had the stout. She looked around at Chinyere and saw that she had a glass of Heineken, as did Sarah.

Funny, she thought, at least they have something in common.

Standing at the edge of the circle formed by the guests chatting with each other, she didn't see Ifeoma. She surmised that, as usual, she was organizing the food. She moved past the dining room, where she noticed bowls and platters holding the food had been placed, and made her way to the kitchen, where Ifeoma stood scooping food from the pots onto more platters that needed to be brought out.

Ifeoma looked up from what she was doing and said, "I thought we should eat first before beginning the discussion."

Ejituru looked at her face, glistening with sweat, and smiled. "Sister, the maid could have done all this. You don't have to do everything."

"Call everybody to sit and eat," Ifeoma said, swiveling to face her.

Ifeoma reluctantly handed the ladle to the maid and wiped her sweaty face with the tail end of her wrapper. She looked around for her unfinished glass of ginger ale and went to call everyone to eat, instructing them to bring their unfinished drinks with them. By the time they all heeded her instruction, Ejituru had already taken her seat at the head of the table. As soon as everybody was properly situated, the loud voice of Emeka calling them to pray temporarily silenced them. In addition to the usual prayer for the food, he thanked God for the safe journey of those sisters traveling soon.

Lulled by the clink of the crockery and the loud voices of those around the table, Ejituru began to relax. She made small talk with Udo, who sat on one side of her, and Ifeoma, who sat on the other. She looked around the table at her brothers, who had opted for yam foo-foo and bitter leaf stew, and at Chinyere, who was busily cutting up a piece of goat meat in her jollof rice plate. She saw that Sarah was content with only a small pile of salad on her plate. "Sarah, dear, is that all you're eating?"

Sarah looked startled to hear her name called out. She sheepishly replied, "I'm just starting. I'll probably have some plain rice with the bitter leaf stew."

This became a subject of discussion, with Chinyere saying loudly, "You must be the only person who mixes rice with bitter leaf stew." Sarah stopped eating and looked at her with fury in her eyes.

Before she could say what was on her mind, Udo, rolling her eyes, said, "Chinyere, let me tell you, I, too, sometimes eat rice with ogbono soup, or any soup that I have at the moment."

"So do I," concurred Ifeoma, frowning.

Ejituru looked up at the ceiling as if calling for help from on high and nodded in agreement.

"To each his own," Chinyere said. "In my household, rice is eaten with stew, not soup."

To defuse the situation, Ejituru called the maid to bring some more drinks and water. At the same time, Michael asked for a toothpick. Soon, the men got up to wash their hands at the sink in the dining room placed there for that purpose. The maid began to clear the table of empty platters and bowls and to replace them with containers of cut-up bananas, pawpaw, mangoes, oranges, and pineapple.

When the last of the fruits were eaten, everyone was satiated, and their minds reluctantly came to the reason for this meeting. Emeka called everyone once again to pray. This time, he again thanked God for the food they'd eaten and then proceeded to ask him to guide their next deliberation. After the prayer, Ejituru felt all eyes on her. "This room is a bit dark and stuffy, since there are no windows. It would be better if we continued in the parlor."

Amid the noise of the scraping of chairs on the wooden floor and the clink of glasses and the clatter of plates being removed by the maid, she quickly slipped back into her room, leaving it to Ifeoma to direct those who needed to use the bathroom to where the facilities were.

When Ejituru reentered the parlor, everyone except Ifeoma was sitting down. Ejituru sat down, holding her purse, and cast her eyes around the room. She could see the anxiety in their eyes as they looked at her expectantly.

"We have no agenda for this meeting," she said quietly. "However, I want to thank everyone for the success of the funeral. It was a good send-off for Mama. Thank you, each and every one of you." She got up and went around the room, shaking hands with everyone. Then she resumed her seat. "However, we need now to wrap things up. Perhaps we should start with Ifeoma giving us an account of the expenses, since those of you who entrusted her with your money will want to know how it was spent."

Before Ifeoma could say something, Sarah forestalled her. "I'd like to know who prepared the church brochure." She glared at Ifeoma. "Imagine my surprise to see that I had become a daughter instead of a granddaughter. At first, I was upset, but on second thought, I am glad I was so listed rather than be reminded of the idiot who is my mother. I just want to get that out. Aunty Udo, forgive me for the hoopla I caused during the repast." Taken aback, both Udo and Ejituru murmured, "Glad you are past it now."

Ifeoma began by listing the amounts of several receipts she laid on the table. Then she said, "I don't have receipts for items I bought in the market because, as you know, market women don't give receipts. Unfortunately, I didn't write down how much each item cost. I paid for them as I bought them. There are still outstanding expenses I haven't met. I have to pay the cooks and pay for the hearse, as well as for some of the soft drinks and native gin. From my estimation, we still owe thirty thousand naira, and I have on hand five thousand." She sat down heavily in her chair, a look of satisfaction on her face.

Immediately, Udo raised her head, looked up at the ceiling as if seeking patience from above, and shouted, "That's a ridiculous report! I expected more from you, an educated person." With fury in her eyes, she adjusted her position in her chair and raised her voice even more. "Even if you have no receipts, you should at least have a record of how much you paid for each item! I expected to see a list of items and their cost, not just to hear a verbal account." She looked around the room, as if expecting support. "Why are you all looking at me like that? You act like I'm being unreasonable." In the corner, Chinyere sat quietly laughing.

The ensuing silence was finally broken by Sarah, who spoke with an edge to her voice. "Aunt Udo, calm down. No need to get yourself in a tizzy. I'm sure that Aunt Ifeoma did nothing wrong. She just never expected that we would require a written account of the expenses. She's not an accountant."

Chinyere laughed. Everybody swiveled to look at her, as if wondering what the joke was.

Udo directed her anger at Sarah. "I can't believe what I'm hearing. Sarah, you're a trained accountant, and you're saying this? Oh my God!" Udo shook her head in disgust.

Ifeoma's mouth sagged as wilted and forlorn as a length of vine cut out of its mother plant. For several minutes she didn't answer, but held her abdomen as if she'd just been punched.

Chinyere seemed to be thoroughly enjoying Ifeoma's discomfort.

Finally, Ifeoma spoke. "I took on this responsibility for the funeral because I felt it was my duty to my beloved mother, and now it looks as if I'm being accused of misuse of funds. I really didn't expect this."

With her eyes closed as if in prayer, Ejituru said in a tired voice, "Sister Udo, I do believe Ifeoma acted in good faith. It was a lot of responsibility, and I don't fault her for not writing down all the items she bought in the market. She's told us of the cost of the major items and the amount of funds remaining. She'll give us a list of the outstanding expenses, and I'll make sure they're met. Let's move on."

"All the same, we need a better accounting," said Udo as her shoulders sagged. She took a deep breath and retreated into herself. Michael, who was sitting there with a look of bewilderment on his face, reached into his pocket for his snuff box, then got up and retreated to the dining room to stuff his nose. Those in the parlor could hear him blowing noisily into his handkerchief. When he came back, he was trembling.

Does he think it will now be his turn to be in the hot seat? Ejituru wondered.

It was as if the atmosphere in the room had changed, and everybody braced for a fight.

Sensing this, Ejituru said, "We have one more proposal to deal with."

Immediately everyone sat up in their seats and, in the dim light of the electric bulbs, watched her as if they were seeing her for the first time.

"We have a new request from the pastor of the church, and he's expecting a response during the memorial service." Ejituru watched the reaction of each of them. This didn't seem to be what they had expected, and no one spoke for a few minutes.

Then Udo said angrily, "What does he want? I for one am stretched out." Chinyere coughed loudly, drawing attention to herself. "I'm out of it. Whatever he wants, nobody should expect me to be part of it. Actually, my view is that Onyeka's children should no longer be involved." She stood up and adjusted her wrapper, marched to the kitchen, and came back with a bottle of beer.

Ifeoma spoke again. "Sister Ejituru, please disregard what Chinyere said.

She likes to sow disunity."

On hearing this, Chinyere shouted, "Get up, you lapdog! Let me tell you who is sowing disunity. It's you!" She marched up to where Ifeoma was sitting and wagged her finger in her face for emphasis. Ifeoma bristled, pushing her away. She got up and retied her wrapper as if preparing for a fight. Those present could see the protruding veins on her face. To stop a fight from ensuing, Emeka got up and held Chinyere, then dragged her to her seat.

Udo immediately stoked the fire by saying, "Chinyere, who made you the spokesperson for the so-called Onyeka children? Just shut your useless mouth for once."

Chinyere raised her right hand as if she was going to slap Udo, but she was forestalled by Michael, who exclaimed,

"Enough! Let us respect each other. Sister Ejituru, you were going to tell us about the church request. Let's hear it."

It took Ejituru a few moments to still her frustration at the turn of events before she calmly answered, "The pastor has suggested that we consider adding a room to the church for Sunday school and other children's activities in honor of both our parents, who were very active members of the church. Ifeoma has the estimated cost."

They briefly discussed the estimate and agreed that the project was worth supporting. Udo offered to contribute a quarter of the cost, and Ifeoma offered a tenth, even Sarah joined in saying, to everybody's surprise, "I'll give five thousand naira. I'd like to contribute more, but I have to think of my credit card bills."

"No," Ejituru said to Sarah. "I won't accept this. You've given enough. It would be unfair to expect you to go into debt just because you feel obligated."

"I was going to ask Auntie Udo to lend me the amount, since I don't have it at the moment, but I'll pay her back as soon as I get back. I want to contribute. Mama meant a lot to me. I owe it to her." Sarah burst out crying. Udo, taken aback, stood up and went to comfort Sarah. In a loud voice, she said, "You don't have to pay me back."

"Sarah, we know you loved Mama," Ejituru said, "but we don't need your contribution. I'll bear the remaining cost."

They agreed on the wording of the announcement. Emeka was so moved by this that he stood up and shook each sister's hand, muttering, "God bless you."

All eyes were now on Michael, whose report was expected. He nervously began by producing the assorted sets of clothing material given during the clothing of the dead. There were twelve pieces, he said, and according to custom, each family member was expected to take what they wanted. "There are eight of us, so I suggest that the remaining pieces be divided among the four sisters."

Sarah, who had now recovered from her outburst, coughed and drew attention to herself. "I object to the distribution.

Chinyere shouldn't be allowed to have any. She's made it clear that she is not a part of this family." She looked around as if daring anybody to contradict her.

Laughter bubbled out of Chinyere, to the surprise of those present. She opened her mouth to say something, but Nwankwo spoke first.

"You can't say that," he said.

"Her very presence here shows that she's a member of the family," Emeka added.

Ejituru sat heavily in her chair, her face drawn and bleak as if she was about to cry. She knew that as far as Chinyere was concerned, she, Ejituru, was not considered a part of their family. In her heart, she also knew that Sarah was right. However, when she dared speak, she pounded the table for attention and voiced her support for Emeka and Nwankwo's views.

They moved on to the rest of Michael's report. He told them that, having handed over a third of the gifts to the kindred, according to custom, he had in hand 20,000 naira.

Sarah at once questioned him, saying that she remembered one doctor from Aba had given a gift of 10,000 naira, and so she was sure the amount was much more than Michael reported.

Udo asked to see the record.

Michael sheepishly said, "I left the book at home."

Udo rolled her eyes. "How could you do that, knowing that Ejituru will have to write a thank-you letter to all those who gave gifts?"

Sarah shrugged her shoulders. "This is unbelievable."

"Actually, Sarah, you're also to be blamed for this," Udo riposted immediately, wagging her finger for emphasis. "We expected this. That was why you were supposed to be with him at all times, but you failed in your duty." Everybody started to shout at each other in no order at all.

Ifeoma pounded the table to get everybody's attention, opened her mouth but closed it, seemingly too dumbfounded to speak.

Michael looked down at the floor, as if not wanting to confront the accusation in his siblings' eyes. "I'll give her the names tomorrow," he mumbled. "I was in such a hurry to come here that I forgot the book."

Chinyere laughed and said, "That's what you get when you ask the fox to look after the chickens. Ha-ha!" She slapped her thighs.

Out of embarrassment, both Emeka and Nwankwo joined in her laughter. Ifeoma remained speechless.

Ejituru felt that there was no way to find out the amount Michael had expropriated, and there was therefore no need to dwell on it. There was no need to make him feel more upset than he was, so she said in a voice that betrayed her anxiety, "Please give the money to Ifeoma, since we still have outstanding payments. I'll get the record and, if possible, the addresses of contributors tomorrow, so I can write the thank-you letters." She got up and came back with the maid, who brought in more bottles of beer. Each person was served with fresh drinks.

Ejituru sat down heavily in her chair and sighed, knowing she still had a very difficult task to perform. There was still one important item to be discussed.

She could see the look of anticipation on everyone's face and waited for their full attention before saying, "I have one more issue to raise. When Mama knew that her memory was failing her, she sat down and wrote a long letter to me in which she put down all her hopes and frustrations." She opened her handbag and pulled out an envelope. Wiping her tear-stained face, she continued. "I won't bore you by reading the full letter because part of it is very private, but in this letter, which I have called her will, she expressed the hope that her death wouldn't mean the end of our family unity. She knew she was the glue that held the family together, since we all have issues with one another, but she hoped that even after her death, we would act as if we're part of one loving family caring for each other. We should let go of our issues and remain united as a family.

"This meeting, therefore, is my attempt to carry out her will. I have nothing against any of you. We share Nwakama's blood, and for what it's worth, we're all siblings. I love and respect you all. I want to say that I would love to be in contact with each of you. Ifeoma has my address, and I hope we'll all continue to be in touch with each other. This is what Mama wished." She refolded the letter and put it inside her handbag. There was complete silence while everyone tried to process what she said. Having all the time been expecting a thunderstorm, it was as if they were left with a passing shower. For a while, nobody spoke. Ejituru wondered if it was because what she had said wasn't what they had expected to hear or because it was a letdown.

"What nonsense is this?" cried Chinyere, the first to find her tongue. "You got us here under false pretense!" Turning to her siblings she cried, "I know it, she is fooling us, just like her mother." "Leave my mother out of it!" shouted Ejituru, gearing for a fight.

"Wo! Wo!" cried Udo. "Are you telling us there is no will?" She burst out laughing, slapping her thighs. "I suspected as much, but even so, this beats everything else. Ejituru! You got us all fooled!! Ha ha ha!"

Amidst the chatter from the men, who were totally unprepared for what they were hearing, Ifeoma clapped loudly, silencing everyone. Just as everyone was beginning to relax and frame their response, Chinyere coughed loudly, breaking the silence. "Let me tell you, Ejituru, you called us here under false pretenses. You are indeed your mother's daughter, users that you both are. Sure, we share Nwakama's blood, but that was because your mother bought our mother and used her as a baby machine to secure her place within his family. That position was given to her when our mother gave birth to that one." She pointed at Michael.

"Leave my mother out of it, Chinyere. I honestly do not want to hear what you have to say."

"But you will hear it!" Chinyere shouted. "Your mother was a user and so are you. Look at how you are using Ifeoma!"

Ifeoma, on hearing her name called, shouted, "Leave me out of it. Nobody is using me!"

"Of course you are being used, Ifeoma, you are a lackey. You just don't realize it.

"Okay. Chinyere, you want to fight? You ungrateful bitch!" Ejituru said, prepared to fight back.

"Who are you calling ungrateful?" Chinyere shouted, glaring at Ejituru. "Yes, you are ungrateful. The only good thing to come out of you is our sister Sarah; but thank God you did not bring her up. So shut up and stay quiet." Ejituru pounded the table in her fury. For a moment, there was silence. Then the three men rose in unison and went over to where Chinyere was smugly sitting.

They were about to lift her up when she rose from her seat, screaming, and pounding the coffee table in front of her. Waving everyone aside, she said, "You can't silence me! You're all hypocrites! Look at her!" She wagged her finger at Ejituru. "She stole our mother's love, and as a result, our mother had none left for us!" By now she was screaming like a madwoman. "What is worse, she had no feeling for the woman who loved and dedicated her life to her! She never had time for her! She didn't even come to her funeral, and here we all are, her children, paying respect to the woman who enslaved our mother!" She pounded the table over and over again as her wig fell off and her wrapper unraveled, revealing her torn underwear. She had to hold it together.

Those present appeared too shocked to act. Ejituru's anger having been spent, she sat transfixed in her seat, unable to move or say anything. Tears ran freely down her cheeks. Udo, as if waking from a trance, got up, marched up to Chinyere and shouted, "How can you say these things about Nkechi? Even though she is not our birth mother, she was more our mother than our birth mother! We owe our success in life to her! Think!" she shouted. "Where would you be today without Nkechi? She helped you get a skill, despite your situation. You talk about Onyeka as if she was an angel. What did you do for Onyeka when she was alive? It is easy to blame other people and to overlook your own fault. Stop dumping everything about your life on Nkechi! Look at you! You never recognized your own child until now when you need help. You are the one who is a user!"

Sarah immediately entered into the fray, getting up and standing in front of Chinyere and poking at her, saying, "You think I do not know why you are cozying up to me now? You think I should support you and your children? Where were you when I was young and needed help? You evil bitch!"

Chinyere pushed her aside, and poking her in return said, "The witch stole you from me and fed you all sorts of crap about me! I am your mother! You cannot deny that!"

"Nonsense!" cried Sarah. "My mother died, and you are not her! Let me not hear you say again that I am your child!" She rushed off from the room to the bathroom.

But Chinyere hadn't finished. Like a furious banshee, she yelled, "Ejituru took our mother's love and gave nothing in return! I speak the truth for all of you! Look, did you see her going at any time to where our mother was buried? That in itself is very telling!"

Just then the driver and the gatemen, hearing the commotion, came up to find out what was happening. Her anger spent she left the room, pushing away the driver and the gatemen, who were trying to restrain her as she rushed out of the house.

For ten minutes, those left in the room sat silently, looking shocked by what they had just witnessed. Then Udo and Ifeoma got up and together went over and embraced Ejituru.

"Sister, we love you and of course our dear mother," said Udo. "We don't share in what has just been said," Ifeoma added.

The boys also went up to her to offer their apology.

Ejituru listened but was unable to feel anything. She wanted them gone so that she could in her own time process what she had witnessed in her own time.

The boys were the first to leave. The driver would take them home, along with Chinyere, who was sitting in the gateman's chair. Ifeoma had called Nkem to come and pick her up. Sarah silently sat near Ejituru, holding her hands, each lost in thought, until Nkem's loud voice jolted them, and she and her aunts silently made their way to the car.

With everyone gone, Ejituru roused herself and went to her room. She lay down and for an hour tried to sleep, hoping to forget everything that had happened. But sleep eluded her. She got up, shrugged on her dressing gown, and opened the door leading to the balcony. She stood there, washed in the bright light of the full moon as she gazed up to the sky with its myriad of stars against a backdrop of a dark-blue sky. Then she saw a shooting star dash across the sky, and she thought it was her mother reminding her that, although she was no longer there in the flesh, she was still with her. She looked at the moon again and felt that the full moon would always in her mind be associated with her mother's death. Perhaps this would be the last time she would experience the full moon here in her birthplace.

She reentered her bedroom, picked up her cell phone, and dialed her husband's number, knowing it would be 5:00 p.m. on a Saturday evening in Silver Spring. He would be relaxing to classical music pouring out of the stereo. When he answered, it was as she envisaged it.

"How did it go?" he asked.

"Not well," she replied. "Chinyere spoiled it all. I can't talk about it now, though. I just wanted to hear your voice."

"It's all right, Ej," he said. "We love you. When are you coming back?"

She could hear the tenderness in his voice. "Tuesday, by Air France, as arranged," she answered with a trembling voice.

"It must be very early morning there for you. Please try and rest." Ejituru heard her children in the background telling their father they wanted to speak to her.

"We'll meet the plane, Mummy," her oldest said. "We can't wait!" they all exclaimed in unison.

Relieved, she went back to bed. It was there that Ifeoma roused her at 7:30 a.m. so they both could meet the others in the church for the memorial service. The family, without Chinyere, who was too tired after her big night to join them, maintained a united front. Ejituru presented to the church a sum of 300,000 naira as a gift for the memorial. After the service, the family stood in line outside to shake hands with church members and to invite them to partake of drinks and snacks at home.

Ejituru went back to the house and after an appropriate period, left to meet her visitors at the new extension house.

Early on Monday morning, she packed up, closed her door, bade farewell to the gateman, drove past her parents' house without attempting to go in, and went to hand over the keys and bid farewell to Ifeoma. As she left, she felt a sense of relief that this, no doubt, would be the end of this phase of her life.

ABOUT THE AUTHOR

Nwanganga Shields grew up in Nigeria and currently lives in Bethesda, Maryland. She studies at the University of St. Andrews and American University in Washington, DC. She is a retiree of the World Bank. The Reading of the Will is her third novel.

NOTE FROM THE AUTHOR

Word-of-mouth is crucial for any author to succeed. If you enjoyed

The Reading of the Will, please leave a review online— anywhere you are able. Even if it's just a sentence or two. It would make all the difference and would be very much appreciated.

Thanks!
Nwanganga

Thank you so much for reading one of Nwanganga Shield's novels. If you enjoyed the experience, please check out our recommended title for your next great read!

Coming Back by Nwanganga Shields

Arochukwu people in Eastern Nigeria believe that death is not the end of life and that the person will return again in the next generation to either re-live his past life or to live a better life than the previous one. This story is about one such return.

Achi, a house slave at the beginning of the 20th century who died in 1950s returns in the form of his American born grandson, Clint. This begins the quest to claim his heritage.

www.ingramcontent.com/pod-product-compliance
Lightning Source LLC
Chambersburg PA
CBHW070911120626

46546CB00001B/220